WASHINGTON STATE
PLACE NAMES
From Alki to Yelm

by
Doug Brokenshire

The CAXTON PRINTERS, Ltd.
Caldwell, Idaho
1993

Library of Congress Cataloging-in-Publication Data
Brokenshire, Doug, 1909-
   Washington State place names: From Alki to Yelm
by Doug Brokenshire.
      p.   cm.
   Includes bibliographical references (p.) and index.
   ISBN 0-87004-356-0 : $14.95
   1. Names, Geographical—Washington (State)   2. Washington
(State)–History, Local.   I. Title
F889.B75   1993
979.7--dc20   93-18926
                                                          CIP

Cover Design by Teresa Sales

E.L. Reedstrom has provided several illustrations for this publication.

Lithographed and bound in the United States of America by
The CAXTON PRINTERS, Ltd.
Caldwell, ID 83605
156485

To my beloved daughter,
Sarah

INTRODUCTION

This is a book in which to browse. Absorb it slowly and it should enhance your appreciation of the region. In this writer's view history is primarily for enjoyment, a means by which to dig down one's roots, to identify with the land and to learn about the trials and tribulations of the people who preceded you here.

Place-names are like the roadwide historical markers past which we all speed in our motor cars, too preoccupied to stop and enjoy them. They are never, of course, mere designators by which to direct our way from here to there. Scratch the surface of most place-names and you will reveal much concerning the customs, habits and interests of the people who inhabited the places they represent.

In my inclusion within the pages of this book the names of so many Washington communities, both large and small, as well as many of the state's other landmarks, it is my hope to convey to the reader some of the lesser known, more intimate details of the state's history. The feeling, the flavor, the legend, and other colorful aspects of Washington's history have too long been neglected. So much of such history is unknown to Washington's present inhabitants. Back east in my native New England, the stories such as are encompassed in these pages would by now be hoary with telling.

But because Washington State represents a comparatively new part of the U.S. in terms of date of settlement, many of its inhabitants are unaware of their rich historical heritage. In this book you will be surprised, I hope, at the wealth of lore it contains concerning the customs, habits, and interests as well as the activities of the people who preceded you here. "What's in a name?" asked Shakespeare in alleging "A rose by any other name would smell as sweet." But the Bard of Avon was not talking about historical aspects of names; rather he was referring to their sounds.

The most prized of all the place-names possessed by us Washingtonians is Strait of Juan de Fuca. World famous it is, given by a Greek navigator whose real name was Apostolos Valerianos. Posing as a Spaniard with the name Juan de Fuca in order to be chosen by the Mexican viceroy to command a Spanish ship, Valerianos (alias Juan de Fuca) sailed, he claimed, into Puget Sound, or waters in a latitude remarkably corresponding to this body of water, just one hundred years after Christopher Columbus discovered the West Indies.

Even before Juan de Fuca's time however, the famous buccaneer Sir Francis Drake sailed into waters which, although only vaguely described by Sir Francis, in all likelihood lay off the Washington coastline. To the entire West Coast of North America Drake gave the name "Nova Albion" or New England. This was long before the part of the United States which today is called New England received its name. The year was 1578, forty-two years before the Pilgrim fathers landed on Massachusetts' Plymouth Rock. Just previous to this, Sir Francis had been engaged in terrorizing the natives of South America, plundering them of their gold, jewels, and ingots of silver. He too was thereby creating alarm on the part of Spain who heretofore had considered all of the dimly-understood west coasts of the Americas as the King of Spain's private domain. Drake continued northward beyond the California coasts hoping like Juan de Fuca to find an opening through the continent through which he could sail eastward back to England. Failing to do so, he then returned home instead by sailing westward around the world.

The oldest and perhaps most interesting of Washington's place-names however are those of the American Indians. They were the oldest inhabitants of our region. According to most anthropologists, the region we now call Washington was probably the springboard from which these Indians spread eastward and southward after having migrated here some ten to twenty thousand years ago from northern Asia. From this latter region, in search of a better place to live, they pushed through the centuries over the land bridge which then connected Asia and America where Bering Strait now lies. Slowly pushing southward as the years passed from Alaska down the coastline of today's Canada, they chose to concentrate for centuries in the area of Washington today known as the Olympic Peninsula.

Here they thrived on the unusually mild weather created by the offshore Japanese Current, creating for them amply supplies of food and trees for shelter. Highly concentrated were these Indian tribesmen on this peninsula, living shoulder-to-shoulder yet unable to speak their neighbor's language, each band having come from widely dispersed parts of Asia.

Indian place-names still to be found on Washington maps are illustrative of this situation—names such as Squak, Pysht, Hoh, Skagit, Puyallup, Sequim, Duckabusg, and Quilcene. Despite their bizarreness, no surer way can be found to annoy native Washingtonians than to mispronounce them even though, as pronounced by the aboriginal

Indians themselves, they doubtlessly resemble a series of hisses, grunts, or hicoughs in no way resembling their current pronunciations. Said one Englishman who in early times was confronted by these names, they must have been formed by placing the letters of the alphabet in a paper bag, shaking it, then emptying them, a few at a time, upon the floor.

This is a sort of "do-it-yourself" history book. If the Washington reader will look up the history herein of his or her own town, then peruse that of neighboring towns, the history of the entire region should emerge in a rather personal way. I hope the readers of my book will enjoy reading it as much as I have enjoyed its preparation.

Doug Brokenshire

For quotations in this book followed by designations such as (IV, 231), the Roman numeral refers to the volume and the Arabic numeral to the page of R.G. Thwaites Original Journals of the Lewis and Clark Expedition, New York, 1904.

The letters and numbers in parentheses following each place name are grid references to the map of Washington on the inside covers of this book.

A

ALKI POINT (H-8)

Just as Plymouth Rock in the harbor of Plymouth, Massachusetts, marks the spot where the Pilgrim Fathers landed from the *Mayflower* (December, 1620), this projection of land at the south end of Seattle's Elliott Bay marks the spot where in November, 1851, Mr. Arthur Denny (1822–1889) and his party of twenty-four men, women, and children stepped ashore after a stormy trip by sea up the coast of Washington from Portland. The name of their ship was the *Exact,* Captain Isaiah Folger in command.

At first Denny and company called their future city by the name New York even though they lived initially in tents here. When however, after the discouragements in getting settled here increased as the winter arrived, this name began to sound too pretentious and so they began calling their settlements New York Alki (in the trade jargon then used in conversing between Indians and whites at this time alki meant tomorrow). Still later, after they had moved to a site on Elliott Bay more suited for their future city and had named it Seattle (after one of the Indians who had helped them immeasurably during the hardships of the winter), New York Alki became just Alki Point. Today Alki Point is a part of West Seattle.

ALOHA (J-3)

Spaniards were the first white men of record to discover the portion of Washington State's coastline where this town now stands, fifteen miles north of Grays Harbor. The first of them was a twenty-four year old Basque from Bilbao named Bruno Heceta who, sailing in his ship *Santiago,* arrived here on July 13, 1775, one year lacking nine days before the founding fathers in Philadelphia signed their Declaration of Independence from England. Senor Heceta had come here from lower California, sent by Spain's viceroy in Mexico City to probe the then-mysterious and as-yet unmapped coastline north to Alaska where Spain's rivals for possession over the Northwest, the Russians, were based. After landing ashore at the promontory immediately north of Aloha, now named Point Grenville, Captain Heceta held a solemn ceremony declaring all the region which we now call Washington State to be a possession of King Carlos III of Spain.

The world aloha after which this town is named, reminds us of the famous Hawaiian greeting from which it is derived, and this in turn reminds of Captain James Cook, the great English explorer who discovered the Hawaiian Islands in 1778, naming them the Sandwich Islands after one Earl of Sandwich, a friend back in England. At this time Captain Cook was enroute to the Northwest's coasts searching in his two ships, *Resolution* and *Discovery,* for an opening along these shores leading through the American continent called the Northwest Passage. It was about one hundred fifty miles up the coast from Aloha, on Vancouver Island's west coast at a place called Nootka, that Captain Cook's sailors discovered the Nootka Indians' immense supply of sea otter pelt, each worth a hundred dollars or more in China. So plentiful were they that these Indians used them to cover their huts. Word of this unbelievable opportunity to become wealthy soon afterward spread not only back to England but all over the world. Coming to Nootka from Europe both by way of the Cape of Good Hope in Africa and Cape Horn in South America were fur trading ships, their crews seeking to become rich. Thanks to the Pacific Ocean's trade winds and currents, virtually all of them stopped in the Hawaiian Islands before reaching the Northwest shores. Thus it was inevitable that Hawaiians, both male and female, during these years of the fur trade in the Northwest, would stow away aboard these vessels.

Thus Hawaiians were among the first non-Indian people to inhabit the Pacific Northwest. Here they became known as *Kanakas,* this being the Hawaiian word for man. Employed by the Hudson's Bay Company, these *Kanakas* proved to be skillful fur trappers, as capable of setting traps beneath icy streams in the Rocky Mountains as were the Iroquois Indians which the Company also brought here from eastern Canada to harvest beaver pelt, another kind of fur which brought wealth to fur traders of the early Northwest. The *Kanakas* in particular were skillful canoe paddlers, and since HBC furs were transported along swift flowing streams across the Rocky Mountains to Hudson's Bay, *Kanakas* became particularly valuable when these canoes loaded with valuable pelt overturned. *Kanakas* saved many a load of this precious cargo, thanks to their skill as swimmers.

In today's southeastern Oregon is a river famous because three Hawaiian fur trappers, while operating along its banks, were surprised by local Indians who killed them; its name: Owyhee River. The word *Owyhee* is the original orthography used by Captain Cook in spelling the word *Hawaii.*

The first Hawaiian female of record to visit the Pacific Northwest's shores was a young girl named Winee. It was in 1787 while the four hundred ton sailing ship named the *Loudon* was anchored off Oahu, that Francis Trevor Barkley and Mrs. Barkley met Winee. Finding the girl possessed pleasing ways, the Barkleys asked of Winee's parents permission for her to accompany them. Mrs. Barkley, too, was the first white woman ever to visit the Northwest. Winee never returned home, dying as she did upon the *Loudon's* return to China, its hull loaded with Northwest furs to be sold in Macao. Barkley's ship *Loudon* is better known in Northwest history under the name *Imperial Eagle.* For, like many other English traders, desiring to avoid the excessive trading license fees then charged by England's East India Company, Captain Barkley sailed his ship under false colors. The vessel carried Austrian papers and was registered under this false name.

AMERICAN LAKE (J-7)

Few residents of Tacoma's southern fringe where American Lake now stands are aware of the remarkable event which took place here in 1841. At this time Puget Sound, indeed all of the Northwest lying north of the Columbia River, was expected (at least by England) to become a possession of King George III, not of the United States. As he sailed his American ship, the USS *Vincennes,* into Puget Sound that summer, Commodore Wilkes wanted to disabuse the Englishmen living at Fort Nisqually, just south of American Lake, of this expectation. The United States, not England, would eventually own the Northwest, he insisted.

In view of this rivalry between the two nations, Wilkes was a little apprehensive upon anchoring his ship off Nisqually concerning the welcome he would receive from Alexander Caulfield Anderson, the British officer-in-charge of this fur post. To his relief, however, Mr. Anderson received Wilkes and his sailors most hospitably, even providing Wilkes with access to a site immediately north of the British post on which his sailors might erect an observatory from which to commence Wilkes' survey of the region.

To dramatize for Mr. Anderson and his Britishers that Puget Sound was not yet a British possession, Commodore Wilkes decided to hold a celebration of the Fourth of July (the date on which Americans achieved independence of British rule) on the outskirts of Anderson's British post. At sunrise on the fifth of July (since the Fourth fell on a Sabbath) Wilkes fired a 26-gun salute from the deck of his flagship, a 780-ton sailing vessel, anchored just off the British post, one salute for each of his nation's twenty-six States.

Leaving only Chaplain Elliott and two sailors on board, all hands landed ashore, the crew dressed "in clean white frocks," as Wilkes describes it. Then in single file they marched through the woods to a meadow closeby American Lake, today a residential community. Here two oxen presented to the Americans by Mr. Anderson had been spitted the day before and had been roasting through the night awaiting the Americans' arrival.

"In a jovial mood," Wilkes records, they thus paraded toward the picnic scene, led by a sailor carrying the Stars and Stripes accompanied by a fife and drum player. First came the officers of the *Vincennes* followed by the crew, the starboard watch, then the marines followed by the larboard watch. Bringing up the rear was a dark-skinned person named Vendovi. He was a prisoner whom Wilkes had taken captive the previous summer when his globe-circling expedition was engaged in surveying the Fiji Islands. Vendovi was being taken back to New York City for trial, charged with having led a massacre which took place prior to Wilkes' arrival in the Fijis, of the crew of an American whaling ship.

Dressed in his native Fijian costume, Vendovi was followed by the *Vincennes'* master-at-arms with the vessel's mascot, a dog named Sydney, bringing up the rear. There followed upon reaching American Lake a football match between the two watches at which the usually unbending Commodore Wilkes served briefly as referee. Then all hands sat down to a sumptuous picnic.

Largely forgotten today is a still earlier Independence Day celebration held to the north of Puget Sound, at Nootka, on the west coast of Vancouver Island where Spain possessed a naval base. Here on the Fourth of July in 1789 Captain John Kendrick, then skipper of the *Columbia-Rediviva,* the same ship in which Rhode Islander Robert Gray was later to discover the Columbia River, held similar ceremonies, particularly mystifying the local Nootka Indians who watched as the American colors were hoisted and guns fired.

It was not long after this event that the Spanish governor at Nootka, the mad Estevan Martinez, so angered the British fur traders at Nootka that England narrowly missed declaring war, claiming that this fur post belonged to England as much as it belonged to Spain.

ANACORTES (D-7)

This is the city, fifty miles north of Seattle, at which people board the ferry that takes them through the beautiful San Juan Islands to Canada's city of Victoria. One day while waiting for the next ferry, I asked the little old lady who was an antique store proprietor at Ancortes how her city happened to get such an unusual name. With a perfectly straight face she replied, "The great Hernando Cortez, conquistador of Mexico, was on a visit to Puget Sound long ago when he decided to name the spot here where Anacortes now stands in honor of his wife whose name was Anna." Of course, no Spanish explorer of record ever set foot around Puget Sound when Cortez was alive.

However, it was in fact a Spaniard named Jose Narvaez who was the first white man to view the site of today's city. In 1791 Jose Narvaez sailed past today's Anacortes in his tiny fragata, the *Santa Saturnina.* At this time, he was searching for an opening in the (to him) mysterious local shorelines which would lead into the Atlantic Ocean.

Senor Narvaez was just one of many Spanish officers who in 1791 were based at Nootka. Now a deserted spot on the west coast of Vancouver Island, Nootka was in Narvaez' day the capital of the Pacific Northwest. Here came the ships of many nations, eager to obtain sea otter skins from the Indians along the Northwest coast. When carried to the Orient these furs brought fabulous sums of money.

In 1789 an erratic Spanish naval officer named Estevan Martinez arrived at Nootka and set himself up there as governor of the place. Hoisting a Spanish flag over the fort which he erected here, Martinez demanded that henceforth all the fur trade captains anchoring their ships in Nootka's harbor, called Friendly Cove, must first obtain his permission to do so. When several British fur trade skippers refused to do so, the governor seized their ships, then sent them south to Spain's naval base in Mexico, the British captains held as prisoners below decks.

Watching all this with wide-eyed amazement, the local Nootka Indians sympathized with the captured Englishmen, and made clear their anger toward the cruel Spanish governor. When a Nootkan chief named Qualicum displayed these feelings by spitting at Martinez, the governor shot the Indian dead. Today the town of Qualicum Beach, located a few miles north of Vancouver Island's city of Victoria, commemorates this Indian leader.

In the event the reader wishes to know the true etymology of the name of this city, Anacortes received its name in 1877 from Amos Bowman, a civil engineer from the State of Maine. Bowman recognized the promising possibilities of the site where Ancortes now stands of becoming a great city. Because it was so close to the Pacific Ocean and because of its deep harbor, Bowman believed it to be the best seaport on Puget Sound. In his opinion the railroad czar Henry Villard, then laying transcontinental tracks toward Puget Sound, would certainly choose Anacortes to become his railroad's Pacific terminus thus causing Anacortes to be the Gateway to the Orient, not to mention to Alaska as well.

Bowman then began publicizing his future metropolis as the Magic City. It was at this time that he gave to it the name Anna Curtiss, this being his wife's maiden name. Gradually over the years Anna Curtiss has become Anacortes.

ANDERSON ISLAND (J-7)

When Charles Wilkes, the American explorer, reached lower Puget Sound in the summer of 1841, he anchored his ship, the US Navy's sloop-of-war *Vincennes*, in the narrow channel between Anderson Island and Fort Nisqually, then went ashore to greet Chief Trader Anderson, the British officer-in-charge of Fort Nisqually, located at the mouth of Nisqually River. Mr. Anderson received Wilkes most cordially even though he must have known that this Yankee had come to Puget Sound to evaluate England's strength in the region. Jointly shared by treaty by both England and the United States, the region was controlled by the British Hudson Bay Company. Indeed throughout that summer Anderson was most generous in affording Wilkes and his Americans every courtesy, even providing them at no expense with horses, equipment, and guides in connection with surveying and mapping this as yet unfamiliar part of the world.

It was in appreciation of these kindnesses that Commodore Wilkes placed Mr. Anderson's name on the charts his surveyors made of these waters that summer, assigning it to designate this island which lies across Nisqually Reach opposite the Nisqually Flats, ten miles northwest of Olympia.

In 1846 when war between England and the United States for possession of the Pacific Northwest seemed imminent, Anderson Island was christened Fisgard Island by the British briefly, this name honoring His Majesty's warship *Fisgard,* 42 guns, which anchored off Fort Nisqually for several months. In 1849 Anderson Island was known briefly, too, under the name Wallace Island—honoring an American named Leander Wallace who was killed that year during Chief Patkanim's attack on Fort Nisqually.

Drayton Passage which lies immediately northwest of Anderson Island, separating Anderson Island from Toandos Peninsula, is named in honor of Joseph Drayton, one of three civilian artists and draftsmen of the Wilkes Expedition of 1841. During that summer Drayton found time to accompany the Hudson Bay Company's annual canoe express up the Columbia on the first leg of its transcontinental trip over the Rockies to York Factory on Hudson's Bay.

Leading the canoe flotilla of that year was colorful, barrel-chested Peter Kene Ogden, explorer of perhaps more territory in the west than any other person. In 1829–1830 Mr. Ogden led trappers the length of California all the way to Baja California's gulf before returning to Fort Vancouver. In his narrative of 1841 Wilkes records that Ogden's nine canoes were manned by sixty French-Canadian voyageurs "dressed in their gayest feathers and ribans etc." and carrying in their flotilla thirty tons of beaver pelt on the two thousand mile trip.

After more than two months of travel along streams, interrupted by frequent portages, the pelt reached Hudson's Bay. As usual, it was loaded aboard HBC sailing ships and carried to England where, in London, it was made into beaver hats, then worn by all stylish Europeans.

When Ogden's fur brigade reached Walla Walla, artist Drayton took leave of it, then, riding mostly on horseback, he returned to Puget Sound and to the USS *Vincennes*, still lying at anchor closeby Anderson Island. Most of the remainder of that summer Mr. Drayton was engaged in sketching the native Indians, their costumes and artifacts for inclusion in the voluminous Wilkes Report submitted to the United States Congress upon the expedition's return to New York City.

Alexander Caulfield Anderson (1814–1884) after whom Anderson Island takes its name, was born in India, the son of a British army officer. Major Anderson retired from the British army in India then engaged in raising indigo on a plantation he owned near Bengal. It was here young Anderson was raised, until at age eighteen he was sent back to England where he was given his schooling. He then joined the Hudson's Bay Company in Canada.

During his twenty-three years with the HBC, Anderson served as officer-in-charge of many fur trade posts, most of them in remote parts of today's British Columbia, which was then called New Caledonia. Anderson's Indian name was *S'gatch Poose* (Scar on the Cheek). One of the more famous of his adventures in this wild region, inhabited only by Indians, was the trip he made in 1853 from Fort Edmonton (in present Alberta) westward over the Rockies by way of Jasper House and Tete Jaune to Stuart Lake, west of today's city of Prince George. He accomplished this trip in forty-six days despite temperatures of 40° below zero encountered most of the way.

In 1854 Mr. Anderson was offered by his superiors the rank of chief factor in these northerly regions but he declined, preferring instead to retire from the Hudson's Bay Company with the rank of chief trader. Before his death Mr. Anderson served as postmaster of the city of Victoria, also as its collector of customs. He was an expert on Indian customs, beliefs, and culture. In retirement Mr. Anderson also wrote several important books on Indian lore.

For many years the Anderson name was perpetuated after his death by a famous side-wheel steamboat which was named for Chief Trader Anderson's lovely daughter, Eliza Anderson. This craft made regular runs between Fort Nisqually and Victoria in British Columbia, stopping along the way at numerous isolated settlements along the shores of Puget Sound. The then-glamorous vessel was the area's only connection with the outside world. Both upon approaching and departing these lonely spots it was customary for the *Eliza Anderson's* captain to play tunes on a steam-calliope with which the vessel was equipped, "Yankee Doodle" being a favorite; that is, except for the residents of Victoria. The Canadian residents of this community abhorred the tune.

One Fourth of July, in fact, when the *Eliza Anderson* chanced to be tied up at the dock in front of Victoria's government building—it being a time when the heated dispute was at its height over the question of whether England or the United States owned nearby San Juan Island— the mayor of Victoria, tired of hearing Yankee Doodle rendered over and over, ordered the little steamboat to leave the dock and put out immediately to sea. After the rendition of several more Yankee Doodles, the *Eliza Anderson's* skipper complied with the mayor's order. But then, just outside Victoria Harbor's entrance, presumably in international waters, he then continued playing the obnoxious tune for the remainder of the day and into the night.

AUBURN (J-8)

The pastoral felicity portrayed by Oliver Goldsmith in his famous poem titled "The Deserted Village" in 1777 scarcely resembles the industrial activity of the valley in which Puget Sound's city of Auburn now lies, ten miles northeast of Tacoma. Also the name Auburn here is in sharp contrast to this town's original name of Slaughter, given to the site in 1855 to honor a local United States Army officer named Slaughter.

In 1852, sailing from New York City, Lieutenant Slaughter departed along with several companies of troops on a ship which took them here to "Oregon country", as the entire Northwest was then known, to fight Indians. Upon his ship's reaching Panama, Slaughter and his fellow soldiers crossed the isthmus on horseback to the Pacific side, then boarded another ship which took them to the Columbia River's mouth where they disembarked. Among the other soldiers accompanying Lieutenant Slaughter on this trip was another army shavetail, Ulysses S. Grant. Upon reaching the Columbia, Grant was assigned duty at Fort Vancouver but Slaughter continued on to Puget Sound where he was assigned duty at Fort Steilacoom. In the memoirs which Grant wrote in later years, following his experiences as commander-in-chief of the Union Army in the Civil War and later as president of the United States, he recalls of his trip via Panama to the Northwest as follows:

> In our regiment there was a Lieutenant Slaughter who was very liable to seasickness . . . I remember him well . . . the picture of despair. At last he broke out "I wish I had taken my father's advice, he wanted me to go into the Navy; if I had done so I should not have had to go to sea so much" . . . Poor Slaughter! It was his last sea voyage. He was killed by the Indians in Oregon.

In October, 1855, the Indians living east of the Cascade Range, being angry over white men invading their lands in search of gold, went on the warpath. Later that month the Indian unrest spread to the Indians around Puget Sound. On 30 October 1855, shots rang out in White River Valley where today's city of Auburn stands. They were fired through the window of a log cabin here in the valley where the Harvey Jones family were residing. While seated at the table inside his cabin, Mr. Jones was killed instantly. His wife, rushing out through the cabin door, also was killed; not before, however, she was able to tell the Jones' two small children to flee.

Thanks to a friendly Indian known to the whites as Tom, the same Tom Kitsap after whom Kitsap County takes its name, they escaped. Hidden under a bear skin rug, Tom Kitsap paddled them in his canoe down the White and Duwamish rivers to the safety of a village called Seattle. The whites in the valley then fled, some to blockhouses hastily erected for their protection, others to Fort Steilacoom, the army post which then stood where the city of this same name now stands.

It was at that time that Lieutenant Slaughter, by then fully recovered from his seasick trip, was dispatched with fifty soldiers to stalk and shoot down Indians. On November twenty-sixth, Slaughter and his men were marching through the rain-drenched forests about fifty miles east of the present Auburn. One of Slaughter's men left us the following description of the events which followed:

> Darkness came . . . Lieutenant Slaughter found a small cabin in an opening in the woods . . . We were all drenched to the skin as we stacked rifles and built a large fire of fence rails around which the soldiers were standing to dry . . . Lieutenant Slaughter was sitting in a nearby log cabin when the Indians fired a volley . . . killing Lieutenant Slaughter

instantly. He made no sound save the sharp intaking of his breath and fell over dead . . . The men ran out and kicked the fires apart. (Denny, A.A. *Pioneer Days on Puget Sound,* Seattle, 1868)

In 1884, in recognition of the efforts of this brave officer, the founders of today's city named their community Slaughter in his honor. With the passage of time, however, the citizens of Slaughter became sensitive to the connotations of the word; particularly when a hotel was built here calling itself "Slaughter House". The more squeamish residents, at this point, decided this was enough. In vain did the old-timers resist the suggestion that their name be changed, but by this time a new "upstart element" had gained the upper hand. The poem from which today's city derives its name goes:

> Sweet Auburn, loveliest village of the plain.
> Where health and plenty cheered the labouring swain,
> Where parting spring its earliest visit paid,
> And parting summers' lingering blooms delayed.

B

BAINBRIDGE ISLAND (H-8)

The first whites to set foot on this nine-mile-long island located eight miles west of Seattle were English explorers of His Majesty's Ship *Discovery,* 330 tons, a little over one year out of Falmouth, England. On 19 May 1792, Captain George Vancouver dropped anchor off Bainbridge Island's south end. On the following morning he landed with some of his crew on the grassy fields immediately westward of Restoration Point past which today ferries constantly ply between Seattle and Bremerton. Here the evening before, he had seen from the deck of his ship large numbers of Indians engaged in some sort of agricultural activity. Now he found them still so engaged. He learned that they were digging into the ground with curved sticks for camas bulbs, a root used as a staple of their diet.

Obviously the Indians were awed by Vancouver and his "giant canoe with the great white wings," never having seen a sailing ship before. By offering them small gifts he gained their friendliness. They responded by offering to the strange whites "refreshments which were very palatable," as Vancouver records. In the afternoon seven canoes full of these Indians put out from their encampment to repay his visit. Eighty more Indians, Vancouver continues, also paddled out to the ship from a point across the water due east of Restoration Point, today called Alki Point. From tiny Blake Island, situated scarcely a mile south of the *Discovery's* anchorage came still more Indians in canoes, causing Vancouver's 100-foot long ship to be completely surrounded with curious Indians.

Bainbridge Island itself was named in 1841 by the U.S. naval officer Charles Wilkes who led his exploring expedition to the Pacific Northwest in the summer of 1841 after many months of exploration in Australia, New Zealand and other islands of the South Seas. Wilkes named Bainbridge Island after William Bainbridge (1774–1833). The American navy was very weak when Bainbridge first joined it. He suffered considerable embarrassment, therefore, at the hands of high-handed Barbary Coast rulers, particularly during the Tripolitan war of 1803 when he and his ship *Philadelphia* were captured. Through a daring raid by a fellow-officer Stephen Decatur, Bainbridge's ship was burned—thereby preventing its use by the Tripolitans—but Bainbridge himself was held prisoner by the Tripolitans until the war's conclusion in 1815.

All was forgiven by the American public in December, 1812, when in a battle off the coast of Brazil, Captain Bainbridge won a remarkable victory over His Majesty's Ship *Java,* 54 guns. The battle lasted two hours and left the British ship a complete wreck with forty-eight sailors dead and one hundred two wounded. Bainbridge's ship on this occasion was the USS *Constitution,* a 44-gun frigate whose subsequent string of victories, as well as this one, prompted the poet Oliver Wendell Holmes to enshrine the vessel in history, its name *Old Ironsides.*

As Commodore Wilkes sailed his ship *Vincennes* into Puget Sound in 1841 he sprinkled names in addition to this one. Port Madison, which is formed by the north shore of Bainbridge Island and the projection of Kitsap Peninsula to the north, he named after the fourth President of the United States, James Madison. Simultaneously he called Port Madison's north entrance Point Jefferson after the second U.S. President, Thomas Jefferson, and to the point guarding Port Madison's south entrance he gave the name of Madison's successor in the White House, President Monroe.

It was at this time that Wilkes surveyors discovered that Bainbridge Island was in fact an island, the narrow waterway separating it from the mainland being Agate Passage, a name which Wilkes chose to honor Mr. Alfred T. Agate, the expedition's artist. In a day when there was no photograph, Mr. Agate was indispensable in capturing for the record the many sights and persons encountered by Wilkes during his circumnavigation of the globe.

Commodore Wilkes, who gave so many of Bainbridge Island's place-names, was the same Wilkes who twenty years later provoked the famous international incident remembered as "the Trent Affair." In 1861, at the outbreak of the Civil War, Wilkes was placed in command of the USS *Jacinto* with orders to search for and capture a Confederate cruiser named the *Sumter,* then operating in the West Indies. While doing so Wilkes intercepted the British mail steamer *Trent* enroute from Havana to Saint Thomas. On this British vessel were sailing two Confederate commissioners, Senators Mason and Slidell, accredited by the Confederates to England and France. Since Wilkes' seizure of them took place on the high seas, a diplomatic crisis followed. President Lincoln was greatly embarrassed by this act, for he feared as a result of it that England, until now neutral in the Civil War, might now declare war on the United States. Recognizing Wilkes' act as an improper one, he ordered him to surrender the commissioners to President Jefferson Davis of the Confederacy, thereby hoping to prevent England's entry into the conflict.

Bainbridge Island's settlement called Winslow, on Eagle Harbor (where today's ferry boats dock transporting commuters to and from Seattle) is named after the son named Winslow of the Hall family, the founders of this community. The Halls were owners and operators of a marine and shipbuilding railway here. Port Blakely, lying inside Restoration Point's northerly side, used to be Puget Sound's leading seaport in the 1880s and 1890s for shipping lumber. Here stood at that time the largest sawmill in the world. Twelve hundred men worked here daily. Ships from all over the world awaited their turn to enter Port Blakely to load up with lumber. As viewed from this vantage point, Port Blakely itself appeared as "a forest of ships' masts," records one of its early settlers.

The Blakely, after whom Port Blakely received its name from Wilkes, is the same for whom Blakely Island in the San Juans, just north of Bainbridge Island, is named. During the War of 1812, Master Commandant Blakely, in command of the USS *Wasp,* captured six British ships in the English Channel within a period of two weeks.

In the past, confusion has existed between Johnstone Blakely and the person after whom Blake Island, located two miles south of the southern tip of Bainbridge Island, is named. In the summer of 1841 when Wilkes named Blake Island he failed to identify the person for whom this honor was intended. It seems likely, however, that he had in mind at this time a fellow naval officer in the U.S. navy, George Smith Blake. In early 1838 when Wilkes' around-the-world expedition was being organized, George Smith Blake was one of those officers, like Wilkes, who was being considered by the secretary of the navy to command this much-sought-after project. When Wilkes was chosen for the command of it in preference to Blake, he asked Blake to serve under him, but was refused.

According to Indian tradition it was on tiny Blake Island, lying here opposite Seattle, that Chief Sealth, after whom the city is named, was born circa 1786. When the first white explorer Vancouver anchored his warship *Discovery* between Blake Island and Bainbridge Island's Restoration Point in May, 1792, Chief Schweabe, young Seattle's father, is said to have allowed his young son to travel with him by canoe from Blake Island out to Vancouver's "giant canoe" to pay "the great white chieftain" a visit.

During the week in which Vancouver's *Discovery* was anchored here closeby Blake Island, Captain Vancouver records that the Blake Island Indians killed a deer. Bringing the meat of this animal by canoe to HMS *Discovery,* Vancouver paid the Blake Islanders for doing so a whole sheet of copper, which the Indians regarded as a most generous reward. It was a portion of this deer meat, made into pasties, which Captain Vancouver enjoyed with his accompanying whites, during the picnic which the explorer held on the shores of Commencement Bay shortly after this.

Also accompanying Chief Schweabe and his young son, Seattle, on this historic visit to Captain Vancouver's ship was Chief Kitsap, another leader of the Suquamish Indians, after whom today's Kitsap County receives its name.

On May 29, Captain Vancouver, having completed his survey of lower Puget Sound, declared a holiday. This was to mark not only the successful survey of every twist and turn of these waters never before seen by white men, but also to celebrate a famous holiday back in England commemorating the date 29 May 1660, when King Charles II, known as The Merrie Monarch, returned from years of exile in France to end the Cromwellian Protectorate. Thousands of gazers, it is said, stood on the white cliffs of Dover, to welcome him back. In commemoration of this event Vancouver gave to the promontory located at Bainbridge Island's southeasternmost point the name Restoration Point.

BAKERS BAY (N-3)

The Columbia River's entrance is guarded by a sandbar which in early times presented a great hazard to sailing ships. The first white man of record to risk his ship by crossing it was Captain Robert Gray of Rhode Island in his ship *Columbia.* Gray anchored in Bakers Bay which lies at the north side of the Columbia's entrance, just inside Cape Disappointment. The question of whether the mysterious Captain James Baker, an Englishman, after whom this bay is named, may have discovered the Columbia River even before the American Gray did so, still bothers historians.

A native of England and an ex-slave trader, Captain Baker operated his ship *Jenny* between Africa's west coast and Barbados for years before coming to the Pacific Northwest to engage, like Captain Gray, in the fur trade. At Nootka, capital of the northwest's fur trade, located on Vancouver Island, Captain Baker met the famous British naval officer and explorer, Captain George Vancouver in the summer of 1792. Vancouver was at the time of their meeting about to sail for the Sandwich Islands via Monterey. Since, as he alleged to Vancouver, Baker was also about to set sail and was proceeding directly back to England, he requested of Vancouver that the explorer take aboard his ship *Discovery* two Hawaiian girls whom the *Jenny's* crew had acquired months ago in the Sandwich Islands, in order to return them to their homes.

Captain Vancouver assented to this request, and enroute southward down the coastline from Nootka toward Monterey, sailing his ship *Discovery* in company with the smaller ship of his expedition, the *Chatham,* Commander William Broughton commanding, Vancouver conceived the idea of making a crossing of the sandbar guarding the entrance to the Columbia which the Yankee Robert Gray had discovered less than six months prior to this time. Anxious to claim the Columbia River for England, Vancouver held the belief that Gray never entered the Columbia River itself but only a salt water bay inside, beyond which, upriver the real Columbia River's mouth lay. After attempting in his own ship without success to cross the sandbar, Vancouver sent his assistant Broughton in the *Chatham* to enter the river. The latter was successful in getting inside.

Here, much to his surprise, Broughton found in the bay which now bears his name Captain Baker himself, his ship *Jenny* at anchor; the same Baker who presumably long since had departed for England. Feigning total unawareness of the discrepancy of his earlier allegations to Vancouver, he was blithely engaged in fur trading with the local Indians as if he never had a thought of returning home to England. After successfully performing a ceremony upstream claiming that he (not the American Captain Gray) was the discoverer of the Columbia, Broughton returned to Bakers Bay to find Captain Baker still here. Being obviously more familiar with the local waters than Broughton, Baker then showed Broughton the way out to sea through the river's sandbar. Then their two vessels parted company.

Later, Broughton recalled that during their conversations together back in the bay, Baker had advised him of having made still another entry into the Columbia ". . . earlier that year." Historians have speculated ever since that perhaps Baker's alleged earlier entry may have taken place prior to May 11 when the American Gray made his entry. It was against this background that Bakers Bay received its name.

BELLEVUE (H-9)

Bellevue lies on the eastern shore of eighteen mile-long Lake Washington. Today those residents of Bellevue whose scene of work lies across the lake in Seattle sometimes complain bitterly of traffic difficulties imposed by bridges across the lake, often blocked by auto accidents. The name Bellevue is derived from the French equivalent, describing the beautiful view which the residents of Bellevue enjoy both to the east where the long line of snow-capped peaks known as the Cascade Range loom in the distance with Sammamish Lake in the foreground, and to the west across Lake Washington of the majestic snow-capped Olympic Mountains.

The founder of Bellevue was Mr. Aaron Mercer, a member of the same Mercer family who founded Seattle. When Aaron claimed free homestead land (640 acres) where Bellevue now stands in August, 1869, cougars roamed the deep woods where skyscrapers now stand. For years thereafter only occasionally did picnickers or rock hunters row or paddle their boats across the waters from Seattle in order to roam the beach along the Bellevue shore.

Bellevue's history however can be traced back to the night of January 25, 1856. War-painted Indians, an estimated 150 of them, assembled on Lake Washington's east side, immediately south of today's downtown Bellevue. Then under the cover of darkness they paddled across Lake

Washington in their canoes to the foot of Capitol Hill in Seattle, the slopes of this prominence then completely covered with a forest of trees. At this time Seattle's population was scarcely two hundred men, women, and children. They lived over the crest of Capitol Hill along the shores of Elliott Bay.

Ever since early October of the previous year when Indians fired through the windows of the Harvey Jones family home in White River Valley, south of Bellevue, and killed Jones and his wife, the residents of Seattle had been expecting trouble with the Indians from east of the mountains. Indeed, on this particular night when the Indians paddled across the lake to attack their settlement, most of the male members of Seattle were away, engaged in protecting white settlers to the south where further trouble with the Indians was being experienced. East of the Cascade Range, Yakima Indians had been on the rampage for weeks, angered as they were at white men invading their lands to hunt for gold.

Probably some of these Indians who climbed Capitol Hill that night were Yakimas. In general Puget Sound Indians seemed friendly. But Seattleites were afraid. From his headquarters at Victoria on Vancouver Island, Governor Douglas of the Hudson's Bay Company had responded generously to Seattleites request for help. He dispatched a load of muskets aboard his steamboat, *Beaver*, to Seattle which arrived the day before this.

A New England-type blockhouse was by now erected where Seattle's First and Cherry Streets now stand. Plans by which the women and children would flee here in case of Indian attack were complete. Anchored in Elliott Bay, Seattle's harbor immediately west of the village, the USS *Decatur*, Captain Guert Gansevoort in command, lay at anchor.

Early on the morning of the twenty-sixth, the Indians from the east side of Lake Washington where Bellevue now stands, had landed on the opposite shore, beached their canoes and climbed stealthily before daylight through the dense forest to the top of Capitol Hill. Seattleites awoke that morning to the thunder of the USS *Decatur's* guns which were lobbing shells over the villagers, the Indians having deployed during the night in an arc around the city.

Terrified by the thunderous noise and of the shells which landed before exploding, the Indians retreated back into the forest. It was a narrow escape for the whites. Had the attack taken place two days before, they would have found Captain Gansevoort's ship careened on the beach, having a hole in its bottom repaired following a grounding in the waters off Elliott Bay. It is theorized that, in launching the attack, the Indians had hoped, due to the ship's helplessness from the grounding, to capture its powder magazine supplies, then to push southward past Seattle in order to seize Fort Steilacoom, a U.S. Army post which recently had been established.

Probably the first whites to roam the site where Bellevue now stands were hunters from Seattle. They came across Lake Washington here by rowboat to hunt cougars which still roamed the woods around Aaron Mercer's homestead site. Near Yarrow Point, just north of the Evergreen Point Floating Bridge's eastern terminus, still stood an Indian longhouse when Mr. Mercer took up residence here. Each week Aaron rowed across Lake Washington to the village of Seattle for his store supplies.

Railroads were the talk of everyone at this time, the chief point of discussion being to what site on the shores of Puget Sound the Northern Pacific's oncoming transcontinental railroad tracks would be laid. Seattleites aspired to achieving this honor; indeed its inhabitants expected to become this terminus, for the lowest opening through which to lay tracks through the Cascades was Snoqualmie Pass, and Seattle lay to the west of it. Doubtless, Aaron too, in choosing the site of Bellevue for his home envisioned these tracks passing by his land. Wherever the tracks were laid, land values boomed.

Not until 1873 were Puget Sounders apprised of the transcontinental railroad's choice of Tacoma for its salt water terminus. When the Northern Pacific refused even to lay a spur line from Tacoma to Seattle, doubtlessly Aaron, as well as all Seattleites, were keenly disappointed. So angry in fact were Seattlites over this news that they decided to lay their own railroad tracks eastward over the mountains to connect with the Union Pacific Railroad which was rapidly approaching Walla Walla. However, in order to do this they needed money, and when huge coal deposits were discovered just four miles south of Aaron's claim at a site called Newcastle, doubtlessly he was overjoyed when Seattleites then built tracks to these mines.

It was not, however, until 1903 that Bellevue got its own railroad. It was called the Washington Belt Line and it was intended not only to serve the budding community called Bellevue but also to serve a steel mill then being planned for erection at the site on Lake Washington north of Bellevue where Kirkland now stands. By this time Bellevue had become connected with Seattle by side-wheel steamboats and it was by this means that commuters between Bellevue and Seattle traveled.

The Mercer Island Bridge connecting Bellevueites with Seattle was completed in 1940, and in 1963 an Evergreen Floating Bridge also connected the two cities.

BELLINGHAM (C-8)

England and Spain were rivals in the Pacific Northwest when in July, 1791, Jose Maria Narvaez discovered Bellingham Bay, seventy miles north of Seattle. He christened it *Seno de Gaston* (Bay of Gaston), naming it after a fellow naval officer who at this time was based near Acapulco, the headquarters for the Spanish navy in the New World. The following June, Captain George Vancouver of the British navy arrived at Bellingham Bay, and he christened it by its present name; this in honor of the man who had been responsible for preparing the Vancouver expedition for its year-long trip here from Falmouth, England, namely William Bellingham, a knight and the chief accountant of the British navy.

The rise of Napoleon in Europe caused both Spain and England to lose interest in the remote part of the world called the Pacific Northwest, preoccupied as these nations were in defending themselves back in Europe against this conqueror. Particularly did the number of English ships sailing these Northwest's coasts diminish, and Yankee ships appeared here in increasing numbers. The harbor from which they operated was called Nootka. It is now deserted, but around 1800 it was visited by sailing ships from all over the world.

In 1844 an American fur trading schooner named the *Platypus* was anchored in the harbor of Nootka (located on the west coast of Vancouver Island) when local Indians attacked the vessel, surrounding it in their canoes and causing the *Platypus's* skipper to weigh anchor hastily and proceed to sea. Inadvertently in his haste he left behind one of the crew, Mr. Robert Jarman, who chanced to be ashore at the time. For the next four years Jarman was held captive by the Nootka Indians.

In 1848 Governor Sir James Douglas (1803–1877), then chief factor of the Hudson Bay Company's trading post at Victoria, hearing of Jarman's plight, arranged for his release by paying the Nootka Indians a ransom of thirty-two blankets, thereby creating the nickname by which Jarman was known for the rest of his life, Blanket Bill. Soon after his rescue, Blanket Bill arrived at the site of today's city of Bellingham where, after falling in love with a local Indian girl, he took up residence with her at nearby Samish Lake. Jarman then prospected for gold in California followed by a visit to Chile and also to the Sandwich Islands, for he was indeed not sedentary by nature.

During the Indian attack upon the village of Seattle in January, 1856, he served as an Indian interpreter aboard the USS *Decatur* which drove away the Indians. In later years Blanket Bill returned briefly to his native home back in England, then retired to live with his niece, Mrs. William Manning at Ferndale, a town located just northwest of Bellingham. Mrs. Manning describes Blanket Bill at this time, age ninety-two, taking daily dips, both in summer and winter, in the local waters of glacier-fed Nooksack River.

Generally regarded as the founder of Bellingham however, was William R. Pattie who in 1852 landed in the vicinity of today's city while seeking spar and piling timber to ship back to his home base in San Francisco. The discovery by Pattie at this time of a rich vein of coal caused him to decide to remain here. Following Pattie's development of coal mines here, more whites arrived, among them Henry Roeder who built a lumber mill closeby Bellingham Bay, thus attracting still more settlers.

Always, however, were these pale-faced newcomers fearful of the Haidah Indians, visitors from nearby Vancouver Island. Traveling in fifty-foot-long canoes, their faces daubed with war paint, they were formidable fighters, on one occasion even attacking Roeder's recently built steamboat. Later, the Haidahs even attempted to board and capture a U.S. navy ship, the *Massachusetts* while it was anchored at nearby Port Gamble. When the founding fathers of Bellingham additionally began to be plagued by attacks from Yakima Indians from east of the Cascades, they prepared a petition to Governor Stevens, head of the recently organized Washington Territory that a blockhouse be erected locally to protect them.

In response to this request Captain George Pickett (1825–1875) arrived here. Possessed ". . . of a head of flowing brown hair, gray eyes, a small mustache, a magnetic smile, and a powerful figure," as one localite describes him, he was the same person who not long after this was promoted to general in the Confederate Army, and who boldly led his four thousand five hundred troops against Union forces during the Battle of Gettysburg. Three-fourths of General Pickett's troops were lost in the charge which Pickett led upon Union positions at Cemetery Ridge. It was an unsuccessful one, but Pickett has since been remembered as a great military leader in the effort. Captain Pickett was already a national hero, moreover, when he assumed command of the Bellingham blockhouse. In 1847 he had achieved national praise when he was the first soldier to gain the heights of Chapultapec, marking the turning point of the Mexican War.

Soon after taking command of Company D, Ninth Infantry here at Fort Bellingham, Pickett married a local Indian girl from nearby Semiahmoo, today called Blaine. In July, 1859, the British in Vancouver Island's city of Victoria began insisting that little San Juan Island, located closeby Bellingham, belonged to England, not to the United States. General Harney, recently having assumed command of U.S. army forces in the northwest, selected Pickett to straighten things out. Harney ordered Pickett and his sixty-eight soldiers at Fort Bellingham to proceed by boat to Griffin Bay, at San Juan Island's southern end and there to build fortifications to assert U.S. control.

Doubtlessly Pickett received quite a shock, soon after he had complied with Harney's order to see a fleet of five British warships anchor closeby his new fort and to point their guns at Pickett and his men. Pickett responded. "Even if fifty thousand British Marines are landed to take us," he is reported to have advised the commander of the British warships, ". . . we will fight to the last man." Fortunately cool headedness on the part of Pickett's superiors and particularly by Admiral Robert L. Baynes, commander of the British navy's Pacific fleet, avoided bloodshed.

In 1861 when news of the Confederate bombardment of Fort Sumter reached Bellingham, Captain Pickett, a loyal Southerner, resigned his commission in the U.S. army and returned east. Left behind at Bellingham was Pickett's part-Indian son, James Tilton Pickett, his

Indian mother having died soon after the boy's birth. For the rest of his life, Pickett kept in touch with young Jimmy Pickett whose upbringing, as arranged before the general's departure for the Civil War, was delegated to foster parents.

General Pickett, his role against the Union being unforgiven, was barred for years after the war from living in the United States. General Pickett died in impoverished circumstances. Pickett's son, young Jimmy, grew up to be a locally-famous artist. Fourteen years after his father's death however, he too died in poverty, having lived his last years in a Portland waterfront boarding house.

With the discovery of gold on Canada's upper Fraser River in 1858, ten thousand people poured into the region around Bellingham from California and the East. The Fraser Gold Rush was threatening to become as unruly and popular as the one on the Sacramento. From Bellingham the prospectors traced northward across the roadless country leading to Chilliwack on the Fraser River, up which they then traced to boom towns around Barkerville above Williams Lake. The Bellingham area swarmed with outfitters, bartenders, storekeepers, and scalawags.

Wishing to gain control of the pandemonium, British Columbia's Governor James Douglas acted. Providing sternwheelers departing Victoria and ascending the Fraser to the turbulent waters of the Fraser near today's town of Hope, he eliminated Chilliwack and the gruesome trip necessary in reaching this point on the Fraser from Bellingham. Victoria thus became the take-off point for the fortune hunters and Bellingham's prosperity disappeared, but not for long. By 1889 four independent and vigorous towns had sprung up here, namely: Old Whatcom, New Whatcom, Fairhaven, and Seahome, each competing with the others for their share of the local fishing and mineral assets. It was at this time that the name of Vancouver's friend, Lord Bellingham was chosen to designate the amalgamation which took place.

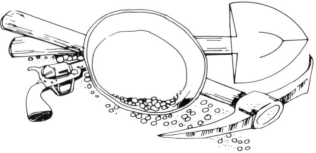

BIRCH BAY (B-7)

The Indians of this harbor, located four miles south of today's Canadian border, had never seen white men before the summer of 1791 when Jose Narvaez, a Spaniard sailing in a thirty-nine-foot schooner named the *Santa Saturnina,* anchored here. Narvaez, prior to reaching here, had been on an extensive sail north of here reaching a latitude of 50° before retreating south down the coast of British Columbia. It still is a mystery that he failed to detect the presence of the Fraser River just north of Birch Bay. Narvaez gave to Birch Bay the name *Punta y Laguna del Garzon* (Point and Lagoon of Herons).

Spain and England both claimed possession over this then-unexplored part of the world; in fact in June, 1792, when Captain George Vancouver of the British navy reached Birch Bay he discovered from the Indians ashore that two Spanish ships had departed the bay just a few hours before the Britisher arrived. These, we know now, were two more Spanish ships, the *Sutil* and the *Mexicana,* their commanders: Dionisio Galiano and Cayetano Valdes respectively.

While his subordinates took astronomical readings on the beach at Birch Bay, so named because of the numerous local trees of this variety, Vancouver himself, rowed by members of the crew, proceeded up the uncharted coastline northward. After passing the site where Blaine, Washington now stands, he too missed discovering that the Fraser River, Canada's mightiest, was flowing into these waters.

Continuing northward past the site where British Columbia's city of Vancouver now stands, they pushed on for about eighty miles before retracing. During the trip they saw "about 17 Indians," Vancouver notes, continuing ". . . they were much more painted than any we had hitherto seen . . . some of their arrows were pointed with slate." He notes, however, that all were "civil and inoffensive in their behavior."

As the Britishers were rowing southward on the morning of June 22 toward Point Grey, where today the University of British Columbia stands, ". . . purposeing there to land and have breakfast," records Vancouver, ". . . we discovered two vessels at anchor under the land . . . a brig and a schooner wearing the colors of Spanish vessels of war." A visit between the personnel of the three vessels followed. Vancouver learned from the Spaniards that, while he had been northward they had already met up with his second ship, the *Chatham,* off Point Roberts. Vancouver continues: ". . . Don Galiano offered us every information, and later sent on board the *Chatham* some milk and cabbages that he had brought from their base at Nootka."

A strange sight ensued two days later, one perhaps unique in the history of exploration. For as agreed during their recent visit together, the rival groups, Vancouver and Broughton in their *Discovery* and *Chatham,* and the two Spanish explorers, Galiano and Valdes in their respective vessels, *Sutil* and *Mexicana,* joined up together, then proceeded in company sailing northward. Little could these rivals have foreseen that thirteen years later Spain and England would be fighting each other in the Battle of Trafalgar.

BLAINE (B-7)

This is the city on Semiahmoo Bay lying just south of the Canadian border closeby Georgia Strait. Quipsters like to allege that the name *semiahmoo* is Indian for "half a cow." The name Blaine dates back to the presidential race of 1892 between the Democratic candidate Grover Cleveland and his Republican opponent James Gillespie Blaine. It is said that the townsfolk then living at today's Blaine agreed to name their town after whomever won this race but that when they awoke on the day after the election to find that their hero, Blaine, had lost, they proceeded to show their fanatical Republicanism by naming their town after him, notwithstanding any promises to the contrary.

Drayton Harbor, the small inlet off Semiahmoo Bay bears the name of Joseph Drayton, an artist who served in Commodore Charles Wilkes' around-the-world expedition which visited these waters in 1841. It was a day when photography had not been developed, so Mr. Drayton's duty while the expedition was visiting Puget Sound that summer was to make sketches of the local Indians, their costumes, and artifacts.

Point Roberts which lies across Boundary Bay to the west of Blaine is named after Captain Henry Roberts of the British navy. Mr. Roberts got his sea legs while understudying the famous Captain James Cook in this great explorer's first three expeditions into the South Seas and around the world. On Cook's final expedition, when Cook met his death in the Sandwich Islands in February, 1779, Roberts was a hero. Gallantly endeavoring to rescue the great explorer from the infuriated natives of Hawaii's Kona Coast, Roberts was seriously wounded in his unsuccessful effort to save Cook's life.

Ten years later the British admiralty chose Roberts to lead his own expedition to the Pacific Northwest with George Vancouver designated to be his second in command. However before the expedition was fully organized, war between England and Spain was about to erupt over the question of which of these two nations owned a remote spot on

Vancouver Island called Nootka. This caused the British admiralty to abandon plans to send Roberts' expedition there, and Roberts was then sent to the West Indies for duty.

Soon after his departure however, the Nootka crisis was peaceably settled and it became desirable to dispatch promptly the expedition which Roberts had organized, but from which he was now absent. Captain George Vancouver was accordingly dispatched in Roberts' place. Thus, by mere chance George Vancouver assumed command of the expedition which was to make him a world-famous explorer. It was he who christened Point Roberts in the summer of 1792.

Point Roberts is indeed a unique part of the United States, owing to the fact that it is surrounded by water on three sides and by Canada on its fourth, the northern side. Thus, American residents of Point Roberts must travel through British Columbia in order to reach the country of which they are citizens. This anomalous situation was brought about by an error on the part of British-American officials surveying the international border past here in 1857.

Boundary Bay, the large body of water separating Point Roberts from Blaine, was first visited by Spanish explorers in 1791. They called it *Ensenada del Engano,* "Bay of Delusion," probably a reference to their disappointment in finding so large a body of water so shallow.

BONNEVILLE DAM (Q-9)

Picture, if you will, a middle-sized man of frank, open expression, dapper though mild in dispossession, quite French in appearance, and you have a picture of Benjamin Louis Eulalie de Bonneville, the person after whom this man-made obstruction in the Columbia River (forty miles upriver of Portland) takes its name. His winning ways chanced to catch the attention of a leading American author of the nineteenth century, Washington Irving, who wrote a book that was a best seller of its day, and served to bring the attention to Americans, then almost all of them living on the east coast, to a new part of the American continent of which prior to this they had no knowledge, namely the Pacific Northwest.

Bonneville was a colorful U.S. army officer and one of the first white men to explore extensively in this hitherto unknown part of America. Born in 1796 in France, Bonneville was brought to the United States in 1810 by the American Revolutionary writer Thomas Paine. He was appointed to the United States Military Academy, with Paine's assistance, as a cadet. He graduated from there in 1815, then was appointed a lieutenant in the army.

In 1824 when France's General Lafayette visited the United States at the invitation of President Monroe, young Bonneville was chosen to accompany him on his tour of America. Upon the conclusion of this trip, Bonneville went to France at Lafayette's invitation to live for several years in the Lafayette home. He then returned to the United States to take up army duty on the western frontier, then a region located scarcely beyond the Mississippi River.

In 1831 Bonneville asked for and was given a year's leave of absence from the army to proceed farther West in order to pursue the life of a fur trader. Bonneville's preparations for this trip were elaborate. Enlisting the financial backing of Alfred Seton, a wealthy New York furrier, it is believed that Seton in turn was able to tap the resources of his friend John J. Astor, one of the wealthiest men in America. Thus young Bonneville was enabled to depart on his venture into the West accompanied by over a hundred veteran fur trappers equipped with most elaborate gear including twenty wagons. The latter were the first wheeled vehicles ever seen in Montana and Wyoming, and they were a particular marvel to the Indians who called them "land canoes." Despite these facilities and three years of effort, Bonneville was not successful in obtaining furs. But probably Bonneville's real goals were other than trapping, though he concealed them as such.

During his three years' effort, Bonneville scouted vast regions of the West, then jointly shared by Great Britain and the United States. He evaluated British military strength in the region and acquired topographical information of value in case of war. So fond of the life in the wilderness did he become that he overstayed his furlough from the army. Declared AWOL, he was court martialled, but nonetheless restored to good standing not long afterward by none other than the president of the United States, Andrew Jackson. In 1853 Bonneville returned to the Columbia River country as commander of Vancouver Barracks, the name of Fort Vancouver for several years after the British relinquished this post following the Oregon Boundary Settlement of 1846.

BREMERTON (H-7)

They called this city (which lies across the waters of Puget Sound, thirteen miles west of Seattle) "Bremer's Town" in 1888 when Mr. William Bremer, a native of Germany (but in this year a prosperous Seattle businessman) heard rumors that the U.S. Congress was about to appropriate large sums of money to build a shipyard across the water where Bremerton now stands. There being no ferry boats, as exist today, to take Mr. Bremer across the water to where the shipyard was rumored to be built, he hastily boarded one of the tiny steamboats which then traveled Puget Sound waters. By this means he reached Port Madison at the north end of Bainbridge Island. Here Bremer disembarked, then set out on foot southward down Bainbridge Island to the entrance to Rich Passage. Here Bremer persuaded an Indian to row him by small boat up Rich Passage and thence to the entrance to Dyes Inlet. On this inlet's south shore he learned that Andrew Williams, a local farmer, owned the land where the U.S. Navy planned to build. Already aware of the sudden importance of his land, Mr. Williams demanded of Mr. Bremer a price even larger than the amount U.S. Congress was appropriating for the whole project.

Gazing into his crystal ball, as it were, the far-sighted Bremer, already envisioning subdividing the property into small lots where the future shipyard's workers would live, decided to pay to farmer Williams his exorbitant price. Thus began what became known as "Bremer's Town" or Bremerton. Mr. Bremer died a wealthy man, in Seattle, December, 1810.

The first white men to view the site where Bremerton now stands were sailors of His Majesty's Ship *Discovery,* commanded by Captain George Vancouver. It was Captain George Vancouver, himself, who, sailing in the *Discovery's* yawl, sailed through Rich Passage (so named later by the American explorer Charles Wilkes) accompanied by Second Lieutenant Joseph Baker (after whom Mount Baker is named) into the extensive waters eastward of Port Orchard on whose shore the city of Bremerton now stands. It was at this time that Vancouver christened Port Orchard, naming it after the ship's clerk, Henry M. Orchard, of his *Discovery.* The date was 19 May 1792. Previous to discovering the site, Captain Vancouver, from his ship's anchorage off the south tip of Bainbridge Island, had discovered by small boat the site where the city of Tacoma now stands.

BREWSTER (F-16)

Left behind in August, 1811, with only a small dog named Weasel for company, Alexander Ross, one of the Northwest's most famous fur trappers, found himself living in a tiny hovel made of driftwood here at the site of Brewster, fifty miles north of Wenatchee where the Okanogan River joins the Columbia. Nearly a month prior to this, Mr. Ross and a fellow trapper, David Stuart, had departed Astoria, the

American fur post downriver of here located where the Columbia River flows into the Pacific.

It was a difficult trip from Astoria upstream, their two leaky canoes paddled by French-Canadian voyageurs. Impressed with the site where Brewster now stands, largely due to the confluence of the two rivers here, Ross and Stuart decided it would be a great place to establish a trading post, to which the Indians might come bringing their furs to exchange with the trade items—beads, buttons, thimbles, etc.—which these traders had brought with them. It was decided that Mr. Ross would remain here alone developing such fur trading possibilities with the local Indians while the remainder of the party, led by Mr. Stuart, would push north up the banks of the Okanogan to investigate trapping possibilities in British Columbia, then called New Caledonia.

Ross and his dog Weasel thus spent the winter of 1811-1812 alone here. In later years Mr. Ross wrote of the experience as follows:

> Only picture to yourself, gentle reader, how I must have felt, alone in this unhallowed wilderness, without a friend or white man within a hundred miles of me, and surrounded by savages who had never seen a white man before. Every day seemed a week, every night a month. I pined, I languished, my head turned gray, and in a brief space of time ten years were added to my age.

Although Stuart and his men were expected to return at the latest by January of the following year, 1812, February passed with no sign of them. It was not until March that they returned.

Even though it was a lonely winter for Mr. Ross, he was proud to report to his colleagues that during their absence up north he had been able to obtain locally a grand total of one thousand five hundred and fifty beaver skins! Exulted Mr. Ross in his book titled *Fur Hunters of the Far West* (Norman, 1956): ". . . these pelt were worth about 2,250 pounds when sold in China . . . and all this for only 35 pounds in trade goods."

Under the name Fort Okanogan, the hovel where Ross spent that winter became a handsome trading post, one over which the American flag flew until December, 1813. At that time, the War of 1812 between Great Britain and the United States having erupted, a British warship arrived at the mouth of the Columbia, and at gunpoint, forced the American post to surrender. As for Messrs. Ross and Stuart, however, this change presented no problem. Both had worked for the British fur company which now took over the former Astoria, renaming it Fort George. They had quit this British company solely because of the higher salaries Mr. Astor offered them. Now they were glad to return to their former employers. Over Fort Okanogan, the Union Jack replaced the Stars and Stripes, but Alexander Ross continued on as officer-in-charge.

Under the British for the next three decades, Fort Okanogan was an important stop along the fur trade routes. Here passed the annual canoe express traveling between Fort Vancouver and the eastern posts of the Hudson's Bay Company at York Factory or Lake Superior. Here, too, the furs harvested in New Caledonia arrived, borne on the backs of long lines of horses, for loading onto the cedar-planked boats—each could carry two and a half tons of furs—to be transported to awaiting ships anchored at the Columbia River's entrance.

When founded in 1896, Brewster was called "Bruster," honoring Mr. John Bruster, formerly of South Dakota. He was the first white to claim land here. In 1862, Brewster became the scene of a gold rush when a strip of sand in the Columbia River nearby, called Rich Bar, yielded large deposits of the precious stuff. Fort Okanogan, long since abandoned, was used by the miners who flocked here by the hundreds. Stripping the historic structure of its wood, they used it for bonfires to keep warm. By 1903, Brewster was a terminus of steamboat service running daily south to Wenatchee. The Columbia and Okanogan Steamboat Company operated for many years.

C

CAMANO ISLAND (F-8)

This island is separated from Stanwood, on the mainland, only by a short bridge. It lies thirty miles north of Seattle. It bears a name which dates back to earliest Puget Sound history. Originally *Camano* was spelled with three *a's* and was the name of a Spanish naval officer. When Senor Jacinto Caamano arrived in the Pacific Northwest, Spain claimed ownership not only of the entire west coast of North America but also of that of South America; indeed of the entire Pacific Ocean. In 1789, Senor Caamano was part of an expedition which Viceroy Antonio Flores dispatched north from San Blas (near present Mazatlan in Mexico) under the command of Estevan Martinez. The expedition's purpose was to hoist the red and yellow colors of Spain over Santa Cruz de Nootka (or Nootka as it appears on modern maps) located 250 miles northwest of Camano Island on Vancouver Island's west side.

Today Nootka is almost deserted, but in Caamano's day it was the capital of the Pacific Northwest. At the height of Spain's power in the Northwest, any non-Spanish ships entering Nootka's harbor, called Friendly Cove, were required to obtain permission of the local Spanish governor in order to drop anchor.

First discovered by Juan Perez in 1774, Nootka was rediscovered by England's famed Captain Cook (1775), then sailing in two ships searching these coasts for the Northwest Passage. By 1787, English ships were visiting Nootka in considerable numbers in order to obtain from the Nootka Indians their precious sea otter pelt. Obtainable from these Indians for cheap gewgaws, such as beads or bits of iron, when sailed to China they could be sold at a hundred dollars apiece. The Nootkan trade flourished.

Meanwhile, the Spanish viceroy in Mexico City was becoming concerned over Russians, then in control of Alaska, who were pushing south down the coast, threatening Spanish sovereignty. The viceroy dispatched a mad Spaniard, named Estevan Martinez, who not only seized several of the British fur traders' ships, but also dispatched the vessels, under Spanish colors, south to San Blas, the Spanish naval headquarters.

War between England and Spain, as a result of this, threatened to erupt. At the last minute, a treaty between the two nations, agreeing to share the base jointly, prevented bloodshed. Meanwhile, a new Spanish governor, Franciso Eliza, replaced Senor Martinez at Nootka. Under Eliza's orders, Senor Caamano sailed his ship *Aranzazu* north into Russian waters to explore and to assert Spanish sovereignty in Alaska. Upon returning from this trip in 1792, Caamano found that during his absence, two high-ranking dignitaries had appeared on the scene, Senor Bodega y Quadra, commander of the Spanish navy in the Pacific, and Captain George Vancouver, dispatched from England by King George III.

These two naval officers had come to arrange the details of how Nootka was to be shared by their two nations under the terms of a Treaty of Nootka, recently signed in Madrid. At this time the Spaniards boasted a non-Indian population of about one hundred and fifty, most of them from Spain and Mexico, but also including Peruvians, Chinese, and Hawaiians who served as laborers.

Also at Nootka, there was a chapel in which three friars held daily services. An infirmary existed to care for the sick. Each morning a bakery oven provided fresh bread. In the village's outbuildings were to be found cows, goats, pigs, and poultry brought here from San Blas. These were much admired by the Nootka Indians, who had never seen such animals before.

The largest of the buildings, of course, was the Spanish governor's mansion, which overlooked the harbor called Friendly Cove. Here, ships from all over the world dropped anchor—Swedish, French, East Indian, and Portuguese, not to mention British and American ones. Among the guests this summer was a youth named John Boit, one of the officers aboard the American ship *Columbia,* and Captain Robert Gray, a fur trader from Rhode Island, being the *Columbia's* skipper. Young Boit has left us a record of this particular evening when, he states, fifty-four guests were in attendance at the Spanish governor's table. During the course of the evening, Boit records, ". . . the solid silver plates on which we ate were sifted five times." Continues the amazed youth: ". . . which makes 270 plates in all. The Dishes, Knifes [sic] and Forks and indeed everything else, was of Silver and always replaced with spare ones. There could be no mistake in this as they never carried the dirty plates or Dishes from the Hall where we dined." (Howay, P.W., *Voyages of the Columbia,* page 411).

The following passage describes events that occurred on 19 September 1792, on the eve of Quadra and Vancouver's departure from Nootka. Although the two had become good friends during their negotiations on behalf of their two governments, they had been unable to reach an agreement. The following is an account written by one of Captain Vancouver's subordinates in which Senor Caamano's temporary assumption of command over Nootka is mentioned:

> . . . On this date Mr. Quadra took his farewell dinner with Capt. Vancouver on board Vancouver's flagship as he intended sailing the next day. Senor Caamano was likewise there. The health of the Spanish and English sovereigns were toasted with great Loalty and accompanied by a salute of 21 guns . . . in the evenin at Quadra's insistence all going ashore & spending an evening in Singing, Music & Dancing . . . and on the following day . . . Seigr. Caamano hoisted his Pendant . . . himself taking up residence in the Government House and becoming Commandante of the place. (*A New Vancouver Journal,* E.S. Meany, Seattle, 1923)

The name Camano Island, spelled with one *a*, was given by Lieutenant Commander Henry Kellett, then surveying Puget Sound for the British navy, in 1847. Kellett evidently preferred the Spanish name for the island to its earlier name of MacDonough's Island, given by the American naval officer Charles Wilkes who surveyed Puget Sound in 1841. Thomas MacDonough (1783-1825) was the American naval hero who stopped the advance of English troops invading the United States in 1814. England had amassed some twenty-five thousand British troops along Canada's border with the state of New York in order to capture Plattsburgh on the western shore of Lake Champlain. Both sides, recognizing in order to capture Plattsburgh that control of this lake was essential, commenced building ships of war. In 1814 with fourteen American ships at his disposal, MacDonough gained a signal victory over the numerically superior British fleet. Congress hailed MacDonough's victory here by promoting him to captain, then the highest rank in the U.S. navy.

On old Spanish charts of Puget Sound, Caamano's name was used to designate the present Admiralty Inlet. They called it *Boca de Caamano.*

CAPE DISAPPOINTMENT (N-2)

This promontory guards the north entrance to the Columbia, the longest river in the Pacific Northwest. Except for the Strait of Juan de Fuca, it is the oldest of the Northwest's place-names. Spanish, English, Russian, and American explorers, attempting to cross the sandbar to enter the waters of the Columbia which lie behind Cape Disappointment, hoped thereby to claim sovereignty over not only this river's lower reaches but also over the vast upper regions which the 1200-mile long stream drains.

First, in 1775, came the twenty-five year old Bruno Heceta, recently arrived at Spain's naval base in lower California from Madrid, where he was a graduate of this nation's naval school. Sailing in his ship *Santiago* from lower California north up the then-mysterious west coasts of America, Heceta was forced to abandon the effort after months at sea when his sailors became ill with scurvy. Heceta did not dare enter the river which today we call the Columbia because if he did so, he records, he feared his sailors were too weak to enable him to exit again. Retreating south down the coast however, he named the Columbia *Rio San Rocque;* Saint Rocque being the saint as listed on the calendar he carried on board his ship for August 17, the date on which he made the discovery.

John Meares, the thirty-two year old English officer who next attempted entry into the Columbia, is remembered in history as a trouble-maker of dubious veracity. He had been allowed by the British navy, as was then quite common during slack periods, to place himself on half pay when he sailed these coasts in order to, he hoped, gain personal wealth through trading with the coastal Indians for their sea otter skins. At the same time he hoped to become famous for discovering land features along these as-yet uncharted coasts.

Taking constant soundings from his tiny ship named the *Felice Adventurer,* Meares saw a white line of breakers from the masthead of this vessel ahead, as he rounded Cape Disappointment. When the waters began to shoal, he hauled out, fearing shipwreck. It was through this incident that the name Cape Disappointment came into being. Meares was fully aware that the Spaniard Heceta had been here before him when he records ". . . we can now assert with safety that there is no such river as the Rio San Rocque as laid down in the Spanish charts." This remark is consistent with other erroneous recordings made by him.

Many other sea captains were to meet with disappointment in attempting to enter the Columbia. Even the great George Vancouver, sailing in HMS *Discovery* five months after Captain Robert Gray's successful effort to enter the river, chose instead to send his second and smaller ship, the *Chatham* to go inside; for shipwreck on these primitive coasts in Vancouver's day meant permanent residence for all hands, if indeed they were not drowned or killed by the natives. Even Captain Gray, in becoming the first to enter the Columbia, did so only after previous unsuccessful attempts to enter.

In 1845, when the long-standing dispute between England and the United States arose in intensity, Cape Disappointment itself came into prominence. For years the English at Fort Vancouver had watched the seemingly ever increasing numbers of Americans arriving on the lower Columbia from their months-long trek from the East over the Rocky Mountains. Land was free for the asking in Willamette Valley closeby, inland of the cape, and England was becoming concerned that prior British settlements here would be overwhelmed by the Americans' superior numbers. By treaty, both the U.S. and England shared equally in possessing the lower Columbia territory, but fears arose that soon the Americans might take the area by sheer numbers. England decided that action must be taken.

A British gunboat, HMS *Modeste,* entered the Columbia and anchored off Fort Vancouver. Also to Puget Sound, where similar fears were arising, the British admiralty dispatched HMS *America,* fifty guns. Fear of war, too, brought new importance to Cape Disappointment with its imposing position overlooking the Columbia River's entrance. Whichever nation controlled this strategic spot, it was believed, would thereby militarily control the entire lower Columbia.

In June, 1845, two British army officers in civilian disguise, posing as carefree hunters and sportsmen, Lieutenants Henry Warre and Mervin Vasavour arrived at Fort Vancouver. They had come here all the way from the London Foreign Office; their orders: to spy and also to organize the mounting of heavy guns atop Cape Disappointment, ones large enough to sink any hostile ships entering the river. To Mr. Peter Skene Ogden, by now retired from his arduous days trapping furs in Snake River country, having replaced Dr. John McLoughlin as the chief factor at Fort Vancouver, was given the task "on behalf of Warre and Vasavour" of secretly gaining title to the site on which the guns would be erected.

As luck would have it, the land was owned by Americans, so Ogden's task was a delicate one. Before he could consummate a deal, however, England and the United States had become friends again; both nations having agreed to divide the Pacific Northwest along the same forty-ninth parallel which now divide Canada and the United States.

CAPE FLATTERY (D-1)

When on March 22, 1778, Captain Cook sailed past this promontory at the south entrance to Puget Sound, he was searching northward in his two ships *Resolute* and *Discovery* for an opening in the coastline which would lead into the Atlantic Ocean. A reward of 20,000 pounds awaited him should he find it. Since making his first landfall on these northwest coasts, ones which as yet had not been mapped, he had been sailing northward in bad weather. He records that the site of this cape ". . . flattered us with the hopes of finding a harbour," doubtlessly so as to rest his crews. Thus Captain Cook was prompted to call this promontory "Cape Flattery." Cook, of course, had heard the tale of Juan de Fuca who alleged that in sailing in this same latitude had found an opening leading into an "inland sea." Of this, Cook writes ". . . we saw nothing like it nor is there the least possibility that any such thing ever existed." Doubtless if he had known that Puget Sound and Georgia Strait lay to the east he would have entered.

Captain Cook then stood out to sea again and when he next approached land he did, indeed, find a harbor—in waters today known as Nootka Sound on the west coast of present Vancouver Island, about 180 miles northwest of Cape Flattery. Here he anchored in an inlet, today called Friendly Cove, received by Indians whose ". . . faces were bedaubed with red and black Paint and Grease," he writes, ". . . the Dress of some being a loose skin thrown round their Shoulders, and which was not seemingly intended to hide their private parts." After holding a ceremony ashore here claiming possession of all the Northwest for England, Cook chanced to come upon one Nootka Indian (Nootka being the name of the place adjacent to Friendly Cove) who was wearing two silver spoons, which he found to be of Spanish manufacture. The incident proved large in the controversy which arose eleven years later over which nation, Spain or England, was entitled to own the Pacific Northwest. Four years before Cook's arrival here at Nootka, a Spanish naval officer named Juan Perez (an ex-Manila galleon skipper, dispatched north by the Spanish viceroy in Mexico to spy upon the Russians in Alaska) had stopped at Nootka, and during this visit he had presented these spoons to a native.

Captain Cook, with his two ships, remained at Nootka for nearly a month preparing for the push north into Arctic waters, where he believed the Northwest Passage would be found. During his stay at Nootka, Cook's sailors acquired over a thousand sea otter skins, a commodity which the Nootkans possessed in such abundance that they roofed their houses and paved their walkways with them. When the expedition reached Bering Strait it was these furs which kept them warm. Freezing of the ice prevented Cook from continuing his exploration. Accordingly, he sailed south to Hawaii where, as is well known, he met his death, stoned to death by natives of these islands.

His expedition, however, continued on westward back to England. When it was anchored in Macao, the sailors were amazed to find that the Nootka furs, now well used, were eagerly sought by Chinese merchants there at a price the equivalent of a hundred dollars apiece. Recalling how the Nootkas had relinquished them for mere bits of iron, a nail, or worthless trinkets, the expedition's sailors nearly mutinied, so anxious some were to return to Nootka and obtain more.

Word spread of the Nootkas copious supply of furs, and of the opportunity for profit in selling Northwest furs in the Orient. Soon ships from all over the world were anchoring in Nootka's harbor of Friendly Cove, and it was by this means that the civilized world became aware of the Pacific Northwest.

Aiding in this development was one James Ledyard (1751–1789) who, during Cook's stay at Nootka, had been serving as corporal of the Royal Marine Guard aboard Cook's flagship, the *Resolution*. When the American Revolution began, young Ledyard, a native of Connecticut and former student of Dartmouth College before joining the British navy, decided rather than fight his own countrymen, to desert the British navy and return to Nootka to get rich. A quixotic individual, he then decided to travel across Europe, Russia, and Siberia to Petropavlosk in order to get there.

While seeking funds to accomplish this, it so happened in Paris he made the acquaintance of Thomas Jefferson, then U.S. minister to France. Jefferson was quite taken with Ledyard, even to the extent of assisting him financially for the eastward overland trip. Although Ledyard reached Petrapavlosk, he was unable to find a ship to take him on the last leg to Nootka. Nevertheless, history credits him with arousing the interest of Jefferson in this then-remote part of America. Before the Lewis and Clark party interested Jefferson in helping them, Ledyard made the trip across the Rockies alone. To Ledyard was great credit given for President Jefferson's sending Lewis and Clark on their famous trek to the Pacific Ocean.

CATHLAMET (N-5)

A frequent visitor to this town, located on the Columbia River twenty miles west of Longview, was Ulysses S. Grant in the 1850s. At this time he was a young army officer stationed at Fort Vancouver. So lonely at the prolonged separation from his recently-wed wife back East, he was thinking of resigning his army commission. Grant used to visit

Cathlamet on weekends to escape the monotony of army life at nearby Vancouver Barracks.

With view to raising some money by which to bring his wife here to be with him, Grant managed to persuade his commanding officer at Fort Vancouver, Colonel Benjamin de Bonneville (another West Point graduate) to loan him some money at two percent interest, by which Grant chartered a schooner to ship ice to San Francisco. Another hairbrained scheme, also concocted by the future Civil War hero and president of the United States, was growing potatoes and raising chickens at Fort Vancouver; neither of them producing enough money to bring his wife west.

Grant resigned his commission in the army in 1854. Not until 1861 did he return to military service to become the hero of Vicksburg, and the eighteenth president of the United States.

The first white to visit Cathlamet's site was the explorer William Clark who in the winter of 1805-1806 was living at nearby Fort Clatsop. Anticipating that his party of men would need another canoe for their forthcoming return home the ensuing spring, Clark came here to procure from the Cathlamets a particularly handsome one which he had seen during an earlier visit. Unable to make a deal, so meager were the trading goods he had to offer, Clark records that the Cathlamets advised him that they never traded such a valuable item except in exchange for wives. Several weeks later, the need for the canoe by now considered greater, Captain Clark's partner, Meriwether Lewis arrived to make a deal, but he too was rebuffed. In desperation he then offered the Indians at Cathlamet his own lace-cuffed official U.S. Army dress uniform, one which he had packed all the way across the Rockies from St. Louis. Later, in confiding to his journal about the transaction which then proved successful, Captain Clark records: "I think the U'States are in justice indebted to Captn Lewis another uniform coat for that which he disposed on this occasion, it is but little worn."

Cathlamet originally was called Birnie's Retreat, after James Birnie (1800–1864) who was an official of the Hudson's Bay Company post called Fort George, located across the Columbia opposite today's Cathlamet, where the city of Astoria now stands. When Birnie retired from Fort George he came across the Columbia to this site overlooking the river with his Indian wife and eleven children.

Also included in the Birnie family was an old Indian slave named George, whom Mr. Birnie, while on a trip to Puget Sound, purchased from the Indians there for the sum of two dollars and fifty cents. Customarily, captains of sailing ships and steamboats, in processing up the Columbia River past Birnie's Retreat, looked forward to a unique ceremony which Indian George performed from the heights where today's town of Cathlamet stands. Using a flat which he had constructed of red white and blue cloth representing the American colors, the old Indian would hoist it on the home-made flagpole located in front of the Birnie home. Quite often the skippers, viewing this ceremony from the deck of their ships through their spyglasses, would salute to him, a response which invariably caused Old George high elation. Resuming his watch, he would again look down toward the Columbia River's entrance for new ships with whom to repeat the ceremony.

James Birnie was a native of Scotland who joined the North West Company of Montreal in 1818. When in 1824 this organization became a part of the Hudson's Bay Company, Birnie was sent to the Columbia River, where he became one of the founders of Fort Vancouver. Service in New Caledonia was followed by Mr. Birnie's appointment as officer-in-charge of Fort George (earlier called Astoria under the Americans) in 1814.

Birnie is remembered at Fort George as a genial host to visitors, and for the gracious hospitality of his charming Indian wife. Doubtless she was happy when her husband chose to retire across the Columbia River from Fort George at the site where Cathlamet now stands.

Mrs. Birnie loved the countryside here and the local Indians. Annually she returned to her own Indian ways by making a trip in a giant canoe filled with sixty of her fellow Indians. Proceeding down the Columbia to the mouth of Chinook River, they ascended this stream to its headwaters, then portaged to the upper waters of the Naselle River, down which they paddled to Willapa Bay (then called Shoalwater Bay). After foraging and relaxing here in traditional Indian fashion for a week, she and her party would return to Cathlamet, the giant canoe loaded with elk meat, clams, cranberries, and other delicacies.

CHEHALIS (L-6)

This city, located about midway between Seattle and Portland, is named after the Chehalis River on whose banks it is situated. The Chehalis flows off the slopes of Mount Rainier past the city of Chehalis, twisting its way westward across the state of Washington until it flows into Grays Harbor, near Westport. It was here at the river's entrance into salt water that great quantities of sand accumulated, giving the Indian village which stood here the name *Chehalis*. This was the original town of this name. The word *chehalis* in Indian means sand.

The first white man to live in the vicinity of Chehalis was Simon Plomondon, a French-Canadian trapper, nearly six foot two, and strong in his proportions. He had been a guide for General Lewis Case in the original territory known as the Northwest, General Cass being the first governor of Michigan Territory. Plomondon, too, had fought in the War of 1812 on the British side. It is unknown just when Plomondon came to the Pacific Northwest, but when Dr. McLoughlin, the white-headed chief of Fort Vancouver on the lower Columbia, gave Plomondon land at the head of Cowlitz River near Chehalis on which to retire as a fur trapper, Plomondon had been with the Hudson's Bay Company for twenty-nine years. Plomondon soon became famous among the handful of whites, then living north of the Columbia, for his practical skills and for the number of his Indian wives. At a family reunion just before his death, no less than ninety of his descendants were there.

Plomondon was followed on Cowlitz Prairie, as the region south of Chehalis is known, by hundreds of Hudson Bay personnel sent here by Dr. McLoughlin to establish a four thousand-acre farm. The supply of furs in the Rocky Mountains was fast becoming exhausted, and by 1840 the Hudson's Bay Company decided to convert most of their efforts to farming. Eleven huge farm buildings were built on Cowlitz Prairie, around which 250 horses and mules were employed in growing huge crops and some 12,000 sheep and cattle grazed. From Puget Sound, farm commodities were then shipped by means of a fleet of ships, which the HBC had acquired, to Alaska to be sold to the Russians living there.

In order to compete with the floods of Americans, who by now were settling south of the Columbia River in Willamette Valley, Dr. McLoughlin and the Company made a concerted effort to similarly attract English settlers to cross the Rockies from Eastern Canada to settle in Cowlitz Prairie, paralleling the covered-wagon Americans crossing over the Oregon Trail to the south. By this means, the British hoped the as-yet undrawn boundary line, dividing the vast region called Oregon Country, might be drawn along the Columbia River. All south of this boundary would belong to the United States; all to the north of the Columbia would belong to England.

To persuade Canadians to emigrate west, McLoughlin promised them free animals and equipment with which to farm, and allotted them two hundred acres on which to grow their produce. Unlike the Americans, however, they were not given title to the land on which they were to farm. Because of this, the British project failed.

In 1841 Commodore Charles Wilkes of the U.S. navy arrived on Puget Sound in his ship USS *Vincennes* to signal to Dr. McLoughlin that the United States was not relinquishing the lands north of the Columbia to England. When he traveled south from Puget Sound to personally indicate this to Dr. McLoughlin, his guide on this trip on horseback was Simon Plomondon. Writing of this ex-trapper, Wilkes states that Plomondon could not tell time, nor could he read or write, but that he was the most capable guide that had ever served him.

With the drawing of the international boundary in 1846 along the present forty-ninth parallel, Americans from over the Oregon Trail commenced pouring north. One of these emigrants was John Robinson Jackson, the first white to claim land in this region which until now had been English. Settling just south of today's Chehalis, his farm and the area around it became known as Jackson's Prairie. Soon many Americans came to live here, angering the British (since the details of the recent boundary treaty had not provided that the area here be relinquished to these Americans). When Americans began appropriating British property for their own use, the situation became so tense that both sides armed themselves. Fortunately no one was killed.

The first white man to visit the site where Chehalis stands, however, was the botanist David Douglas (after whom the most famous fir tree of the Pacific Northwest is named). He was suffering from a swollen leg at the time he passed here, caused a week before when, at Fort Vancouver, he stepped on a rusty nail. Ignoring the injury, he had traveled by canoe down the Columbia to its mouth, then north up the coast until he reached Grays Harbor. By this time Douglas was ill. At a Chehalis Indian village here, Chief Tha-amuxi attempted to treat him, but as he ascended the Chehalis River his leg got worse. The Chehalis River, as he was being paddled up stream by local Indians, reminded Douglas of the streams in England. He writes that along the stream's lower reaches it was "nearly as wide as the Thames." Douglas decided not to follow the Chehalis to its source. Instead, at the site where the city of Chehalis now stands, he paid off the Indian canoe men, giving them ". . . twenty shots of ammunition, two feet of tobacco, a few flints, and some vermillion." Then he struck out cross-country to the headwaters of the Cowlitz River, down which he drifted to the Columbia, thence paddling upstream back to Fort Vancouver, having been away almost two weeks.

CHELAN (G-15)

This Washington resort community, nestled in the eastern side of the snow-capped Cascade Range, attracts people from all over the world to the shores of beautiful, deep, sixty-mile-long Lake Chelan. The city itself is located thirty miles northwest of Wenatchee, at the lake's southern tip. The lake here flows into the Columbia River through a one-mile stretch of water called Chelan River. The river's entry into the Columbia is over a beautiful cataract, called Chelan Falls, located closeby the city of Chelan itself.

Traveling up the Columbia River past Chelan Falls in late August, 1811, came the first white men ever to pass this way. Progress up the waters of this swift stream was slow, for the group, lead by Alexander Ross and his colleague David Stuart, were paddling their way in two leaky canoes. They were leading a party of nineteen French-Canadian fur trappers, also two Sandwich Islanders, into the as-yet unexplored interior regions of the north.

Two weeks prior to their passing upstream at Chelan Falls, they had commenced their journey at the Columbia River's mouth, where recently a fur post called Astoria had been built. Ross and Stuart's mission, in ascending the Columbia River into the interior, was to find sites to establish trading posts, where they hoped the Indians would bring their furs. Furs, at this time were like gold; a source of great wealth.

The group of which Stuart and Ross were members called themselves Astorians, because they were employees of John J. Astor. A wealthy and shrewd New York businessman, Astor had decided to challenge a rival British fur group, the North West Company of Montreal, in their rush westward to trap furs beyond the Rocky Mountains. In order to beat them to this goal, Mr. Astor dispatched his trappers from New York City, around Cape Horn by sailing ship, to the mouth of the Columbia, where they commenced building Astoria in April. Scarcely had Astoria been completed, when the Astorians became aware that trappers of the North West Company were operating, barely three hundred miles inland of them, a British fur trading post called Spokane House.

The rivalry which then arose between the trappers of Spokane House and those at Astoria was a most unique one. Mr. Astor, lacking American trappers to sail to Astoria had, on the eve of his sailing ship's departure from New York City, lured away from the Montreal group some of their trappers to work for him; indeed, most of the Astorians, though working for the Americans, were British citizens and good friends of the trappers now operating inland at Spokane House.

When in December, 1813, Astoria was captured by a British warship (incident to the War of 1812 between England and the United States) these former Nor'Westers (including Ross and Stuart), now working at the captured fort, were at a loss what to do. Many chose to remain in the Pacific Northwest, working with their former Montreal associates at nearby Spokane House. Despite these startling events, after the fall of Astoria to the British, the business of trapping furs went on as before; the only change being that the Union Jack flew over Astoria, whose name then changed to Fort George.

The city of Chelan began in 1879 as a U.S. army post, its mission being to protect the whites of the Chelan region against Indian hostility.

CLARKSTON (N-24)

Were the famous exploring team of Lewis and Clark alive today, they would doubtlessly be pleased to have two towns, located almost side by side, named in their honor. Located in the southeastern corner of Washington State is this city called Clarkston, commemorating William Clark (1770–1838) while across the Snake River, connected by a bridge, is the city of Lewiston, honoring Meriwether Lewis (1774–1809).

Originally, Clarkston was named Jawbone, after the dry character of the local soil. When the president of the Union Pacific Railroad, Mr. Charles Francis Adams, of Boston, decided to extend his railroad into this region in 1896, he conceived the idea of simultaneously building an irrigation project at the site of Jawbone, utilizing the nearby waters of the Snake. Building his own residence nearby, Adams christened the planned city, which he anticipated would spring up beside his railroad tracks, with the name Concord, after the town of Concord in his native Massachusetts.

Then in 1900, local townspeople changed the name to Clarkston, this name particularly appropriate because it was a fitting counterpart to Lewiston, the name of the town to the east of Clarkston, located on the Snake River's opposite bank.

The Lewis and Clark party spent three years in preparing for the expedition, crossing the Rockies to the Pacific, and returning again to St. Louis. They accomplished this feat through untracked wilderness, much of which had never been seen before by whites, with the loss of only one man—his death, moreover, caused by illness, not accident. During the long journey, Lewis and Clark operated together in complete harmony, operating as co-equals in commanding the group.

Both of them were natives of Virginia, raised around Charlottesville which was then located on the westernmost fringes of civilization. Both got to know Indians living closeby in their youth, and thereby understood them better than most whites.

In 1780 when Clark was ten, he moved with his parents to Kentucky, then a territory bordering on Spanish country. In 1790, British troops aided by the Indians, began invading these regions from Canada. William Clark, by then twenty, found himself fighting them under "Mad Anthony" Wayne.

Meanwhile, Meriwether Lewis had become a volunteer in quelling Pennsylvania's Whiskey Rebellion. Soon afterward, Lewis, enamored with military life, became an ensign in the regular army. By chance, his first assignment to duty was as a subordinate to William Clark, four years his senior. Together they fought the British and the Indians between Detroit and Pittsburgh. During this campaign they became close friends.

Lewis, in his early youth, had lived in Charlottesville; his family and the Jefferson family were close friends and neighbors. It was natural, therefore, that when Thomas Jefferson became President in 1801 he appoint Meriwether Lewis, age twenty-seven, to serve as his personal secretary in the White House. In 1803, Jefferson organized an expedition to explore the Louisiana Purchase and the upper reaches of the Missouri River ". . . and such principal streams of it, as, by its course & communication with the waters of the Pacific Ocean, may offer the most direct and practicable water communication across the continent." He appointed Captain Lewis to command it. Captain Lewis, in turn, wrote a letter to Captain Clark, his former commanding officer, as follows:

> . . . I make this communication to you with the privity of the President, who expresses an anxious wish that you would consent to join me in this enterprise; he has authorized me to say that in the event of your accepting this proposition he will grant you a Captain's commission . . . and . . . your situation if joined with me . . . will be in all respects precisely such as my own . . . If therefore there is anything under those circumstances, in this enterprise, which would induce you to participate with me in its fatigues, it's dangers and it's honors, believe me there is no man on earth with whom I should feel equal pleasure in sharing them as with yourself . . . (VII, 230)

Clark then responded:

> . . . This is an amence undertaking, fraited with numerous
> difficuelties, but my freind I can assure you that no man lives
> with whome I would prefur to undertake & Share the
> difficuelties of such a trip than yuorself. (VII, 259)

More of the unique and quaint spelling for which Clark still remains
famous is illustrated in the following passage, descriptive of the
primitive conditions under which this epochal journey was made,
through lands never before seen by white men:

> Fryday, July 19th, 1805 . . . proceeded on in Indian Parth
> river verry crooked passed over two mountains. Saw several
> Indian Camps which they left this Spring. Saw Trees Peeled &
> found poles &c. at 11 oC I saw a gange of Elk, as we had no
> provisions. Concluded to kill some my feet is verry brused &
> out constantly stuck full [of] Prickley pear thorns, I puled out
> 17 by the light of the fire to noght Musquotors verry
> troublesome. (II, 250)

Perhaps due to his red hair, but also to his genial disposition,
Captain Clark was especially admired by the Indians encountered
along the route through the wilderness. The lone girl of their party,
Sacajawea, wife of Charbonneau (the group's interpreter) particularly
admired Clark. Clark, in turn, was especially devoted to Sacajawea's
baby boy, born to her and her French-Canadian husband soon after the
two joined the explorers in February, 1805, at the Mandan Village in
present South Dakota. The months-old child—carried on foot, horseback, and canoe the rest of the trip west—was affectionately known to
the thirty-odd men of the group as Pomp, although his real name was
Jean Baptiste Charbonneau.

The return of the expedition in the early fall of 1806 was joyous, for
they had been away from civilization for over two years. As they drifted
down the Missouri River in their canoes, they met in the general
vicinity where Kansas City now stands, one Captain Robert McClellan,
later famous as a part of the Hunt Expedition which followed Lewis
and Clark's to the Pacific. McClellan told them that people in the
United States had long since given them all up as dead, and that they
were "almost forgotten." It was he who gave them their first drink of
whiskey in almost fourteen months, and a royal celebration took place.

At St. Charles, they came in sight of the first white females they had
seen in two years. Greeted as a hero in St. Louis, Clark was made a

brigadier general and was rewarded with 1600 acres of land, and the grand sum of $1228. In his haste to get back to Virginia to propose to his future wife, Julia Hancock, he missed President Jefferson's invitation to a special dinner at the White House.

Clark's partner, Meriwether Lewis, was made governor of the northern part of Louisiana. He never married. He mysteriously met his death near Nashville, Tennessee, supposedly murdered. Captain Clark lived on to the age of sixty-eight, the father of six children. His favorite son, named Meriwether Lewis Clark honoring his beloved exploring partner, became a graduate of West Point.

COLUMBIA RIVER (B-23/N-2)

This is the longest and the mightiest of the Pacific Northwest's rivers. It is fourteen hundred miles long. From its source in southeast British Columbia's Canadian Rockies, the Columbia flows initially northward as if it were headed for the Arctic. About one hundred fifty miles from its source, the river then suddenly reverses its course and flows south for more hundreds of miles into northeastern Washington. After making a giant U-shaped sweep westward, it then rushes through the deep chasm in the snow-capped mountains, called the Cascades, past Cape Disappointment into the Pacific Ocean.

Spanish explorers knew of this river's presence as early as 1753, under the name "River of the West." Claiming possession over the entire west coast of America, they feared Russian advance southward from Alaska. To investigate, the viceroy of New Spain in Mexico City dispatched Bruno Heceta north from San Blas in the eighty-two-foot-long ship *Santiago*. He was the first explorer to probe the coastline of today's state of Washington. In so doing, he discovered the Columbia River. He named it Rio San Rocque, after a church saint. Heceta, however, failed to enter the river, his sailors at the time being too ill of scurvy to risk the attempt. Next in 1778, the British explorer James Cook, and then in 1792 the Britisher George Vancouver probed these coasts, but they failed to detect the Columbia River's presence.

It remained for an obscure American sailor named Robert Gray, from Tiverton, Rhode Island, to cross the treacherous sandbar guarding the Columbia's entrance, thereby becoming the first white person to venture inside. A hard-bitten Yankee, Gray was probably little aware of the significance of his almost routine anchoring inside. Later it would afford the United States a major claim to all the interior regions which this river drains. In vain would the British claim he had not entered the river itself, only an estuary along the coast leading to it. His feat would become perhaps the most important basis by which the United States successfully gained sovereignty over the Pacific Northwest.

Thanks to careless descendants of Captain Gray who lost all of his records in a fire, we have only the impressions of the historic moment when Gray anchored inside the Columbia's entrance, as described by a seventeen-year-old youth named John Boit. He was then serving as third mate aboard Gray's 212-ton ship *Columbia,* after which the river takes its name. Recalls Boit as their vessel dropped anchor off the tip of what is now called Chinook Point at the entrance to Bakers Bay:

> . . . The men of the Columbia's River are strait limb'd, fine looking fellows, and the women are very pretty. They are all in a state of Nature except the Females who wear a leaf Apron. They are very numerous, and appeared very civill not even offering to steal. During our short stay we collected 150 Otter, 300 Beaver, and twice that number of land furs. The river abounds with excellent salmon, and most other River Fish, and the words with plenty of Moose and Deer, the skins of which they brought us in great plenty. (John Boit, *Logs of Boit and Gray,* annotated by F.W. Howay)

Canadian fur trappers, searching for a stream down which to ship Rocky Mountain furs to the Pacific, were the first to discover the Columbia River's upper stretches. The first to search for them was Sir Alexander Mackenzie, then twenty-eight years old. In doing so he traced down a stream which, to his disappointment, reached the Arctic Ocean. Today his find is known as the Mackenzie River. In 1792, still searching for the Columbia, he discovered another stream, called *Tacoutche-Tesse* by the Indians, which he believed to be the Columbia. Following it for weeks in his twenty-five-foot long canoe, he reached a point where the river swept over rocks with such fury that two holes were smashed in his canoe's bottom. Striking out overland, Mackenzie nonetheless reached salt water at a point called Bella Coola, two hundred miles up the coast from the present city of Vancouver in British Columbia. Thereby, Mackenzie became the first white man to cross the American continent.

In 1805, the American exploring team of Lewis and Clark had duplicated Mackenzie's feat, and in so doing discovered a source of the Columbia in Idaho, namely: the Salmon River. Still the true source of the great river remained a mystery. In 1807, Simon Fraser traced down the same stream which Mackenzie had followed. This time he circumvented the tempestuous portions of its lower reaches and reached the ocean, near today's Canadian city of Vancouver, only to find through latitude measurements that the stream's mouth was considerably north of Lewis and Clark's Columbia. Today this stream, the mighty Fraser River, bears his name.

First to discover the source of the Columbia was Mr. David Thompson (1770–1857). English by birth and a skilled geographer as well as explorer, he arrived on the upper waters of the Columbia in July, 1807; but since the stream flowed northward initially from its source, he failed to recognize it as the great River of the West for which his colleagues Mackenzie and Fraser had sought in vain.

Almost before Thompson had completed Kootenai House, the fur trading post from which he planned to operate, Indian messengers brought to him a letter. Dated July 10th, 1807, it notified Thompson that all the headwaters of the Columbia belonged to the United States, and that he was trespassing on American soil (Kootenai House actually was located in southeast British Columbia). The letter directed him to fly the American flag over Kootenai House and to abide by U.S. regulations. Ignoring the document, Thompson set about encouraging the local Indians to bring in their furs. Six months later he received another letter by Indian messenger. This time the unknown writer ordered Thompson to desert the area or be expelled.

Clearly, American rivalry for Rocky Mountain furs was beginning, and Thompson must have realized that his North West Company of Montreal must act promptly in these mountains to establish a string of British fur posts here before the Americans gained the advantage. Historians have criticized Thompson for not racing down the Columbia River to the Pacific Ocean to set up a claim as soon as he unravelled the twisting course of this river's waters upstream. Had he done so, they argue, today all of the Pacific Northwest lying north of the Columbia River, including the present state of Washington, would fly the Canadian Maple Leaf flag instead of the Stars and Stripes.

During each of the three summers in which these historians claim he dilly-dallied, Thompson returned east over the Rockies to Fort William in order to deliver the furs he had acquired during the previous trapping season. Doubtlessly, on these trips he learned of attempts by the American executive John J. Astor to persuade his North West Company colleagues at Fort William to join with him in establishing the fur post called Astoria at the Columbia River's mouth.

Mystery, however, still surrounds the incident which occurred on 10

July 1810. At this time Mr. Thompson was returning east as usual on his summer trip to headquarters when at Rainy Lake (on the Canadian-U.S. border between present Manitoba and Minnesota), he was met by a messenger from Fort William bearing urgent instructions. Whatever this message contained, it caused Thompson to immediately turn back westward to his trapping grounds. Did it direct him to rush down the Columbia to its mouth in order to precede the American John J. Astor's expedition heading there to establish his American fur post? Or was it a directive which, though informing Thompson of the Astorians' impending arrival downstream, advised him to make every effort to stop these Americans from gaining a foothold amongst the Indians upstream by establishing American fur posts in the interior regions? In support of this latter belief is the famous notice which Mr. Thompson posted on 9 July 1811 at the inland juncture where the Snake River joins the Columbia (where the city of Pasco now stands). "Keep your American trappers downstream of here," the notice advised, "because all trapping rights upstream of here belong to my North West Company."

The name Columbia is a Latinized version of Columbus, coined by one Phillip Frenau in 1775 in a popular poem, which became popular during the days of the thirteen colonies as a synonym for the more cumbersome United States. Columbia was popular, too, with the British, as evidenced in 1857 when Queen Victoria suggested its use in the name British Columbia. To all Americans who traveled the Oregon Trail, the present Columbia River was known as the Oregon River.

COLVILLE (D-22)

Many historians regard this city, fifty miles north of Spokane, as even more colorful in its background than Astoria. It began in 1826, twelve miles northwest of today's city, at Kettle Falls on the Columbia River, where Old Fort Colville was built as a replacement for Spokane House. The older post, the Hudson Bay Company believed, was too far away from the main highway of travel, the Columbia River, which the canoe brigades traveled between Fort George at the Columbia's mouth and York Factory on Hudson's Bay. Both Kettle Falls and Old Fort Colville have now disappeared beneath the backwaters of Columbia River dam projects.

The original name for the city of Colville was Pinckney City. This name was chosen in honor of Major Pinckney Lougenbeel. He was the U.S. army's commanding officer of the American military post called Fort Colville which was established three miles northeast of the present city of Colville in 1859. This American Fort Colville was built to quell the Indians in northeast Washington, who went on the warpath to prevent white gold seekers overrunning their lands.

No blood was ever shed around Major Lougenbeel's fort, however; in fact, the occupants of this army post regarded it as an exceedingly dull place. Some idea of the monotony of its life can be gathered from the following extract from the diary of a young Englishman, Charles Wilson. At this time, Wilson was a member of the British team, who with their American counterparts, were surveying the nearby boundary between the United States and Canada, running just north of here. Wilson's headquarters were located where the town of Marcus stands, but he regularly traveled to Lougenbeel's army post to take his meals.

> August 1, 1860 We were honored today by the presence of two ladies, wives of the officers of Fort Colville. They appeared at dinner in a gorgeous array of crinoline and low dresses, enough to frighten a man out of his senses in such a remote area as this . . . Early on New Year's morning [1861] the Indians began firing a salute with their muskets, bang, bang, bang, in every direction, during the day we went up to Old Fort Colville [the British one] to pay a New Year's visit, and we had capital fun there; I believe I was the only one bold enough to follow the custom of the place and kiss the old squaws right around . . . There are quite a number of Indians about here, some of them fine looking fellows; they are all mounted & ride splendidly, sometimes bareback with nothing but a rope in the horse's mouth for a bridle, at other

times they use a small leather pad or some pieces of buffalo robe, always at a full gallop with their hair & streamers flying back in the wind; traveling soberly along you suddenly hear a scream behind you & an Indian passes in a cloud of dust, like a flash of lightning, leaving you uncertain as to what the row is all about. (Sir Charles Wilson, *Mapping of the Frontier,* Toronto, 1970)

The town of Marcus, situated thirteen miles northwest of Colville, is named for Marcus Oppenheimer. He was the first merchant to settle here. The structure in which he operated his store was built in 1860 as living quarters for the Anglo-American Boundary Commission, of which Mr. Wilson was a British member. Mr. Marcus' store was opened in this same structure in 1863, the international boundary line along this region by now having been surveyed.

Originally Old Fort Colville spelled its name with only one *l,* the man after whom it was named being Mr. Andrew Colvile (1779–1856). A brilliant young man named George Simpson (1787–1860) gave Colvile's name to this fort in gratitude for Colvile's having made him governor of the Hudson's Bay Company in Canada when Simpson was only twenty-eight years old. Colvile was able to promote young Simpson over the heads of many older members of the HBC because of the high position he held in this organization's ranks. Colvile at the time of Simpson's promotion, was one of the most influential members of the committee in London, the select group who ruled the company.

When in the spring of 1826 young Simpson named Fort Colville, he was engaged in inspecting the many far-flung fur trading posts under his recently-acquired command across Canada. On such inspection trips, of which he made many, Simpson sometimes traveled in a single canoe and, except for the French-Canadian voyageurs who paddled his craft, he accompanied himself by only a doctor and a bagpiper, the latter serving to ceremoniously announce his arrival and departure from each fort. Recalling such trips, Simpson writes:

> . . . Weather permitting our slumbers would be broken about one in the morning by the cry 'Levé, levé, levé!' In five minutes, woe to the inmates that were slow in dressing; the tents were tumbled about our ears; and, within half an hour, the camp would be raised, the canoes laden, and the paddles keeping time to some merry old song. About eight o'clock, a convenient place would be selected for breakfast, about three quarters of an hour be allotted for the multifarious operations of unpacking and repacking . . . the equipage, laying and

> removing the cloth, boiling and frying, eating and drinking and, while the preliminaries were arranging, the hardier among us would wash and shave . . . About two in the afternoon we usually put ashore for dinner and, as this meal needed no fire . . . it was not allowed to occupy more than twenty minutes of half an hour . . . Such was the routine of our journey, the day, generally speaking, being divided into six hours of rest and eighteen of labor.

In 1841, Sir George (he was later made a knight by the queen for his Hudson's Bay Company services) made a record crossing of Canada by canoe from York Factory on Hudson Bay to Fort Colville, a distance of nineteen hundred miles, in forty-seven days, excluding the days he spent at the various posts along the way while inspecting them. Normally such a crossing took almost three months.

Perhaps the most colorful of all the chief traders in charge of Old Fort Colville during its half century of existence was Mr. Angus McDonald (1816–1889), not to be confused with his uncle, Archibald McDonald (1790–1853). Angus was born at Craig House, Loch Torridon, Ross Shire, Scotland. He entered the service of the HBC in 1838.

The following year Angus was transferred to Fort Hall (by this time a famous stop along the Oregon Trail) where he married Catherine, a cousin of Nez Perce Chief Eagle-of-the-Light. Twelve children were born to the McDonalds from 1854 to 1871. Angus became chief trader at Fort Colville in 1853 and his services here continued until 1871. The following is a description of Angus in 1853 when he was thirty-seven, as described by Edward Higgins, a fellow fur trader from Fort Nisqually:

> . . . I had heard a great deal about MacDonald, and was anxious to see him, which desire was soon gratified, for Doctor "Tolmie," Chief Trader at Fort Nisqually . . . brought him to the packing room where I was working and gave me an introduction to him. He was a rather good looking man, about six feet in height, straight and slim, but was said to be wiry and strong. . . . He wore a dressed deer skin shirt and pants, a ragattor or roving shirt, and had a black silk handkerchief tied loosely around his neck. He had a black piercing eye, and a deep sonorous rather musical voice . . . He could talk several Indian languages and lived a long time amongst the Blackfeet . . . He was a good French linguist, but his native language was the gaelic of the Scotch Highlanders, and he was very fond of singing, or chanting in a deep, not by any means musical voice: Gaelic songs or verses improvised by himself.

Angus' most prized possession, other than his wife and family, was his bagpipe; one which he had brought with him from Scotland back in 1838. Being married to an Indian, Angus loved to go on trips with her people, living on such occasions in Indian lodges. Often on such trips he would play his bagpipe, which the Indians knew by an Indian word translated "bag that whistles". Angus was welcome at the Indians' hunts and he was regarded as a sage in their councils. Angus recalls nights spent on the trail listening to the coyotes howling outside his tent while contentedly inside he read favorite passages from Shakespeare by the light of the campfire. He continues:

> . . . In this plain. . . we hear no more the voices of hundreds of men and women, keeping time to the sad strain of the San-k-ha, the red man's farewell before he leaves to battle. To hear it sung by five or six hundred voices in a calm starry night . . . is a rare thing, never perhaps to be heard again . . . In 1850 at a great gathering of Indians to dance this staid insisting strain, I stripped with leading men, painted with vermillion by upper body and, mounted on my black buffalo charger with full eagle feathered bonnet, cantered round and round with them to the song. (Angus McDonald, *A Few Items of the West,* F.W. Howay, Washington Historical Society, July, 1917)

COMMENCEMENT BAY (J-8)

Also known as Tacoma Harbor, this is the body of water on the shores of which in May, 1792, Captain George Vancouver, a British explorer, and his fellow-crewmen, held their famous picnic. With the snow-capped fourteen thousand-foot-high Mount Rainier looming overhead to the southeast as a background, and with a group of local Chebaulip Indians for guests, Vancouver and his group devoured English pasties made of deer meat.

Forty-nine years later, in May, 1841, another group of explorers, this one being American, visited Puget Sound in two ships, the warships *Vincennes* and *Porpoise,* to similarly survey Puget Sound. Since they commenced their survey here closeby today's city of Tacoma, its waters are accordingly known today as Commencement Bay. From his flagship, USS *Vincennes,* Commodore Charles Wilkes, spent the summer of 1841 evaluating Puget Sound as a future possession of the United States.

Towards this end, Lieutenant Cadwallader Ringgold in the USS *Porpoise* surveyed north from Commencement Bay up Admiralty Inlet past the San Juans to the mouth of Canada's mighty Fraser River. Lieutenant A.L. Case of USS *Vincennes* mapped Hood Canal. Lieutenant Robert Johnson, with a party of six, climbed on horseback into the Cascade Range of mountains to ascertain what lay beyond, and Midshipman Eld led a group to explore Grays Harbor and the coastline south to the Columbia River's entrance.

Even as they were proceeding on their assignments, American and British diplomats were negotiating over the question of how to divide "Oregon country," as the Pacific Northwest was then known, between their two nations. The Americans insisted that the forty-ninth parallel of latitude already dividing the two nations eastward of the Rockies be extended westward all the way to the Pacific Ocean, thereby giving Puget Sound to the United States. England's diplomats, however, insisted that the international boundary, upon reaching the Columbia River on the forty-ninth parallel, be drawn down this river to the Pacific Ocean, all lands north of the Columbia including Puget Sound thereby belonging to England.

During that summer of 1841 Wilkes also dispatched a party up the Columbia to map this stream's upper valleys. Also, at the head of a horse brigade, Lieutenant George Emmons, U.S. Navy, explored south of the Columbia into Spanish country where a Buenaventura River was rumored to flow, like the Columbia, into the Pacific. At the conclusion of these efforts, Wilkes predicted that the Pacific Northwest would ". . . control the destinies of the entire Pacific." Of Puget Sound itself, he records: "Nothing can exceed the beauties of these waters, and their safety; not a shoal exists . . . that can in any way interrupt navigation by a 74-gun ship. I venture nothing in saying that there is no country in the world that possesses waters comparable to these."

Commodore Wilkes himself, that summer, rode south to the headwaters of the Cowlitz River down which Indian paddlers carried him by canoe to the Columbia and Fort Vancouver. Here he paid his respects to Dr. John McLoughlin, then known as "King of the Columbia."

After inspecting British installations at Astoria, Wilkes rode horseback over to Willamette Valley. Here he visited recently-arrived fellow-Americans, fresh from their trip over the Oregon Trail; also Americans of the missionary station in Willamette Valley recently established by Reverend Jason Lee. Already these Americans were becoming restive under the British monopoly over their lives being exercised by Dr. McLoughlin. A handsome, kindly, and highly capable administrator, this British leader was showing marked compassion in assisting those Americans who were arriving on the lower Columbia depleted of all their worldly goods as a result of their three moonth trip over thhe Rockies. However, once settled, he nonetheless strictly maintained these same Americans' dependence upon his British company insofar as possible. Dr. McLoughlin's Hudson Bay Company store became these Americans' only supply of tools and clothing. Even the seed required in order to raise their own food had to be purchased from his British store.

In an effort to provide his fellow-Americans with some measure of independence from the British, Mr. Joseph Gale, a former American trapper who had chosen to settle in Willamette Valley, hit upon the idea of building a sailing ship. With it Gale planned to sail south to Yerba Buena (today called San Francisco) where, after selling the vessel, he hoped with the proceeds to purchase a herd of Spanish steers. Driving these animals overland back north to Willamette Valley, Gale hoped to establish a source of American-supplied beef, thereby establishing at least this food source independent of Dr. McLoughlin's Hudson's Bay Company.

In his every attempt to build the ship, Gale was opposed by McLoughlin. In vain did he request of the chief factor an anchor, a logline, and a spyglass necessary in order to make the trip. According to tradition, at this point the exasperated Gale then threatened Dr. McLoughlin, adding: "I have a rich uncle back East who will get me anything I want." Replied McLoughlin: "and who may that be?" whereupon Gale is said to have blurted: "Uncle Sam, that's who!"

Commodore Wilkes, whose visit to Fort Vancouver happened to coincide with Gale's frustration, proved to be Gale's "Uncle Sam." From his ships' stores, Wilkes supplied the necessary items for going to sea; moreover, he provided Gale with a master's license, thereby making the trip a legal one under U.S. regulations. With masts cut from the local forests and other lumber, the first ship built on the Willamette River was constructed and successfully sailed to San Francisco, and there traded by Gale for a herd of 350 cattle. With the help of others, herds of 1,250 cattle, 3,000 sheep, and 600 horses were driven overland to Willamette Valley.

Later that summer, as recorded in his narratives, Wilkes attended a formal dinner in the great hall of Fort Vancouver, attended by Sir George Simpson (1787–1860), governor of all Hudson's Bay Company activities in Canada, who chanced to be passing through the lower

Columbia. Records Wilkes: "It was a very stiff and formal affair. Sir George occupied the head of the table with myself on his right and with Hudson. . . [Wilkes' second-in-command] . . . on his left." Wilkes then goes on to complain that the three of them carried on the only conversation which took place during the entire dinner. Wilkes observed that those sitting "below the salt" including Dr. McLoughlin himself ". . . were silent as in feudal times." Describing his own junior officers who also had been invited to the affair, Wilkes records that their behavior was ". . . stupid . . . wanting in manners and maintaining a mawkish silence." In writing later of the affair, Sir George records that Wilkes himself ". . . was by no means communicative on the object of his surveys during the summer past."

It was at this dinner that Wilkes startled Governor Simpson by expressing the view that the United States should claim territorial rights in the Northwest extending north all the way to Alaska. Sir George wasted no time afterwards in rushing this piece of news to his superiors in London, adding: "His Majesty's Government should not consent to any boundary that would give the United States any portion of Oregon Territory north of the Columbia River."

COUPEVILLE (E-7)

So named after colorful Captain Coupe, veteran sea captain. He is remembered today more for his years spent here at Coupeville in retirement than for his earlier years as a skipper. When he lived at Coupeville he was more of a country squire than a nautical man. In his one-horse gig he used to spend much time riding amidst the beautiful scenery and natural open spaces on this Puget Sound island, comparable in length to New York State's Long Island.

Born on the Isle of Man in the Irish Sea, Coupe sailed his own ship to Maine at age twenty-two. Here in 1840 he married Martha White of the town of Bath. They had raised a family of four in 1849 when the California Gold Rush caused Captain Coupe, by now the owner of a full-rigged schooner named the *Rochester,* to sail around the Horn to San Francisco, where he sold his cargo of merchandise to gold prospectors at high profit.

Purchasing a large cargo ship named the *Success,* Coupe then sailed this vessel from San Francisco to Puget Sound, where he found unlimited supplies of lumber, free for the cutting, amongst the forests growing along the seemingly limitless shoreline of this body of water. With this cargo he sailed back to San Francisco, where merchants eagerly purchased the lumber to erect docks and stores in this booming city. More trips to Puget Sound in his vessel brought Coupe even greater profits. It was while pursuing this activity in the *Success* that he came upon the site where Coupeville now stands, on the south shore of Penn Cove.

The great beauty of Whidbey Island, and especially of the site where Coupeville now stands, prompted Captain Coupe then to send back to Bath, Maine for his wife and children to come here. The voyage which they took to arrive here via Cape Horn took six months. Tradition has it that Martha, Coupe's wife, upon gazing at her husband's choice of the future Coupeville at which to live, agreed to do so only if he promised to give up his life as a sea captain and retire to become a farmer. Coupe consented.

Still famous is the grandiose manner in which Captain Coupe sailed his ship *Success* through Deception Pass, just north of Coupeville, on its last voyage under his command. It was a feat of daring seamanship which, in retrospect, seems unbelievable; for Deception Pass is scarcely fifty yards wide in spots, yet he is said to have crossed through it with all sails of his full-rigged ship flying.

Fully justified was Martha in refusing to live at the future Coupeville without her husband, for although today the site is populous, and Whidbey Island in fact was becoming filled with people at the time the Coupe family settled there, packs of timber wolves roamed the surrounding region and over sixteen hundred Indians lived on Whidbey Island.

Moreover, they were members of two tribes, the Skagit and the Skykomish clans, and war between these two groups was common. Their rivalry, about the time the Coupes arrived at Coupeville, was on the rise, thanks to a Skykomish chief named Patkanim who had distinguished himself by collecting the scalps of enemy Indians and taking them to Washington Territory's capital at Olympia, where he sold the scalps to the whites.

Still further adding to the unrest around Coupeville at this time were Haidah Indians, who in increasing numbers were arriving in Puget Sound from their native homes in the Queen Charlotte Islands. Traveling in elaborately-carved, fifty-foot-long, high-prowed canoes paddled by fifty or more Haidas, their faces hideously painted in silver and black, these warriors not only conducted raids at random on white settlements all over Puget Sound but also attempted to capture white people; on at least two occasions with success.

On the night of August 11, 1857, about midnight, two canoes full of these Indians knocked on the door of Mr. Isaac Ebeye, who lived four miles from Coupeville on the island's west side. Upon opening the door of his cabin, Mr. Ebeye was seized by these Indians and killed, then beheaded. This horrid act was traced to a recent event at Port Gamble, which lies on the mainland closeby Whidbey Island. The whites there killed twenty Haidahs who were attempting to seize the USS *Massachusetts,* a warship of the U.S. navy which recently had arrived on Puget Sound to protect the white settlers. One of these Haidahs who was killed at the the famous Battle of Port Gamble had been a "big chief" of the Haidah tribe. It was, therefore, a matter of honor that the Haidahs, in response, kill a white "big chief." Mr. Ebeye at the time of his death, qualified for their requisites, for he was U.S. Collector of Revenue for Puget Sound.

Little is known concerning the Mr. Granville Penn, after whom Penn Cove (on whose shores Coupeville stands) is named; except that it was Penn who witnessed the discoverer of Whidbey Island, Captain Vancouver's Last Will and Testament (dated 8 April 1798) and therefore must have lived near the place where Vancouver died. This was in Vancouver's native city of King's Lynn, north of London in East Anglia. Vancouver never married; indeed from the time of his entrance at age thirteen into the British navy until his death at age forty, this great explorer engaged almost continuously in sailing the high seas.

Point Partridge, which lies four miles west of Coupeville, was named by Vancouver for one Martha Partridge of Hockham Hall, located near Vancouver's birthplace of King's Lynn. Martha was married to Vancouver's brother, John.

COWLITZ RIVER (N-6)

Today this is the stream along whose banks automobiles speed from Portland to Puget Sound, a trip of only three hours. In early times however, persons wishing to make this trip had to embark in a schooner, proceed down the Columbia to the Pacific Ocean, sail up the Washington coast to the Strait of Juan de Fuca, and thence they could reach Puget Sound in a matter of four days at best. The voyage often involved seasickness.

Bolder persons wishing to proceed north, however, crossed the Columbia from Portland downstream to the mouth of the Cowlitz River, where the cities of Kelso and Longview now stand. Here they embarked in a dugout canoe paddled by Indians. In his book titled *Canoe and*

Saddle (Portland, 1913) Theodore Winthrop, then a recent graduate of Yale College in Connecticut describes this trip in 1852 as follows:

> Next day we went up the Cowlitz . . . with four Indians to paddle or pole. The stream flows through forests thick as those in the tropics . . . rich but almost gloomy in their solitude. The current was very rapid . . . and we progressed at something like two miles an hour . . . At the Cowlitz head of navigation [where the Cowlitz turns eastward toward its source on the slopes of 14,000 foot high Mount Rainier] . . . we spent a tedious day waiting for horses until evening when we rode out of Jackson's Prairie, eight miles [Mr. Jackson had settled here quite recently, the first American to venture onto land claimed by England]. We passed the Hudson Bay Company's beautiful Cowlitz farms, rich with ripe grain [where the British grazed thousands of sheep and cattle] . . . nearer than ever rose graceful Mount Saint Helens [from which the south branch of the Cowlitz flows] and now first fully seen was the immense bulk of Mount Rainier . . . it stood grand, grand above the plain.

The twenty-seven-year-old Winthrop then notes that by riding horseback fifty-two miles continuously the next day they reached Tumwater. It was then the only American settlement on Puget Sound.

The Cowlitz Indians, after whom the river takes its name, were much feared by the early whites. In the spring of 1818, they killed one of the Hudson Bay Company's fur trappers who was bold enough to seek furs along the above stretch of river. They did so because he had been making improper advances to one of the females of their tribe. Sent to punish them for his death, Peter Skene Ogden, at this time just beginning his distinguished career in the Northwest as a mountaineer, allowed his followers to run amok. They killed not only Cowlitz males suspected of killing their fellow white, but also some Cowlitz women and children, as well.

Consequently for many years, white men traveling north between the Columbia and Puget Sound avoided the Cowlitz River route. Instead, they traveled north via Willapa Bay along the coastal beaches to Grays Harbor. From here up the Chehalis River, by way of Black Lake, they reached the site on Puget Sound where the city of Olympia now stands.

With the arrival of steamboats on the Columbia, a faster means of proceeding north was assured. In 1854, a Stuart Express Company boasted that their passengers could go from Portland to Olympia in thirty-six hours! Their advertisement proclaimed: "We believe this is a feat which has never been accomplished." In fact, however, the boast was overblown. Omitted from the advertisement were the modes of transportation involved. From Portland the passengers, indeed, traveled across the Columbia by steamboat. However, upon disembarking at the mouth of the Cowlitz, the same old canoes propelled by Indians awaited them. A stage coach awaited them at Cowlitz Landing (one mile downstream from today's town of Toledo) in which, for the remainder of the trip, they painfully jounced their way over the primitive roads, stopping every fifteen or twenty miles for a change of horses.

The word cowlitz is said to come from the Cowlitz tribal word *coweliske* translated "capturing the medicine spirit." This refers to the custom of the tribal elders requiring their young males to fast and pray for prolonged periods, the site where this took place being along the banks of the stream. This practice was considered a prerequisite to these youths becoming full-fledged warriors.

CYPRESS ISLAND

Passengers on a holiday trip to the Suan Juan Islands, after embarking on the ferry boat which takes them there, will observe this island on their starboard hand shortly after leaving Anacortes, fifty miles north of Seattle, their point of departure. In June, 1792, Captain George Vancouver, the thirty-seven-year-old explorer from Kings Lynn, East Anglia, who was then exploring these waters, upon observing the trees on this island from the deck of his three-masted sailing ship

Discovery, thought they were cypress trees, and accordingly gave the name Cypress Island here.

Upon landing ashore here, however, he was delighted to find that the trees existing in the greatest numbers were spruce trees. From their needles, after setting up a distillery ashore, he was able to brew "spruce beer," a drink which he insisted that his sailors imbibe plentifully in order that they might avoid becoming ill with scurvy. By strange coincidence, even as Vancouver anchored his ship *Discovery* off Cypress Island, a strange ship was sailing off this island's opposite shore, unbeknownst to Vancouver.

It was a vessel belonging to the Spanish navy called the *Sutil,* commanded by one Senor Dionisio Alcala Galiano. A few days later the rival explorers in their respective ships came within speaking distance of each other off Point Roberts, northward of Cypress Island on today's Canadian border. Courtesies between the rival ships were exchanged, then the two vessels sailed together northward up the coast of present British Columbia for a brief period.

Senor Galiano called Cypress Island by the name *Isla de Vicente,* Vincent being one of the many given-names of a recently appointed Spanish viceroy, whose last name was Revillagigedo. In Mexico City, Revillagigedo had recently arrived from Spain in order to take over the job of ruling the New World, as Spain called her vast possessions along the Pacific Coast of both South and North America. Disputing Spain's claims to these coasts, Captain Vancouver's expedition to Puget Sound had come here to assert England's claims to possession over these same areas.

In 1789, three years previous to Vancouver's arrival here on Puget Sound, at Spain's headquarters in the Northwest—a place known as Nootka, on Vancouver Island, northwest of Puget Sound—a hot-headed Spanish governor seized British ships for failing to salute his Spanish flag before anchoring in the local harbor, called Friendly Cove. In retaliation for this offense, Governor Martinez sent the offending British ships, under Spanish crews, to lower California, the British commanders and their British crew prisoners. War between the two nations, as a result of this drastic act, was narrowly avoided through a diplomatic agreement called the Treaty of Nootka, signed by both nations, agreeing to henceforth share Nootka. To arrange the details of Nootka's joint occupation, Vancouver had come to the Northwest not only to explore Puget Sound, but also to meet at Nootka with a Spanish counterpart to himself, Senor Bodega y Quadra, appointed by the Spanish king.

For two weeks after departing Cypress Island, the *Discovery* and the *Chatham* sailed northward through the waters now called Georgia Strait. While rounding Vancouver Island's north tip, Captain Vancouver's ship *Discovery* went aground but was refloated without damage on the high tide. When their expedition reached Nootka, located on Vancouver Island's west coast near Gold River, Vancouver was pleased to find Senor Bodega Y Quadra awaiting him.

D

DECATUR ISLAND (D-6)

This island lies east of Lopez Island in the San Juan archipelago. It bears the name of one of the greatest of the founders of the American navy, Stephen Decatur (1779–1820). Decatur's first famous act of heroism took place in the harbor of Tripoli on the Barbary Coast of North Africa. While cruising here in command of the USS *Enterprise,* in 1803, he received word that Captain William Bainbridge (after whom Puget Sound's Bainbridge Island is named) had gone aground on an uncharted reef with the USS *Philadelphia* in the harbor of Tripoli.

Bainbridge had boldly entered this harbor to bombard 25,000 Tripolitan troops defending this city. Word of the grounding also included the humiliating news that Captain Bainbridge, along with the entire crew of American sailors, had been made captives of the Bey of Tripoli. To make matters worse, Decatur heard, the Tripolitans were now engaged in refloating Bainbridge's grounded ship in order to man the vessel with Tripolitan crewmen.

Decatur decided to act boldly. On a dark night, at the head of a small raiding party of American sailors, their faces blackened and carrying tomahawks, he entered Tripoli Harbor in a small rowboat. Continuing inside until they were under the guns of the Tripolitan shore batteries, the valiant group boarded the *Philadelphia* and, after hand-to-hand fighting, recaptured the vessel. Decatur then set fire to it, thereby assuring that it would not fall into Tripolitan hands. Astonishingly, they returned without the loss of a man.

As for Captain Bainbridge and his crew, they remained prisoners of the Tripolitans until the conclusion of the Tripolitan War in 1805. News of Decatur's bold raid particularly delighted the English, for Tripolitan pirates had for years been raiding this nation's vessels, as well as those of the United States, demanding ransom payments for their crews' return.

During the War of 1812, Decatur distinguished himself fighting against the British as commander both of the frigate *United States* and the frigate *President.* Following the war, ten ships under the command of Decatur sailed into the harbor of Algiers to end a resurgence of depredations being inflicted on foreign ships by Barbary pirates. Forcing at gunpoint the ruler of this nation to free more American seamen similarly seized for ransom, Decatur demanded and obtained from him the payment of $25,000 to the United States as an indemnity.

On the occasion of Decatur's return to the United States after this episode, Decatur was lionized by the entire nation. It was at one of the many banquets given in his honor at this time that Decatur made his famous toast: "Our country! In her intercourse with foreign nations may she always be in the right; but our country, right or wrong!" As one of the three commissioners of the U.S. Navy, not long after this, Commodore Decatur opposed the return to active duty of Commodore James Barron, a fellow officer who had been found guilty by court-martial of surrendering his USS *Chespeake* to a British ship in 1807. Barron challenged Decatur to a duel and killed him.

DES MOINES (I-8)

Past this Puget Sound metropolis, located immediately south of Seattle, came Chief Patkanim, head of the Snoqualmie nation, in April, 1855. At this time he was traveling by canoe, seated in the bow of a fleet of such vehicles numbering twenty-five, proceeding southward toward Olympia—then, as now, the seat of the legislature. Recently the whites on Puget Sound had been under attack by the Indians; indeed white lives had been lost. Chief Patkanim, however, was leading his flotilla south to convince the legislators in Olympia that his Indians, henceforth, would be friendly toward the whites.

The little town called Seattle, two months before this, had survived an Indian attempt to capture it, thanks largely to the presence of a U.S. Navy warship, the *Decatur.* As Patkanim returned several days later, still accompanied by his Snoqualmies in their fleet of canoes, the residents of Des Moines, had they been alive then, would have seen Patkanim head for the *Decatur,* still anchored in Seattle's harbor. Chief Patkanim was about to board this warship to pay his respects to Captain Gansevoort and his crew. He wanted to convince them, too, of his and his Indians' new friendliness. As the little chieftain crossed the gangway upon climbing aboard, everyone was astonished, for apparently as proof of his new loyalty, as described by one witness:

> . . . he now was arrayed in citizen's garb including Congress
> gaiters . . . [these were a covering of leather at this time worn
> by fashionable males over their shoes], white kid gloves, and
> a white shirt with a standing collar which reached half way
> to his ears, the whole finished off by a flaming red neck tie.
> (*History of Washington*, E.S. Meany, New York, 1909)

The name Des Moines goes back to the days of Marquette and Joliet, those explorers of the Mississippi River who (*circa* 1673) named Des Moines River, which flows past Iowa's city of Des Moines, with the sobriquet *Riviere des Moingouenas,* after the name of a local Indian tribe. Years passed, and Marquette and Joliet's Indian *Riviere des Moingouenas* became changed by local French fur trappers into the French *Riviere des Moings,* the word *moings* being French for monk or priest; hence "River of Monks." Still more time passed leading to the further corruption of *des moings* into our present Des Moines.

DESTRUCTION ISLAND (H-2)

This name dates back to the days when explorers and fur traders sailed the coast of Washington. This particular island, forty miles south of Cape Flattery, relates to an English sea captain named Charles Barkley (1760–1832). Accompanied by his seventeen-year-old bride, Francis Hornby Barkley (1769–1845), he sighted Destruction Island in September, 1787.

Anchoring his ship *Loudon*—a vessel of 400 tons, ship-rigged and mounting twenty guns—off the island's east side, Barkley then sent a ship's boat ashore with instructions to its crew to obtain fresh water from the mouth of nearby Hoh River. While his sailors were thus filling the *Loudon's* fresh water casks, Hoh Indians suddenly appeared out of the nearby forest and killed them all. To commemorate their tragic deaths, Barkley gave here the name Destruction Island.

The *Loudon* at this time was a British ship masquerading under the Austrian flag, and thus was calling itself the *Imperial Eagle.* This subterfuge by Captain Barkley was prompted by his desire to escape the necessity of securing a license from England's East India Company, whose licensing fees were exorbitantly expensive.

The above display of ferocity by the Indians then living along these coasts was not new. Down the coast a few miles, where the town of Moclips now stands, these Indians had attempted to drive off two

Spanish ships commanded by Bruno Heceta and Bodega y Quadra in July, 1875. Heceta, at the time of this tragedy, was ashore holding a ceremony claiming all of the Pacific Northwest for Spain. Meanwhile, Heceta's assistant, Senor Quadra, having sent sailors of his ship *Sonora* ashore nearby to obtain fresh water, found them similarly attacked and killed by the Indians. After this tragedy, Quadra in his ship *Sonora* was continuing northward past Destruction Island, as it is known today, when, in memory of his recently killed men, he named it *Isla de Dolores,* or Island of Tears.

While Captain Barkley in his ship *Loudon* (alias *Imperial Eagle*) was anchored in Calcutta, a year after the Destruction Island tragedy, the East India Company seized Barkley's vessel for its violation of the company's licensing laws. Nothing seems to be known of Barkley's career during the next thirty years; however, based upon journals kept by his wife Francis, the couple were none too prosperous. As of May 16, 1832, Mrs. Barkley's diary records: "On this date I lost my beloved husband—in his 73rd year—worn out more by care and sorrow than by years." Captain and Mrs. Barkley were the first whites after Juan de Fuca to visit the Strait of Juan de Fuca. Mrs. Barkley was the first white woman to visit the Pacific Northwest.

DUNGENESS SPIT (F-6)

When George Vancouver anchored his ship *Discovery* inside this tongue of land (fourteen miles east-northeast of Port Angeles) on 30 April 1792, he was unaware that two years prior to this the Spanish explorer Manuel Quimper, captain of the *Princessa Real* had preceded him here. Captain Vancouver chose to name it Dungeness Spit after a famous headland called Dungeness located on the south coast of Kent,

England, to which this Dungeness Spit, he notes, bore a resemblance. Senor Quimper's earlier name here was *Punta de Santa Cruz.* Whereas Vancouver remained here only briefly before pushing on to Port Discovery to the east, Senor Quimper remained here for two weeks trading bits of metal and iron hoops with the Indians for their plentiful supply here of fish, crabs, clams, and venison.

E

ELLENSBURG (K-15)

This eastern Washington city is located eighty miles southeast of Seattle. Its site was known to the Indians as *Che-we-lah.* Ever since gold was discovered around Colville to the northeast of Ellensburg the Indians of *Che-we-lah* were plagued with white men overrunning their lands. Discovery of gold in Fraser River country, as well as in the Okanogan, served to accentuate their troubles.

Taking full advantage of this traffic was Ellensburg's first white resident, a disreputable character named Bud Wilson. Assembling a band of local Indians as his followers, Bud erected a small log cabin, Ellensburg's first white residence. Due to his nefarious practices it was called Robber's Roost. Many a gold prospector passing through the future site of Ellensburg lost all his money, or his gold, to Bud Wilson operating from Robber's Roost. As additional white men took out land claims around Robber's Roost, Wilson found himself an object of their scorn.

In 1864 they demanded that he leave. Stealing a herd of local horses, Wilson departed with the animals one night, pursued the following morning by an armed posse. When he was last seen, Wilson and his stolen animals were swimming the Snake River headed into Idaho's Sawtooth Mountains.

In 1866 Mr. Jack Splawn (1845–1917), who later became the first mayor of Yakima, arrived at Ellensburg. He established a store in the cabin formerly occupied by Bud Wilson. Placing a bull's head over its door and a sign marked Robber's Roost, he began operating a trading post. To attract the Indians, Splawn presented the local Chewelahs with three hundred steel traps free-of-charge in return for their promise to use them to trap local animals and to bring their pelt to Robber's Roost. Soon Splawn's store was thriving, engaged in swapping ". . . red paint, brass rings and spotted handkerchiefs" (as Splawn described his trading goods) for beaver, fox, marten, and other skins. Mr. Splawn's book of memoirs concerning these days is titled *Kamiakin, Last Hero of the Yakimas* (Portland, 1917), one of the classic accounts of the history of eastern Washington.

Due in no small measure to Mr. Splawn's congenial manner of dealing with the Indians around the future Ellensburg, from the outset the other founding fathers of Ellensburg enjoyed similar cordial relations with the natives. Not far from his store Splawn built a race track where the Chewelahs loved to gather, particularly in the springtime when the nearby camas grounds were in blossom. Records Splawn of these times:

> Knowing that the Indians would congregate in June at Che-ho-lan . . . [this was the name of their camas grounds] and in preparation for the sporting events which followed this annual gathering, I bought a number of race horses and one hundred decks of cards . . . then . . . made a half-mile track to which the Indians came in flocks to play games with me . . . I did not do so well in their bone games [this was a form of Indian gambling involving carved bone sticks] . . . but I could hold my own at cards . . . and I skinned them at horse racing.

Mr. John A. Shoudy—after whose wife's name, Ellen, today's city of Ellensburg takes its name—was born in 1842 in Illinois. He fought in the Civil War. Then with his wife, Mary Ellen Shoudy, accompanied by his brother-in-law, Dexter Horton, he traveled by sailing ship and the Isthmus of Panama to Seattle. Here he became a successful merchant store operator, aided by Dexter who became a banker.

Shoudy's first interest in eastern Washington came about through plans by Seattleites to build a road through Snoqualmie Pass into this then-remote area. Such a road had not yet been built when, in 1872, Mr. Shoudy dispatched a thirteen-mule pack train over the trail through Snoqualmie Pass to *Che-we-lah,* the future Ellensburg, loaded with items he would attract these Indians. In moving his family to the site however, Mr. Shoudy chose a more circuitous route. They went by steamboat up the Columbia to The Dalles, thence by stage coach they traveled a primitive road past Goldendale to Robber's Roost, as Ellensburg was still known.

Mr. Jack Splawn, whom the Shoudy's encountered upon their arrival at Robber's Roost, was still engaged in swapping gewgaws with the local Chewelahs, but as Splawn records in his book:

The call of the mountains and the plains was too constant
and strong for me to remain in any one place. In the early
summer [1872] . . . I sold my stock of goods at Robber's Roost
to John A. Shoudy . . . and . . . afterward I made him a
present of my squatter's rights to the 160 acres of land
comprising the present site of Ellensburg.

During the Shoudy's first years at Ellensburg, Indian troubles were
frequent; indeed Mr. Shoudy narrowly missed losing his life in an
encounter with them, saved however by Jack Splawn and his good
Indian friend, Chief Moses—the latter's name now commemorated by
the name of a neighboring town, Moses Lake. When he died in May,
1901, Mr. Shoudy was fifty-nine.

The first white man to view the site where Ellensburg now stands
was Alexander Ross (1783–1856) of Cairnshire, Scotland. He marched
past here in May, 1814, leading a group of five other fur trappers. A
week before this they had departed their fur post, called Fort
Okanogan, to the north of here. They were headed into Yakima country
to attend the annual fair held by the Yakima Indians, hoping to obtain
the horses they needed at Fort Okanogan with which to carry on their
trapping.

In the book *Adventures on the Columbia* (London, 1846) which Ross
wrote in later years, he describes eastern Washington at this time as
populated mostly by bears, wolves, snakes, and coyotes; adding,
however, that the Indians in this region numbered in the thousands. In
passing through the site where Ellensburg now stands, Ross records that
the local Chewelah Indians were ". . . the handsomest of Indians" and
he noted that they were ". . . the southernnmost members of the great
Oakinacken [sic] nation." They dressed, he continues, "both male and
female in deerskin robes decorated with porcupine quills." Mr. Ross
was later to marry a woman of the Chewelah band.

On the day after they passed the site where Ellensburg now stands, Ross and his men found themselves caught up in a huge mass of Indians attending the Yakima fair. Here on the plains near today's city of Yakima, they found themselves held captive for three days, surrounded by howling, dancing Yakima Indians so numerous, Ross records, that they covered an area ". . . more than six miles in every direction." Finally they came upon a Yakima chief who was friendly to them, and through his help they were able to obtain twenty-five beautiful Yakima horses with which they safely returned to their fur post (located where the town of Brewster, Washington now stands).

ELLIOTT BAY (H-8)

This is the commodious body of water which constitutes the city of Seattle's busy harbor. The name relates to five sailing ships, known as the Wilkes Expedition, which visited here in the summer of 1841. Actually, only two of the five ships dropped anchor in Elliott Bay. Prior to arriving on the Northwest's coasts, the Wilkes Expedition visited both coasts of South America, Samoa, the South Seas, Antarctica, and Hawaii.

There were three Elliotts in the Wilkes Expedition. Elliott Point, located twenty miles north of this harbor where Seattle stands, bears the name of Midshipman Samuel Elliott, in 1841 serving aboard Wilkes' ship named the *Porpoise.* Wilkes probably named Seattle's harbor after Reverend Jared L. Elliott, the expedition's Chaplain. Chaplain Elliott's long-winded sermons aboard Wilkes' flagship USS *Vincennes* were mandatory affairs; which no one was excused from attending each Sunday, even at sea, except when the seas were too rough. In port, it is remembered, Chaplain Elliott's services had to be attended by all hands; the crew dressed in white frocks with blue collars, the officers in their best blues. Throughout the sermon all stood with heads uncovered.

ENUMCLAW (J-9)

The name of this city, located twenty miles east of Tacoma, is linked historically with Stampede Pass, the 3,725 feet high opening through the Cascade Range which lies eastward of here. Plans to lay transcontinental railroad tracks over the snow-capped Cascade Range had been a dream of all northwesterners since 1873, when the Northern Pacific Railroad chose Tacoma, just east of Enumclaw, as its Pacific Ocean terminus. When in December, 1880, Mr. Virgil Bogue began surveying a railroad route from the site where today the city of

Enumclaw stands to go over the Cascades to connect at Pasco with transcontinental tracks, excitement ran high in the Puget Sound country. Thus the city of Enumclaw traces its beginnings to the railroad base which was established here.

It took Mr. Bogue's surveyors over two months to penetrate the rugged and wild countryside through which they then pushed their way up the banks of Green River until this stream was but a rivulet in the high mountains. Here on March 19th, 1881, they discovered Stampede Pass. At the time of this discovery it was snowing and Bogue's men were exhausted and frozen. Angry at a foreman who nonetheless demanded they work faster, some of Bogue's workmen then "stampeded" back down the slopes and returned to the comforts of Tacoma; hence the name "Stampede Pass" which this opening in the Cascade Range into eastern Washington now bears.

It was not until 1886 that the boring of a railroad tunnel beneath Stampede Pass commenced. In the meantime tracklayers from Pasco in Eastern Washington, while laying tracks eastward across Eastern Washington toward Idaho, had met up with the west-bound tracklayers of the Northern Pacific who for months had been pushing across the plains and prairies of Wyoming and Montana. The two groups had joined together in September, 1883, at Deer Lodge, Montana, causing a great celebration. From Pasco tracks by this time had been laid down the Columbia River's south side to Portland. So the honor of becoming the transcontinental railroad's first western terminus in the Pacific Northwest went to the town of Portland, not Tacoma.

The word *enumclaw* is Indian, translated "place of evil spirits." This name applies to Enumclaw Mountain located closeby the city of Enumclaw. Apparently the name refers not to the mountain itself but rather to some evil incident now forgotten which was suffered by local Indians while traveling on the slopes of Enumclaw Mountain.

Probably the first white structure built where Enumclaw now stands was a blockhouse to which the white families living in the neighborhood fled during the Indian troubles which occurred in the summer of 1855. Some blamed the Brritish at Fort Nisqually for causing the Indians to attack the American settlers. The real cause, however, appears to have been numerous Americans overrunning Indian lands east of the Cascade Range in search of gold. In doing so as they passed through Yakima country, they killed several Yakima Indians, and it was warriors of this Indian nation who caused the fighting against whites to spill westward over the mountains into the region around Enumclaw.

Mr. A.J. Porter who lived immediately south of today's Enumclaw was sleeping in a shelter near his house on the night of October 27, 1855. Having vacated the cabin anticipating it would be attacked that night by Indians, suddenly he awoke to realize that some Indians indeed were engaged in looting his home. Hastily Porter spread the alarm by paddling his home-made canoe down the nearby White River, warning the settlers downstream as he progressed, advising them to abandon their cabins and flee. Today he is remembered as "The Paul Revere of Puget Sound."

EVERETT (G-9)

The history of this city, twenty-seven miles north of Seattle, dates back to 3 June 1792, when the British explorer Captain George Vancouver, sailing in HMS *Discovery,* anchored in adjacent waters (off present Elliot Point at Mukilteo) accompanied by his second ship, the armed tender *Chatham,* Lieutenant William Broughton in command. For several weeks prior to this, Broughton and Vancouver had been exploring the waters of what we know today as Puget Sound. Attempting to unravel its complicated topography; Vancouver in his *Discovery* probed the waters south of here while Broughton attempted to map the many islands of the San Juans. On the evening previous to this the two vessels had made a successful rendezvous here, the *Chatham* firing a gun to reveal her presence to the *Discovery.* On the morning of June 3 the two vessels moved in company to the north end of today's Everett Harbor off the tip of Tulalip Inlet. At this point Vancouver notes "All hands were employed in fishing with tolerably good success," then he continues in his journal:

> . . . On Monday the 4th the crews were served as good a dinner as we were able to provide them, with a double allowance of grog, to drink the King's health, it being the anniversary of His Majesty's birth; on which auspicious occasion I had long designed to take formal possession of all the country we had lately been exploring . . . To execute this purpose, accompanied by Mr. Broughton and some of his officers, I went ashore about one o'clock, pursuing the usual formalities on such occasions, and under the discharge of a royal salute from the vessels, took possession accordingly.

To the general region between here and the Columbia River, Vancouver gave the name New Georgia, honoring his monarch King George III, and he continues: ". . . to the inland sea . . . behind the supposed Strait of Juan de Fuca I gave the name Gulf of Georgia . . .

This branch of Admiralty Inlet obtained the name Possession Sound; and its western arm, after Vice Admiral Sir Alan Gardner . . . I distinguished by the name Port Gardner," this being the first name given to today's city of Everett and one by which Everett's harbor is still known.

At this time Admiral Sir Alan Gardner was a member of the prestigious Board of Admiralty back in England. Vancouver had recently served under him in the West Indies, both aboard HMS *Europa,* fifty guns, which Gardner commanded in 1786 and HMS *Courageux,* seventy-four guns, in 1790. During this period Vancouver had distinguished himself as a bright young officer, and it was to Admiral Gardner that Vancouver owed his appointment as leader of the exploring expedition to America in which he was now engaged. In later years Admiral Gardner served in the British Parliament where, as Baron of Uttoxeter, he was knighted.

Upon departing Port Gardner the next day, headed northward, Lieutenant Broughton ran his vessel aground near present Stanwood in Port Susan, which separated Camano Island from the mainland. No damage was done, and the next day Vancouver in the *Discovery* and Broughton in the *Chatham,* commenced their explorations northward along the coast, including the islands not yet explored enroute. The two vessels by now were headed for Nootka, a spot now deserted on Vancouver Island, but at this time the busiest harbor in the entire Northwest.

In 1789, the Spanish governor at Nootka had so insulted British sea captains trading for furs there, that war between England and Spain nearly erupted when news of it reached London. England, at this time, was displeased with Spain in her possessive attitude over all of America's west coast and decided to seize the incident to assert equal claims over the region. Spain's lessened position of power back in Europe was reflected in the Treaty of Nootka signed in 1790, wherein this nation agreed henceforth to share Nootka equally with the British.

Accordingly, Captain Vancouver was proceeding northward to work out the details of joint occupancy. Vancouver was not surprised, therefore, when in the vicinity of Birch Bay, seventy miles north of Everett, he and Broughton encountered two Spanish ships sailing closeby. Together the four vessels, after exchanging courtesies, continued north into present Georgia Strait. Separating only before reaching Johnstone Strait, Vancouver and Broughton, bidding them farewell, rounded Vancouver Island's northern tip to anchor in Nootka's harbor, called Friendly Cove (located on the island's coast due west of the present city of Campbell River).

Chiefly responsible for the establishment of today's city of Everett was the Great Northern Railroad which was being laid toward Everett from the east in the 1880s. It was the approach of the track-layers of this giant project, directed by James Jerome Hill, its president, which prompted two Ohio men, Messrs. W.J. and B.J. Rucker to take out land claims on the shore of Port Gardner in 1886. Well aware that by virtue of Port Gardner's location at the mouth of the Snohomish River, the Great Northern would most likely lay tracks from Stevens Pass here, the two brothers envisioned their site becoming a future New York City. After all, the magic wand of another transcontinental railroad, the Northern Pacific, had similarly touched Tacoma (located closeby to the south of here) and they felt certain that because of Port Gardner's closer proximity to the ocean, their site would be preferred over this neighboring harbor.

Not long after this, Henry Hewitt arrived at Port Gardner, likewise enthused over the site. A wealthy lumberman from Wisconsin who had come to exploit the seemingly unlimited supply of Douglas fir in the Northwest, he joined in the land speculation which was going on.

Next to join in the fever were the Wall Street capitalists Charles and Gardner Colby, two brothers and both of them friends of John D. Rockefeller, then the richest man in America. With news from the Colby brothers that Rockefeller himself was investing in the future of the Port Gardner site, optimism ran rife. The quick riches to be made by purchasing land here was publicized throughout the East and thousands of small investors became involved.

Organizing Port Gardner Land Company, the promoters drew up a blue-print model community here, complete with sawmills, a huge shipyard for building ocean-going steam vessels, extensive docks, paper mills, a nail factory, even electric street cars (then a total novelty in the West). Predicted Gardner Colby, treasurer of the burgeoning land company, ". . . the time is not far distant when this town will be to the Pacific Coast what Boston is to the East."

In order to provide enough land to the innumerable small purchasers who were by now arriving on the scene, a paper town adjacent to the future city (its name: Lowell, after the then-thriving metropolis back East, adjacent to Boston) was also blueprinted.

Exuberance reigned supreme when in 1891 "giant deposits" of gold, silver, and other precious ore were discovered forty miles to the east of here in the Cascades. The site was promptly christened "Monte Cristo," after the island off the coast of Italy to which, in Dumas' famous novel, its hero finds the treasure with which to pay off his debts. Mr. Rockefeller's own money was added to build tracks to this bonanza, and a huge smelter on the shores of Port Gardner was added to the blueprint for the future city.

The name Everett was chosen at a dinner party in 1888, held at the home of Charles Colby, his mansion situated on New York City's Fifth Avenue. Attended by both Colby brothers, as well as other eastern capitalists representing Rockefeller interests, also by Henry Hewitt who by now was president of the Everett Land Company; the group was in a festive mood, news of the recent Monte Cristo mines having been recently received.

After-dinner cigars and brandy were being served, and Mr. Colby was in the act of lifting his glass to a toast, the story goes, when it suddenly occurred to him, to his astonishment, that the forthcoming city as yet had no name. It was then that Charles Colby allegedly noticed the young son of his brother, Gardner Colby, sitting rather bored at the foot of the long banquet table. Everett Colby was his name; thus it occurred to him, as he lifted his glass, to propose a toast to "Everett," a name which has endured to this day.

When he grew up, Everett Colby became a famous man. Educated at Brown University and Harvard Law School, he attracted national attention when he successfully prosecuted and broke up the corrupt Jersey City political machine of Mark Fagan, then the mayor; a machine which had for years past defied all governmental effort to bring about its downfall.

Only thirty-two when he achieved this notoriety, Everett Colby went on to become a State Senator; then in 1917 Chairman of the U.S. Food Administration, and was a member of the executive committee of the World Court. In a famous book of this period titled *Shame of the Cities*, written by Lincoln Steffens, Everett Colby is hailed as having been the inspiration by which President Theodore Roosevelt launched his famous Muckraker Movement, one of the more famous reform movements in U.S. history.

The Everett Land Company's boom ended with the arrival of the Panic of 1893, when the entire nation was swept into the worst financial disaster in its history. Soon afterward, Rockefeller withdrew his financial support for the whole affair; the Colby brothers followed suit, and Hewitt and the Rucker brothers were left impoverished.

Especially hard hit were the thousands of small investors involved, their lifetime savings lost in the holocaust. Even harder hit were the hundreds of laborers, many of them immigrants from Europe, who, having been promised employment if they traveled here, were left stranded without adequate means of survival.

To make matters worse, Mr. Hill's Great Northern Railroad decided to choose Seattle, not Everett, as its ocean terminus. The founders of Everett were not ones to despair, however. By 1900 the town had rebounded, and not long after Everett boasted the largest lumber mill in the world. A decade later it possessed over ninety manufacturing plants, all of them prospering.

F

FERNDALE (C-7)

This town lies ten miles northwest of Bellingham, not far from the Canadian border. When Ferndale began *circa* 1872 its founders were surrounded by Indians of the Nooksack tribe. In their language the word *nook* meant people and *sa-aak* meant ferns; hence their tribal name meant "people of the ferns." From this source the name Ferndale was given to the town. Past Ferndale flows the Nooksack River. It empties into salt water on Lummi Bay, eight miles to the town's southwest.

Spanish explorers were sailing past Lummi Bay in June, 1792, headed northward up the coastline looking for an opening in the shoreline which led into the Atlantic Ocean. They were sailing in the two small schooners, the *Sutil* and the *Mexicana*. The date was June, 1792.

Suddenly they began hearing violent rumblings and saw huge clouds of smoke issuing from the beautiful snow-capped peak they saw to the east, which today we call Mount Baker. Then they saw in the distance to seaward two strange craft under sail. As they shortly were to learn, these were boats from two English ships, namely His Majesty's Ship *Discovery*, commanded by Captain Vancouver and the armed tender *Chatham*, commanded by Lieutenant William Broughton. The commanders of the *Sutil* and *Mexicana*, Lieutenants Dionisio Galiano and Cayetano Valdes of the Spanish navy, were not aware until now that there were rival explorers sailing in these waters.

England and Spain at this time were rivals for possession of this new region of the world. This, however, did not constrain the two groups about a week later from making cordial visits upon each others' ships. During these visits, Vancouver and Broughton were impressed with the superb quality of the navigational instruments they found aboard the Spanish ships. Also, they were impressed with the luxurious style in which the Spaniards lived, even though their vessels were much smaller than their English ones.

Amazingly, upon the completion of these visits, the rival groups agreed to explore together northward up the coastline. One cannot help but wonder which of their respective nations—Spain or England—would have claimed ownership in the event that the opening to the Northwest Passage they were jointly seeking had suddenly loomed ahead.

The British government, in dispatching Captain Vancouver to these coasts the previous year had given orders for him to meet at Nootka, a Spanish naval base northwest of here, with Spain's diplomatic representative, Senor Bodega y Quadra, to negotiate a settlement over the question of how the two nations were to share this base. Nootka, at this time, was capital of the Pacific Northwest, located at a now-deserted spot on the west coast of Vancouver Island. Nootka was visited by sailing ships from all over the world.

The rival explorers continued sailing north into Georgia Strait. When north of Texada Island, the Britishers separated from the two Spanish vessels, continuing north independently. Just prior to reaching the northern tip of Vancouver Island, Captain Vancouver in his ship *Discovery* went aground. Fortunately, at high tide his ship floated free and reached Nootka, a few miles north of the present town of Gold River, where he found Senor Quadra awaiting him. Then the two commenced diplomatic negotiations which lasted most of the ensuing summer.

FIDALGO ISLAND (D-7)

This is the island, sixty miles north of Seattle, on which the city of Anacortes now stands. Lieutenant Salvador Fidalgo never sailed the waters near the island bearing his name. However, he was already a distinguished Spaniard when in June, 1791, his superior in the Spanish navy, Francisco Eliza, applied his name here. Both Eliza and Fidalgo at this time were recent arrivals in the New World, having arrived at Spain's naval base in San Blas, lower California from Madrid in 1789. Before coming here to New Spain, as the entire west coast of America was then known, Fidalgo had made a name for himself by mapping the Mediterranean. When his name was given to Fidalgo Island, he had creditably led ships north from Nootka—the Spanish naval base on Vancouver Island of which Eliza was the Commandant—into Alaskan waters to spy upon the Russians there, whom Spain feared were pushing southward to invade the Spanish coasts. At the time Eliza bestowed his name on this island, however, Lieutenant Fidalgo had not yet been assigned the job, which one year later would make him famous in Northwest history; for it was Senor Fidalgo who, in early 1792, established the first white settlement in what is now called Washington State.

Called Fort Gaona, for a Spanish admiral of that time, this Spanish post was fortified with guns by which to bar all non-Spanish ships from sailing into the waters we today call Puget Sound. Fort Gaona was located just inside the Strait of Juan de Fuca at what is now called Neah Bay.

The details of how Fidalgo Island received Lieutenant Fidalgo's name relate to fellow Spaniards who became the first white men to explore the then-mysterious waters lying inside the Strait of Juan de Fuca. First of these explorers was Manuel Quimper, sailing in the ship *Princesa Real.* From the body of water we now call Dungeness Bay, Quimper, in 1790, dispatched Juan Carrasco by longboat to probe the as-yet unexplored waters they saw to the northeast. Senor Carrasco, in becoming the first white man to view Fidalgo Island, failed to recognize it as an island, believing it to be a part of the mainland. To the waters adjacent to Fidalgo he gave the name *Boca de Fidalgo.* In the following year another Spanish naval man, Jose Narvaez, recognizing that waters adjacent here were not a bay, gave them the name *Canal de Fidalgo.*

For nearly a half century after this, no white explorers took an interest in these waters. Then in 1841, the U.S. explorer Charles Wilkes, a naval officer, recognized Fidalgo Island to be, in fact, an island (it is separated from the mainland by a waterway scarcely one hundred yards wide). He called it Perry's Island, honoring Oliver Perry (famous for his words "We have met the enemy and they are ours" while fighting the British on Lake Erie in the War of 1812). It was six years later that a British surveyor, Commander (later Admiral) Henry Kellett, finding this American name distasteful, resurrected the Spanish name *Boca de Fidalgo,* to give this landmark its present name: Fidalgo Island.

FORKS

Forty miles west of Port Angeles is this mountain community, situated on the western side of Olympic National Park. Founded in 1912, Forks is so named after the three rivers which converge closeby, namely, the Calawah, Bogachiel, and Soleduck rivers. Forks is famous as the settlement to which John Huelsdonk, the first white settler of nearby Hoh Valley, traveled whenever he became short of supplies. He was a fur trapper, logger, and all-around lover of remote wilderness. Huelsdonk first arrived in the Forks area in 1892. He and his stalwart wife, Dora, traveled sixty miles—by canoe and on foot up the Quillayute and Calawah rivers, and then by trail not even passable by horse—in order to stake out the site of their home, located in a small clearing in the forest. Here they lived for the next half century.

Periodically Huelsdonk made shopping trips to the store at Forks. Once a neighbor of Huelsdonk came upon him, returning over the rugged trail from Forks to his home, carrying a new kitchen stove he had just purchased. "Isn't that stove too heavy a load for you?" he asked of the giant man. "No," Huelsdonk replied, "except that one hundred pound sack of flour rolling around inside the oven keeps shifting," Huelsdonk complained. The Huelsdonk family's only other connection with the outside world was over a primitive elk trail down the banks of the Hoh River to the Pacific Ocean and thence northward along the beach to the town of La Push.

FORT COLVILLE (D-22)

Now submerged by the backwaters of Roosevelt Dam, this Columbia River fur post stood one-half mile below the original Kettle Falls, tallest drop in the entire twelve hundred-mile flow of this stream from the Canadian Rockies all the way to the Pacific Ocean. Fort Colville was established in 1825 by Governor George Simpson in order to replace nearby Spokane House, not only because this new site was located more directly on the line of travel of the fur brigades traveling between Fort Vancouver to York Factory in eastern Canada, but also because it was better situated as a resupply station for outlying fur posts to the north in New Caledonia. This fort, which lasted for almost fifty years, became one of the most colorful of the trading posts in the Pacific Northwest.

In naming Fort Colvile (spelled with one *l*), Simpson was honoring his mentor and sponsor, Andrew Colvile (1779–1856), a wealthy and powerful figure in the London headquarters of Simpson's Hudson Bay Company. Through Colvile's efforts, Simpson, at age twenty-seven, became Governor of the HBC's activities in all of Canada. "To you, sir," Simpson wrote in later years to Lord Colvile, "I am solely indebted for my advancement in Life."

The first chief factor of Fort Colville was Archibald McDonald (1790–1853). He is remembered as presiding over this fur post like a Scottish laird, regaling visitors with skirling bagpipes and Scotch whiskey. Previous to coming here, Archibald was private secretary to Lord Selkirk (1771–1820) who controlled the Hudson Bay Company for several years, and founded the Red River Colony in present-day Manitoba.

In 1823, Archibald was sent west from Red River over the Rocky Mountains to officially take over the North West Company's fur posts on the Columbia under the provisions of a recent merger of this company with the Hudson's Bay Company at Fort Vancouver.

In 1824, Archibald fell in love with the oldest daughter of Chief Comcomly, powerful head of the Chinook nation. Shortly after Archibald's marriage to Princess Raven, as she was known, she died at the birth of their son Ranald. When Ranald was twenty-three he ran away to sea as a Pacific whaler, and was shipwrecked on the coast of Japan. Archibald remarried Jane Klyne, a daughter of the head of Jasper House in the Rockies. Their daughter, Jane, is remembered for her skill as a horseback rider on the race track which Archibald built at Fort Colville.

Chief Factor Archibald McDonald should not be confused with a later equally-famous chief factor at Fort Colville. His name was Angus McDonald (1816–1889), a nephew of Archibald. Very fond of the Indians, Angus was known to them affectionately under the name of *Oops-chin,* translated "whiskers," for he sported a heavy red beard. He was long remembered by Governor Isaac Stevens, the first Governor of Washington Territory, for the reception he gave the governor one night in 1853 at Fort Colville. The governor arrived after traveling for over a month, by horseback and on foot all the way from Minnesota over the

Rocky Mountains. After entertaining the governor and his assistant, Captain George McClellan (later commander of the *Patomac* in the Civil War) and drinking late into the night, Archibald presented the governor, upon his departure for Puget Sound on the following day, with fifty more imperial gallons of whiskey.

FORT OKANOGAN ⌐-17)

Fur trappers were tₕₑ pioneers of the Pacific Northwest, and one of the more famous of them built this trading post where today the town of Brewster, Washington, stands, forty miles upriver of Wenatchee on the Columbia River. Alexander Ross (1783–1856) was a school teacher prior to becoming a fur trapper. A British citizen, he trapped initially for The Honourable North West Company of Montreal after arriving in Canada from his native Scotland. In 1810, however, he shifted his allegiance from the Canadian company to a rival fur company operated by the New York City fur mogul John J. Astor. Then in early 1811, Ross arrived at the mouth of the Columbia River by sailing ship, having sailed here at Mr. Astor's direction from around Cape Horn. Here Ross and fellow cohorts established an American fur post called Astoria to be Mr. Astor's fur headquarters in the Northwest.

It was in the summer of 1811 that Mr. Ross with a group of trappers, after spending two weeks paddling up the then swift-flowing Columbia in two leaky canoes, arrived at the site where Brewster now stands to establish here a sixteen-by-twenty foot hovel made of driftwood, calling it Fort Okanogan. It was located upstream on the Okanogan River one-half mile from the juncture of this stream with the Columbia River. It was here that Ross spent the winter of 1811–1812 all alone, except for a dog for company, cultivating the good will of the local Indians and buying their furs while the remainder of the party, led by another Scotsman, David Stuart, proceeded on north into Canadian country to obtain furs.

In December, 1813, as a result of the War of 1812, Astoria was seized by a British warship, and Fort Okanogan, being a satellite of the seized Astoria, became a British post instead of an American one. Alexander Ross, his citizenship being still British, and because he was a former employee of the Montreal fur company who then occupied Astoria, stayed on at Fort Okanogan. Now that it was a British post, Ross became its first officer-in-charge under British auspices.

With the Union Jack flying over it, Fort Okanogan flourished. Copious amounts of fur harvested north of Fort Okanogan in Kamloops country were delivered on the backs of long lines of horses to Fort Okanogan. Here they were loaded in fleets of canoes whose jolly French-Canadian voyageurs, wearing their traditional glazed blue hats and red capotes, transported the furs up the Columbia River to the point in this stream called Boat Encampment, where the river suddenly turns south. From here the furs were again loaded onto the backs of horses and carried over the Canadian Rockies. Thence they were transported by stream and horseback eastward across today's provinces of Alberta, Saskatchewan, and Manitoba to Hudson's Bay. Sailing ships then carried the pelt to London to be made into beaver hats and clothing, then worn by all stylish Europeans.

In 1816, Alexander Ross left Fort Okanogan to become second-in-command of Fort George, this being the name of Astoria following the post's seizure by the British. Two years later Ross was further promoted by the 300-pound Donald McKenzie, a fellow Scot, to become McKenzie's chief assistant at a fur post called Fort Nez Perce, located where the Walla Walla River joins the Columbia River at Wallula. At this time Fort Nez Perce was on the edge of an unexplored territory known only as Snake country (now called Southern Idaho) lying to the east beyond the Blue Mountains, it being a region teeming with hostile Snake Indians. While Ross remained at Fort Nez Perce, the base of the Snake country operations, the herculean Donald McKenzie began leading his famous fur brigades. Accompanied by hundreds of horses and a small army of mounted fur trappers, McKenzie's famous series of trapping expeditions traversed country never before seen by white men. Remaining away from Fort Nez Perce as much as a year or more at a time, the burly Scot and his followers lived off the land, constantly dodging hostile Indians while setting traps along the Snake River and its tributaries. When they had acquired all the furs which their horses could carry, they would return to Fort Nez Perce and to Alexander Ross. Three such expeditions were made by McKenzie, ones which extended into Spanish country where Utah now stands and into the Rockies and the region presently known as Wyoming.

By 1823, Alexander Ross had succeeded Donald McKenzie in leading such expeditions; the base from which Ross departed, however, being one called Flathead Post, located in western Montana. From here Ross led giant fur brigades of trappers south along the Continental Divide into the same Snake country in which McKenzie had been so successful.

By this time, however, rival American trappers coming from Bear River country in Utah and the territory around the Grand Tetons were increasingly active in Snake country. They were curious as to how successful their British rivals were in the harvesting of furs, and as to where the British base was located. Competition with Ross's trappers increased, the Americans often shadowing the British. In the Spring of 1824, a contingent of these Yankee trappers, led by Jedediah Smith, followed Ross back north to Flathead Post to spy upon the British operations there. In vain did Mr. Ross attempt to shake the Americans as he was enroute north.

When, despite all efforts, Ross and his brigade reached Flathead Post, the Yankees still trailing him, it so happened that the very head of the Hudson's Bay Company, Sir George Simpson, was paying the post a visit. The presence of these Americans following on Ross's heels so angered the vitriolic Sir George, that he fired Ross, even though this former Fort Okanogan trapper had made every effort to shake the Americans, and despite the fact that Ross's trappers (during the previous winter of trapping Snake country) had broken all records for the number of pelts acquired.

Mr. Ross's later years were spent at Red River, near present Winnipeg in Manitoba, with his Indian wife, an Okanogan girl, and their children, engaged in farming the 100-acre parcel of land given him by the Hudson's Bay Company. By this time Fort Okanogan, which Ross had built in 1811, had been moved a short way from its original site to one overlooking the Columbia. This fort continued under British management even after the international boundary line, in 1846, was drawn north of here. Fort Okanogan was finally abandoned in 1860.

FORT SPOKANE (H-23)

When, in 1808, the wealthy John J. Astor, America's leading fur trader, decided to extend his business by selling furs to China, he chose to establish a fur depot called Astoria at the Columbia River's entrance to the Pacific Ocean. Here, he planned, furs harvested in the interior regions of the as-yet unexplored Pacific Northwest would be delivered, then shipped across the Pacific to Macao where the pelt was in high demand. Lacking American fur men by which to implement this plan, Mr. Astor then lured Canadian fur men, members of the North West Company of Montreal, to work for him, offering them higher wages than their Montreal employers wished to pay them. Mr. Astor then dispatched these recently-engaged Canadians around Cape Horn by sailing ship, and it was they who established Astoria, as it was known; the first permanent white establishment of the Pacific Northwest.

The Astorians were scarcely established on the lower Columbia when, to their surprise and dismay, they suddenly became aware (through the Indians) that their former Montreal colleagues—many of them old friends—had also moved west and built a rival fur post inland of Astoria called Spokane House, located about 260 miles northeast of their own fur post. It was in order to compete with this British post, that in the summer of 1812, John Clarke, one of Mr. Astor's partners, journeyed from Astoria up the Columbia, Snake, and Palouse rivers and erected Fort Spokane (situated within a few hundred yards of his former North West Company associates who were now his rivals). The two side-by-side trading posts, one American and the other British, presented an amazing spectacle in the wilderness, about eight miles north of the present heart of downtown Spokane.

John Clarke was a pompous and conceited executive. He constantly strutted—accompanied by aides wearing feathers in their hats—before the local Spokane Indians, who were duly impressed. Having come to Astoria recently on a supply ship the *Beaver*, Mr. Clarke possessed an immediate advantage over his former colleagues of Spokane House; the *Beaver* brought in its hold a fresh supply of trade goods which Clarke had now brought with him to his new trading post. They were goods far superior to the dwindling number of items the British had to offer the Indians for their furs.

Although this rivalry for the local Indians' favor was intense, outwardly the two posts were friendly. Horse races were held and conviviality existed on the surface. However, following an argument between Francois Payette of Clark's team of traders at Fort Spokane with one Nicholas Montour of Spokane House over the relative merits of certain furs, a duel between the two was fought. Happily it ended fortunately. After the usual ten paces were marched by its participants one early morning at the appointed scheme, the two whirled about and fired at each other; Payette's pistol grazing Montour's arm, Montour's pistol shot, in turn, shooting off Payette's pantleg.

In the late fall of 1812, word reached the two posts, brought overland by John G. McTavish of Montreal, that the United States and Great Britain were at war, and that a British warship was on its way to the mouth of the Columbia to capture Astoria. Months passed, however, and still the expected warship did not arrive. Meanwhile, the British occupants of Spokane House (having exhausted their supply of trade goods with which to obtain the local furs) marched down the Columbia to await the British warship's arrival, gleeful over the prospect that with the vessel's capture of Astoria, their pesky rivals at Fort Spokane would cease to bother them.

Mr. Duncan McDougall, Astor's chief representative at Astoria, was likewise a former North Wester who had succumbed to his boss's offer of higher pay. As the weeks passed with no sign of the warship, he began discussing with his former associates from Spokane House, now his competitors, about the possibility of making a deal. It would be better to sell Astoria, claimed McDougall, thereby obtaining at least some financial reward for Mr. Astor, than to have the post seized as a prize of war.

Whether by collusion or by a sincere desire to serve Mr. Astor's best interests, on October 13, 1813, a deal was struck with Spokane House's McTavish wherein the North West Company of Montreal agreed to pay forty thousand dollars for the seventeen thousand pounds of beaver pelt stored at Astoria, along with other emoluments. The following month when HMS *Raccoon,* twenty-nine guns, anchored off Astoria, its commanding officer, Captain Black, found to his disgust that he had no American post to capture, it already having become a British possession.

FORT VANCOUVER (Q-7)

This historical spot was situated where the city of Vancouver now stands, opposite Portland across the Columbia River. Fort Vancouver, itself, consisted of some thirty buildings which included a blacksmith shop, a jail, a school, and two churches. Outside the palisade which surrounded this British fur post were located peripheral activities related to the purpose of Fort Vancouver which was to administer the harvesting of furs throughout the Pacific Northwest. Among these were salt works, a shipyard, a sawmill, and fisheries. Included in the farm's stock at various times during the post's thirty years' life were 450 cattle, 100 or more horses, 300 hogs, 200 sheep, and 40 goats. Outside the stockade, too, lived hundreds of laborers of many nationalities forming, as one visitor recalled ". . . a little village where there is quite a Babel of tongues, as the inhabitants are a mixture of English, French, Iroquois, Sandwich Islanders, Crees, and Chinooks."

When Charles Wilkes USN visited Fort Vancouver in 1841, his American warships at the time anchored in Puget Sound (he had ridden horseback from Puget Sound to the lower Columbia to visit Dr. McLoughlin here), he was quite impressed with the great industry displayed at this Hudson's Bay Company post. He records:

> . . . The routine of the day at Fort Vancouver is perhaps the same throughout the year. At early dawn [five A.M. in summer and one hour later in winter] . . . the bell is rung for the working parties, who soon after go to work; the sound of hammers, click of anvils, the rumbling of carts, with tinkling of bells, render it difficult to sleep after this hour. The bell rings again at eight for breakfast; after which they resume work which continues till one, then an hour is allowed for dinner, after which they work till six, when the labours of the day close.

Center of social life at Fort Vancouver was the Great Hall, located in the middle of the palisade. Visitors upon arriving to see the chief factor were shown into a large waiting room, its walls decorated with impressive trophies of the chase, rifles, and broadswords. Here a tall Scot Highlander, dressed in kilt and tartans set, notoriously paced the room, apparently unaware of the guest's presence.

A giant of a man, Dr. McLoughlin wore his hair long, its whiteness combining with his florid pink complexion to create an appearance which greatly impressed all newcomers. In the Great Hall, protocol and manners were strictly observed, particularly at meal time. Food was served on the finest china and toasts were drunk with the finest wines, as bagpipes skirled and Kanaka servants dressed in special uniforms quietly attended.

Probably the most dramatic event at the fort was the arrival of an annual canoe brigade from York Factory on Hudson's Bay, after several months of travel across Canada. When they reached a point a few miles upstream on the Columbia above the fort, it was customary for them to send an advance messenger overland to the fort, advising Dr. McLoughlin of their impending arrival. The personnel of the brigade, meanwhile (numbering as many as one hundred) changing their rough clothes of the trail into finery suitable for the ceremonious occasion soon to take place. Dignitaries donned frock coats and top hats, made of beaver of course; clerks and the lower hierarchy of the brigade changed to similar attire, including ruffled shirts and black ties. The French-Canadian canoemen, called *voyageurs,* donned their dress uniforms; striped shirts, glazed blue hats, and red-lined capes. Bagpipes skirled as the flotilla, usually of six to ten canoes, rounded the bend of the river above the fort where all hands were assembled awaiting their arrival. Guns were fired, and upon the completion of the landing, warm embraces and the drinking of toasts followed. Dr. McLoughlin then customarily declared a holiday sometimes lasting for days.

The departure of the canoe brigades was equally impressive. Commander Charles Wilkes, USN, describing his own leave-taking in 1841 to return north up the Cowlitz River to Puget Sound where his flagship USS *Vincennes* was anchored, recalls:

> On the morning of the 17th June, 1841, the Fort was in a stir at an early hour, and preparations were making. Now and then we saw a voyageur decked out in his ribands and feathers all attention to his duties. About ten o'clock we were all summoned by Dr. McLoughlin to the Hall to take a parting cup customary in this country and observed as far as I could learn throughout among themselves . . . I like this hanging to old customs . . . On reaching the river we found one of Mr. Ogden's boats. Wilkes here refers to the famous Peter Skene Ogden of Snake River country fame . . . manned by fourteen voyageurs, all gaily dressed with their plumes of various colors tied in large bunches over their oil skin hats. With another warm shake of the hand we embarked & off we flew against the Stream under the fine chorus of a Canadian boat song. After paddling upstream for some distance we made a graceful sweep to reach the centre, then passed the spectators of the fort with great animation. The boat and voyageurs seemed a fit object to grace the wide-flowing stream. On merrily we went, while each voyageur in succession took up the song, all joining in the chorus . . . (*Narrative of the U.S. Exploring Expedition* (1839–1842) Phila. 1850)

Founded in 1824, Fort Vancouver was intended by Governor George Simpson of the Hudson's Bay Company (who chose the site) to replace Fort George, the earlier fur post which had been operating downstream on the Columbia River where the city of Astoria now stands, since 1813. Governor Simpson chose to name the new post after George Vancouver (1757–1798) to emphasize that it was this great explorer who formally claimed possession of the Northwest for England back in 1792. Captain Vancouver, moreover, continuously surveyed the coasts of the northwest from April, 1792, to December, 1794, interrupted briefly each winter by trips to the Hawaiian Islands where he conducted surveys there. Writing of the joyous occasion when he and his sailors were about to leave this remote region to return to England, Vancouver records:

> . . . they [the crews] . . . were served such an additional allowance of grog as was sufficient to answer every purpose of festivity on the occasion. This soon prompted a desire for mutual congratulations between the two vessels [Vancouver's two ships, H.M.S. Discovery and the armed tender Chatham] expressed by three exulting cheers from each; and it may be easily conceived that more heart-felt satisfaction was scarcely ever more reciprocally experienced, or more cordially exchanged.

Vancouver and his two ships sailed from Monterey in California on December 22, 1794, and arrived in the British Isles December 13, 1795, after four and one-half months at sea, having been away from England for nearly five years.

John McLoughlin, chief factor at Fort Vancouver from 1824 to 1848, was a leading figure in the history of early Oregon, as the Northwest was first called. Born at La Riviere du Loup near Quebec in 1784, he was trained to be a physician, but early in his life chose instead to follow the career of fur trader. He was already a partner in The Honourable North West Company of Montreal in 1812 when he married Margaret Wadin McKay, eight years his senior, a woman of considerable charm, who throughout the remainder of McLoughlin's years, aided him with her calm and forceful temperament. She was born of a Scottish father and a part-Chippewa Indian mother, and was educated in an Ursuline convent in Quebec. She was previously married to the famous Alexander McKay, an Astorian official who crossed on foot the Canadian continent before Lewis and Clark. McKay was killed in 1811 aboard the fur-trading ship Tonquin when Indians boarded the vessel at Clayoquot Harbor, Vancouver Island, and killed all aboard but two.

Sir George Simpson, governor of the Hudson Bay Company in Canada (the organization which McLoughlin joined to become chief factor at Fort Vancouver) describes Dr. McLoughlin as: ". . . a very bustling man who can go through a great deal of business but is wanting in system and regularly sets himself up for a righter of wrongs . . . Very anxious to obtain a lead among his colleagues with whom he has not much influence owing to his ungovernable violent disposition."

When Reverend Herbert Beaver (an Episcopal clergyman, thirty-six-years old and described as "a pompous little man") arrived from London at Fort Vancouver with his wife Jane to serve as this fur post's chaplain, he irritated Dr. McLoughlin; not only by complaining over the lack of physical comforts available at the fort, but also because he was intolerant of Catholicism, the religion taught Dr. McLoughlin in his youth and one to which he had recently returned.

When Reverend Beaver refused to baptize a small daughter of one of McLoughlin's good friends, Alexander Caulfield Anderson, because she was, like some of McLoughlin's own children, born out of wedlock, McLoughlin became particularly miffed. When the cleric referred soon afterward to Dr. McLoughlin's wife as ". . . a female of notoriously loose character," he struck the Reverend Beaver with the gold-headed cane, which it was his custom to carry, then apologized. Soon after the incident, Chaplain Beaver and his wife departed by sailing ship back to England.

FRIDAY HARBOR (D-6)

This is the largest of several communities which are to be found on this westernmost of the San Juan Islands, that group which lie immediately north of Puget Sound, and to which escapees from the crowded cities like to flock. Friday Harbor is named after a man named Friday, who used to live here in a hut. Friday was a Hawaiian laborer who worked for the Hudson's Bay Company, which in the 1850s operated a huge farm on the island. Friday tended some twelve hundred sheep here in the general vicinity of Friday Harbor. Originally this giant organization was engaged in harvesting furs for shipping to England and China. When the supply of these furs became exhausted due to over-trapping, the HBC began operating farms such as the one on this island (called Bellevue Farm). Here they raised sheep and cattle, and grew farm produce, then sold such items to the Russians in Alaska.

Before sailing to the Northwest, Captain James Cook (the first Englishman to do so) discovered the Hawaiian Islands of which Joe Friday was a native. Captain George Vancouver (the explorer who followed Captain Cook to the Northwest by four years, arriving in 1792) was always happy, after months of survey work during spring, summer, and fall, to sail to the Hawaiian Islands to spend the winter months. In doing so he cultivated a close relationship between the Northwest and the Islands which still exists. In the fall of 1793, Vancouver returned two young girls (who had been living aboard the fur trading ship *Jenny*, and brought to these northwest coasts) to their homes on the Island of Kauai. The *Jenny's* skipper, James Baker (an ex-slave trader) claimed the two young girls were stowaways aboard his vessel, but Vancouver thought they had been kidnapped. While returning the girls to their parents, Vancouver, in his ship *Discovery*, stopped in Spanish California. There he acquired a cow and bull, which upon reaching Oahu, he presented to Kamehameha, then the king of the islands. They were the first such animals ever seen by the Hawaiians, and created a great sensation. So pleased was the Hawaiian king with this gift, that in February, 1794, he officially ceded the Hawaiian Islands to Vancouver's monarch, the King of England.

G

GRAYS HARBOR (K-3)

The first recorded white to view this harbor, located midway down the Washington coast, was John Meares sailing in his tiny schooner *Felice Adventurer*. He was at this time headed south, skirting the coastline and inviting Indians in their canoes to come from the shore to swap their sea otter skins (worth large sums of money in China) for worthless items—beads and bits of iron—offered them by Meares in exchange. When Meares viewed the line of breakers guarding Grays Harbor, he chose not to risk his vessel in proceeding into the harbor itself. Captain Robert Gray, after whom Grays Harbor is named, similarly was trading for furs with the coastal Indians when he sighted Grays Harbor from his 212-ton ship *Columbia* in May, 1792. He was a different sort of skipper, bold and aggressive. After penetrating the breakers at Grays Harbor's entrance he anchored inside.

Gray and the crew of his *Columbia* had just come here from

Clayoquot Sound, which lies 100 miles northward up the coast from here on Vancouver Island's west coast. Here at Clayoquot Sound, Gray had been experiencing great trouble with the local Indians who had plotted to seize Gray's ship, and to kill Gray and all of his crew. Fortunately the hard-fisted captain had gotten word of the nefarious plan through Atoo, a Hawaiian member of his crew.

Two years prior to this, Gray had taken Atoo aboard his vessel in Hawaii, at Atoo's request, and Atoo then had sailed with Gray back to Boston. There he created quite a sensation, dressed in his Hawaiian costume of brilliant feathers. However, by the time Gray reached these Northwest coasts (this time the second occasion for his doing so) Atoo was restless and had gone ashore to live with the Clayoquot Indians without Gray's permission. When, however, Atoo learned of the Clayoquots' plan to kill Captain Gray, he rushed back to advise his captain.

Hastily Gray weighed anchor and moved the *Columbia-Rediviva* (the same vessel in which he was soon to discover the Columbia River) to another anchorage several miles away from the Clayoquot's village. When, some time later, the Clayoquots followed him there to attack his ship, Captain Gray was fully ready to repel them. Not only did he ruthlessly kill the Indian attackers, but he returned to the Clayoquot village anchorage and burned the entire village to the ground.

The following is a description of the Indians who, soon after Gray anchored his ship inside, put out in their canoes from the shore in great numbers and began to circle Gray's ship:

> They appear'd to be a savage set, and was well-arm'd, every man having his Quiver and Bow slung over his shoulder. Without doubt we are the first civilized people that ever entered this port, and these poor fellows viewed us with the greatest astonishment. (John Boit Gray's Third Mate aboard the *Columbia* at this time)

Trade was brisk; but as darkness fell and the Indians departed, all aboard the *Columbia* felt that they were in unfriendly territory. At this point we return to Third Officer Boit's account of what followed:

> This evening heard the hoot of the Indians, all hands was immediately under arms, severall canoes was seen passing near the Ship, but was dispers'd by firing a few Musketts over their heads. At Midnight we heard them again, and soon after as 'twas bright Moon light, we see the Canoes approaching the Ship. We fir'd severall cannon over them, but still they

persisted to advance with the war Whoop. At length a large
Canoe with at least 20 Men in her got within 1/2 pistol shot
of the quarter, and with a Nine pounder, loaded with
langerege and about ten Musketts, loaded with Buck shot, we
dash'd her all to pieces, and no doubt kill'd every soul in her.
The rest soon made retreat. I do not think they had aney
Conception of the power of Artillery. But they was too near
us to admit of any hesitation how to proceed.

Strangely, Boit records, on the morning following this disaster, the
Indians returned in their canoes and trading was resumed as if the
previous night's tragedy had never occurred.

Captain Gray and the *Columbia* remained at anchor in Gray's Harbor
until May 10, when in the evening he put out to sea and resumed
sailing south along the coast. The next morning found Gray and his
Columbia sailing off the mouth of the Columbia River. Bad weather had
previously prevented him from entering this river; indeed the previous
April he had spent nine days off the river's mouth waiting for the
opportunity to sail over its treacherous sandbar. On this particular
morning the weather still was not perfect. Courageously Gray headed
his vessel into the long line of breakers and emerged inside the
sandbar, the first white seaman ever to sail a ship into this great river.

Meanwhile, to the north of Grays Harbor, history was also being
made at a place—now deserted—named Nootka, located on Vancouver
Island's west coast to the north of Clayoquot Sound. Here a fracas had
taken place between Englishmen and Spaniards vying on behalf of
their respective nations for possession. Nootka at this time was capital
of the coastal fur trade, and when a Spaniard naval officer seized
Nootka's Harbor preventing its use by English fur traders, England and
Spain threatened war. By the time of Gray's visit here, however, peace
had been restored; but rivalry between England and Spain continued,
especially over which nation owned the waters which today we call
Puget Sound. Representing England in this rivalry was Captain George
Vancouver, who during this same summer (1792) named numerous
landmarks around Puget Sound, and, with the assistance of Master
Joseph Whidbey, surveyed extensively. It was Whidbey who gave the
present name Grays Harbor to what Captain Gray called Bulfinch
Harbor. Later this same year two Spanish explorers, Galiano and
Valdez, visited Grays Harbor. In charting it they confirmed Whidbey's
name, placing it on their charts as *Puerto de Gray.*

H

HOOD CANAL (H-6)

On May 6, 1792, Captain George Vancouver of the British Royal Navy, with his two warships HMS *Discovery* and the armed tender *Chatham*, dropped anchor in Port Discovery. At 7:00 a.m. on the following day, Vancouver departed Port Discovery to commence his survey of the waters we know today as Puget Sound. He traveled in the *Discovery's* yawl, and was accompanied by two other boats; the *Discovery's* launch commanded by Peter Puget, and the *Chatham's* cutter commanded by Sailing Master James Johnstone of the *Chatham*.

The crews of these boats had loaded them the previous evening with enough supplies to last for five days, and were setting out by oar and sail, into waters they believed never had been seen by white men. Without maps they were to proceed into many dead-ended waterways, so complicated is the coastline here. The most important of them is Hood Canal, which extends for about eighty miles south of where they were anchored before it reaches its dead end.

The first night away was spent on Marrowstone Island, east of Port Townsend, which Vancouver so named because the soil of this island was of a type with which he was familiar back in England, known by the name marrowstone. To the tiny harbor at Marrowstone Island's south end Vancouver gave the name Oak Cove, after the stand of oak trees near which they spent this first night away. On the next day, following the coastline southward from here past presently-named Port Ludlow, they sighted Indians "slowly paddling under the lee of a rocky point with an apparent intention of waiting our approach. In this they were gratified," continues Vancouver, "and on our arrival they did not seem to express the least doubt of our friendly disposition towards them."

Spanish explorers had preceded Vancouver in anchoring in Port Discovery, a fact of which he was unaware, and possibly these same Spaniards (although they left no record of it) had preceded Vancouver into these waters. "Having landed about nine o'clock to breakfast," Vancouver continues, "our friends the Indians, seventeen in number, landed also from six canoes . . . They now approached us with the utmost confidence, without being armed, and behaved in the most respectful and orderly manner. On a line being drawn with a stick on the sand between the two parties, they immediately sat down, and no one attempting to pass it, without previously making signs, requesting permission to do so." The explorer continues: "They had not anything to dispose of excepting bows and arrows and some few of their woollen and skin garments . . . these they exchanged for trinkets . . . conducting themselves in a fair and honest manner."

For four more days they continued down presently named Hood Canal (Vancouver so named it after Samuel Hood, one of England's most beloved naval leaders of that day), awed at the "pristine stillness." Upon discovering it ended in a cul-de-sac they retraced to Point Foulweather—which marks the eastern entrance to Hood Canal—on the 14th of May, one week having passed since leaving their ships. It was at this point that Vancouver first noted the waterway today called Admiralty Inlet (leading to lower Puget Sound southeastward). Supplies being low, however, he decided to lead his party back to their ships. Everyone received them joyfully, great anxiety having been entertained for their safety.

Lord Samuel Hood (1724–1816) also was honored by Vancouver with the naming of Portland's Mount Hood in his honor. The only blot on Admiral Hood's long and distinguished career was the failure of his ships, in 1781, to relieve British land troops under General Cornwallis at Yorktown during the American Revolution.

HOQUIAM (K-3)

Past the site of this Grays Harbor city, located midway on the Washington coast, trudged a party of fur trappers of the Hudson's Bay Company. The time was May, 1824, and they were traveling in three boats loaded with guns and ammunition and enough supplies to last the thirty men in their party for a month; flour, peas, oatmeal, grease, rum, butter, sugar, and pemmican. They had come here from Fort George, the British fur post at the mouth of the Columbia River on its south bank, the site which today is called Astoria. From here, after a difficult crossing of the Columbia, they had pushed their canoes and otherwise managed to negotiate the difficult inlets and beaches along the Washington coast from Cape Disappointment to Grays Harbor. Mr. Work and his fellow trappers were among the first whites to view the site where the city of Hoquiam now stands.

From Hoquiam they rowed and sailed their canoes up the Chehalis River until they came to the mouth of Black River, then up this stream's banks they plodded to lower Puget Sound. Northward up the Sound they sailed and rowed their boats, past the sites where Tacoma, Seattle, Bellingham, and Blaine now stand, until they reached their destination, the Fraser River; their purpose in completing this historical trip: ". . . to discover the mouth of the Fraser River and to ascertain the possibilities of navigation up that stream." Here on the Fraser River they found many Indians living "some in villages numbering more than one hundred houses."

John Work, at this time, was already a famous figure in the Northwest's fur trade. Described as ". . . a staunch Scotch-Irish Presbyterian," he was noted in his younger years for his fondness for comely Indian females; that is, until he married Josette, to whom he was devoted for the remainder of his life.

Josette used to accompany Mr. Work on the famous "Spanish brigades" which this rugged Irishman led for several years from Fort Vancouver into California, this region having not as yet become a U.S. possession. On such trips, he and Josette would depart the Columbia southward at the head of a column of as many as two hundred horses, on whose backs were loaded tents, cooking gear, and enough supplies to last their one hundred or more trappers for the winter season.

Beaver, as well as Indians, were plentiful, especially in the Sacramento Valley. It was Mr. Work, on one of these trips, who discovered beaver to be especially plentiful in San Francisco Bay. Several times they returned from such expeditions with as many as 4,000 beaver pelt to show for their efforts.

The name Hoquiam is applied to this city because of its location at the mouth of the Hoquiam River. It is an Indian word, alleged to be derived from *ho-qui-umps,* and having to do with the large accumulations of driftwood still to be found here.

I

ILWACO (N-3)

The founder of this city at the north entrance to the Columbia, was a scoundrel, Elijah White (1806–1897). This fact, however, was unknown for many years to the early settlers of Willamette Valley. White came west in 1836 as an important leader, whose intent was to work for the missionary, Jason Lee, at Salem. Within a year of his arrival however, White had quit his job as a missionary, accused of finagling the mission's finances; also of taking improper liberties with an Indian girl. One might have thought that White was through as a respectable resident of the region.

Undiscouraged, however, White hastened east to lobby in the national capitol as an "expert" on this new region of America. Shortly he had gained a congressional appointment to Oregon as its first U.S. Indian Agent. Moreover, in proceeding west to assume this lucrative job, White managed to have himself elected as leader of the wagon train of 1842, numbering some one hundred souls. Midway along the three-month long trek, however, White was removed from his position as leader of the group, and by an almost unanimous vote.

Undaunted, Dr. White (he had by now assumed this title for vague reasons), upon reaching Willamette Valley, not content with his already having the position of Indian agent, tried to establish himself as the region's governor. Moreover, as Indian agent, he made promises to the Indians which he was unable to fill. He also borrowed money from the British at Fort Vancouver which he failed to repay.

Again in 1845 he returned to the national capitol carrying a resolution signed by one faction of Willamette Valley's American settlers petitioning the U.S. Congress to assume jurisdiction over "Oregon country," as they called the northwest region as a whole. The move, however, was suspected by White's opponents in Willamette Valley to be his way of gaining from the Congress appointment as Oregon's first Territorial Delegate.

Word of Dr. White's malfeasance as Indian agent preceded his arrival in Washington. Upon his arrival he was dismissed from U.S. Government service. Dr. White returned to Oregon in 1850 with a wagon train which numbered over fifteen hundred men, women, and children, signaling the commencement of the "Oregon fever" which was beginning to sweep the nation. Within the next five years more than thirty thousand Americans arrived. It was against this background that Dr. White conceived of the phony land deal which marked the establishment of today's city of Ilwaco.

Filing a land claim here in the shadow of Cape Disappointment, he thus obtained title to 640 acres of free land under the existing homestead laws of that time. Then White subdivided this parcel of land into lots which he proceeded to sell to unsuspecting absentee purchasers. Initially he called his "paper city" by the name Lancaster City. Later he changed it to Pacific City. In the exaggerated write-up he distributed to prospective victims, White falsely alleged his settlement to be already in existence complete with such facilities as a hotel, library, and even a park filled with deer.

Meanwhile, in no way anxious to see a rival city springing up across the Columbia River from their own, the citizens of Astoria became increasingly concerned. When Mr. Joseph D. Holman, later to become one of the first trustees of Willamette University, joined in White's project by building an elaborate hotel here, Astorians managed to have this rival project across the river taken over by the United States Government as a military reservation; that is, all except the portion of the project which Mr. Holman managed to retain for himself. It was on Mr. Holman's land and around his sumptuous hotel that there arose today's city of Ilwaco.

The name Ilwaco was chosen by Mr. Holman to honor a local Indian leader of this name. Better known locally as "Ilwaco Jim," he was a minor chief who owed most of his local prominence to his marriage at that time to the eldest daughter of the famous ruler over the Chinook nation, one-eyed diminutive Chief Comcomly (1760–1830), dubbed by the author Washington Irving in his book *Astoria* (Boston, 1977) as "the Mephistopheles of Astoria." Chief Comcomly had been dead for half a century when Ilwaco was founded, but the memory of this rich and powerful Indian ruler had not disappeared.

From Chief Comcomly's palace atop Chinook Point, lying across Bakers Bay from today's city of Ilwaco, six miles to the southeast, exciting events took place in 1811 with the arrival of the ship *Tonquin.* In March of that year a party of whites, unloaded from this vessel, commenced building a fur post called Astoria immediately south of Comcomly's village and across the river on its south side. Known as Astoria, it was named for John J. Astor of New York City. Although it was an American fur post, Mr. Astor chose to man it with Britishers, experienced fur men of The Honourable North West Company of Montreal, for the New York fur executive lacked experienced fur trappers from his own nation.

This unusual situation caused considerable bewilderment to Chief Comcomly when in November, 1812, a British warship entered the Columbia River to capture Mr. Astor's American post. The War of 1812 having erupted between the two nations, His Majesty's Ship *Raccoon* commanded by Captain Black, wasted no time in pointing its guns at the American fort and demanding its surrender.

By this time Astoria's fur men were well ensconced at Astoria under the post's officer-in-charge, a dour Scotsman named Duncan McDougall. Initially, McDougall had been plagued by the Indians under Comcomly across the river, but diplomatically he had solved this problem by marrying the oldest of chief Comcomly's many marriagable daughters. With the arrival of the warship, however, McDougall's behavior greatly puzzled his father-in-law, Chief Comcomly. Comcomly did not know that his son-in-law, McDougall, had known for months of the warship's impending arrival and was not at all dismayed by the event.

Being himself an ex-Britisher for the Montreal Company, McDougall had figured it would be more helpful to his American boss, Mr. Astor, if he sold all the furs thus far accumulated at Astoria to his former colleagues, now his competitors, who a few months prior to this time had built a rival fur post inland of Astoria near today's city of Spokane. Weeks prior, the wily Scot had sold his post's furs to his former colleagues, and the deal was completely consummated before HMS *Raccoon's* arrival.

In the book *Astoria,* accordingly, Washington Irving portrays Chief Comcomly as completely bewildered when, from his "palace" across the river on Chinook Point he viewed the warship's arrival. "King George has sent a great canoe to destroy your fort," Comcomly tells his son-in-law at this point. The chief then offers McDougall the services of one hundred of his finest Chinook warriors to do battle with the British warship. "I will send them out in our war canoes to capture the warship's captain" he tells his son-in-law, McDougall. The latter's failure to be excited and to accept his father-in-law's generosity in this crisis puzzled Comcomly, and he became convinced his oldest daughter had married a "squaw man."

Chief Comcomly watched in complete amazement the formal surrender to Captain Black, skipper of the warship, by Duncan McDougall of the recently established fur post, gazing at the hauling down of the Stars and Stripes over the post and the raising instead of the British flag. It was this ceremony, Irving writes, which suddenly revived the Indian chief's political acumen.

On the following day, it was Duncan McDougall, viewing his father-in-law through a spyglass from the upper ramparts to Astoria, who gazed at the Indian chief in amazement. Suddenly that morning McDougall saw his father-in-law appear at the boat landing at Chinook Point dressed in his finest feathers. Seating himself on the high pedestal platform amidships in his famous forty-foot-long war canoe, its high prow decorated with ornate carvings and colors, Comcomly set out, propelled swiftly by his finest Chinook paddlers, to pay a call on Captain Black anchored in his warship *Raccoon* off McDougall's Astoria.

McDougall watched as his father-in-law ascended the vessel's ladder where he was received by Captain Black, then taken below decks. An hour elapsed, then Comcomly reappeared, still attended by Captain Black. After shaking hands all around on the *Raccoon's* quarterdeck, the one-eyed chief then descended the ship's ladder into his awaiting canoe of state, by now wearing, to McDougall's total amazement, a British naval officer's dress uniform complete with laced sleeves, cocked hat and epaulettes. Comcomly then headed back to his native village, the Union Jack flying from the bow of his canoe and a sword given him by Captain Black resting on his knees.

ISSAQUAH (I-9)

Today, in view of the concentration of business activity in the vicinity of this city, twenty miles southeast of Seattle, it is difficult to picture the heavy Indian fighting which took place here in 1855. Two of Issaquah's founders lost their lives that year, just weeks before the Indians launched their attack upon Seattle.

Another three decades passed and Issaquah Valley was an agricultural one, the principal commodity being grown: hops, used in the making of beer. The quality of the hops grown here was considered very high, and much of it at this time was being shipped all the way to England. Principal grower of the hops that year was the Wold family, and when they suddenly fired all the white hops pickers in the valley and supplanted them with Chinese pickers, rioting broke out.

Anti-Chinese feelings were already rife elsewhere around Puget Sound and they arose to a particularly high pitch here, the resentment of the white pickers intense at these "foreigners" who were willing to work for lower wages. On the night of 30 September 1885, some of these displaced white workers fired into tents here in the valley where Chinese were asleep, killing three of them and wounding three others.

The first Chinese formally introduced into the Pacific Northwest were sailed from Macao in September, 1788, by Captain John Meares, a British naval officer on half pay who had decided to become a fur trader in then-undiscovered America. In his tiny ship named the *Felice Adventurer* he loaded fifty-three Chinese males for the long voyage across the Pacific to Nootka, then a spot on Vancouver Island where sea otter skins could be obtained from the Indians for beads, buttons, or other trivia.

Some historians allege that enroute to Nootka, while his ship was anchored off Oahu, Meares took on board his sailing ship Hawaiian girls, a number of them equal to the number of Chinese laborers he was carrying on board. At any rate, Meares established the first non-Indian settlement on our Northwest coasts. It was through the skill of his Chinese laborers that the first sailing ship built in the Northwest was launched at Nootka.

While Meares was away on a trip back to China, Spaniards seized Meares' ship and property at Nootka causing him, upon receiving this news, to sail directly from China back to England. A skillful agitator, in London Meares created enough furor, particularly in the British Parliament, to cause England's prime minister to mobilize the British fleet. At the last minute, Spain backed down and peace was restored.

With their coolie hats and the long queues which they wore down their backs, the early Chinese of the American West were a colorful addition to the scene. But for their immigration from China, the railroad tracks across America might never have been laid. Such folk were also in great demand in the early West as farm laborers, gardeners, and laundrymen. They also served a useful role working the West's gold fields.

Various meanings have been ascribed to the name Issaquah but the true one is now lost. The name is related to the word *squak* which, as allegedly pronounced by the Indians, sounded as if spelled *isquoh* or *issaquah.*

K

KALAMA (O-6)

In 1870, this Washington community on the lower Columbia River, twenty-five miles downstream of Portland, was being touted as the future New York City of the Pacific Northwest. Railroad tracks were being laid north from Kalama to Puget Sound. Word had just been received that the Northern Pacific Railroad would soon connect Kalama with transcontinental tracks over the Rocky Mountains to Lake Superior. Ocean-going ships began tying up to Kalama's dock. "Where Rail meets Sail" became the town's motto.

But the transcontinental tracks, instead of being laid down the north banks of the Columbia to Kalama, came down the opposite side of the river to Portland. From Pasco the tracks also crossed through Stampede Tunnel in the Cascade Range directly into Tacoma on Puget Sound. The final blow took place in 1890, when the railroad ferry connecting Kalama to Goble on the Oregon side of the Columbia, until now busily carrying railroad passengers from Tacoma to Portland, was abandoned in favor of a Portland-to-Vancouver bridge built upstream.

The word *kalama* is an Indian one, believed to stem from the same source as that of the town of Cathlamet nearby. Both names are believed traced to an Indian word which means stone. The first white person to live at Kalama's site was Mr. Ezra Meeker (1830–1928), distinguished early champion of Indians' rights and a wealthy hop grower in later years, remembered as founder of Puget Sound's city of Kent.

KELSO (O-6)

In 1884, Mr. Peter Crawford claimed free land at the site of this city, located where the Cowlitz River joins the Columbia. Being a native of Scotland, he named the small settlement (which soon arose here) after his native home of Kelso, back in Scotland. Years passed, and then, springing up almost overnight opposite Kelso, across the Cowlitz, was a new community called Longview; the first planned city in the Pacific Northwest.

When not long afterward a bridge was built across the Cowlitz River connecting Longview with Kelso, residents of the two communities began meeting to discuss a merger of these two communities into one. Being the older of the two communities, Kelso's citizens believed that the new enlarged community being proposed should bear the name of their town. However, theirs being a "model city," its facilities having been laid out overnight and being far superior to those of the Kelsoites, the citizens of Longview adamantly insisted the merged town be given their name.

The issue became heated and tempers flared. In vain did the Longview citizens then propose the name Monticello as a compromise (this being the name of a local community long since disappeared which was the first capitol of Washington Territory). When Kelso's citizens rejected this compromise, Longviewites abandoned all hope, sarcastically then proposing that Kelso change its name to East Longview. At this point, according to the book *Longview* (Portland, 1917) written by historian J.M. McClellan:

> If there was any hope for a reconciliation, it died on the society page [of the local newspaper] . . . Came inevitably the time when someone gave a party on one side of the river to which no one on the other side was invited. From then on it was a rare thing to see in the social columns of the rival newspaper a guest list that didn't reflect a sharp social dividing line, one that seemed invariably to follow the approximate course of the Cowlitz River.

Five years before Peter Crawford founded the city of Kelso, its site became an important one for travelers wishing to proceed overland from Portland to Puget Sound. Recently the invention of the steamboat had captured everyone's imagination, particularly when a 160-foot long sidewheel steamboat was built near Portland upstream on the Willamette River. Until now most travelers between the lower Columbia and Puget Sound did so by ship, but with the arrival of the steamer *Lot Whitcomb,* the overland route between the two places became a more feasible one.

After crossing the Columbia River from Portland aboard this sleek craft, Olympia-bound passengers landed at the site where the city of Kelso now stands, then embarked in canoes operated by a newly organized transportation group calling themselves The Cowlitz River Bateau Line. At this time the Cowlitz River flowed quite briskly downstream to the Columbia, making the passengers' trip by canoe up this stream a little less than rapid. The last leg of the journey, from Toledo to Olympia, was even worse. It was made by horse carriage traveling over corduroy roads. Traveling without stop over this route, nonetheless, was considered sensational, the elapsed time being only thirty-six hours.

KENT (I-8)

Just as today's business population would doubtlessly like to make the valley where this city stands (between Seattle and Tacoma) a major industrial area, likewise in 1900 Mr. Ezra Meeker (1830-1928), the founder of Kent, doubtlessly would have liked to make it the world's largest grower of hops, that ingredient so necessary in the making of beer. When he chose the name Kent, Meeker had just returned from the County of Kent in England, where he had been conferring with the hops growers of that area.

Long before his hop-growing success, however, Ezra Meeker was prominent in the life of Puget Sound. Particularly is he remembered for the courageous stand he took on behalf of an Indian named Leschi, accused of having been the leader of the Puget Sound Indians in the many Indian attacks on the whites during the period 1855-1858. Many whites had lost their lives as a result of this fighting, and Leschi was generally believed to be the leader in the attacks.

When Chief Leschi was brought to trial, following the return to peace, and charged with murder, Ezra Meeker objected vigorously to this charge. If, indeed, Leschi was guilty of taking lives during this time, Meeker stoutly maintained (despite great disapproval on the part of most whites), he should be accorded the rights of a prisoner of war and tried, not as a murderer, but as an honorable combatant. Despite his efforts, however, Leschi was hung.

It is difficult to picture the deep forest which covered Kent Valley when the whites first arrived. Today the trees are gone and large factories cover the area. Even then, however, logjams in the nearby White River were being created by the lumber interests. So swift was the river, carrying tremendous amounts of water from the snow-capped Cascades to the east that, blocked by these fallen trees, an inland sea formed which covered the entire valley. On its waters, sternwheel steamboats traveled for a number of years, carrying passengers between the sites where Kent and Auburn now stand.

Because Kent is situated about midway between Seattle and Tacoma, its citizens found themselves, commencing in 1880, caught between a crossfire of rivalry between these two cities. By this time the Northern Pacific Railroad had made Tacoma the leading city of Puget Sound by virtue of the tracks this organization laid south from Tacoma to Kalama on the Columbia River, thereby connecting it with transcontinental tracks leading eastward all the way over the Rocky Mountains to the Great Lakes.

Ever since this transcontinental connection occurred, President George Wright, head of the Northern Pacific, had sought to perpetuate Tacoma's leading-city status by isolating its rival, Seattle, as much as possible. First Mr. Wright vetoed the citizens of Seattle's request that his railroad tracks be extended to their community, even though the distance involved is scarcely twenty miles. Whenever Seattle's citizens wished to travel to Portland they found themselves forced to embark on a steamboat owned and operated by Wright's Northern Pacific Railroad. Invariably the boat would take them from Seattle to Tacoma too late to board Wright's railroad train which daily left for Kalama and Portland. Forced to stay overnight in one of Tacoma's hotels, their patience exhausted, they finally caught the train south the next day only to find at Kalama, the Northern Pacific's railroad barge had left, forcing them to stay overnight for a second time before finally reaching Portland the third day.

In 1881, however, the Northern Pacific was taken over by a more public-spirited president, Mr. Henry Villard, who proceeded to operate the railroad with more regard for Seattle's residents. From a spur track already laid from Tacoma to the Wilkeson and Carbondale coal mines, south of Kent, Mr. Villard projected another spur line north through Stuck Junction (as Auburn was then known) past Kent (then called Titusville) to Renton at the south end of Lake Washington. Here Villard's spur connected with Seattle's own railroad, the Columbia and Puget Sound, recently built by private contributions in a feeble effort to connect the struggling community by rail with the outside world. Thus by this linking of the two rails at Renton, Seattle at last became connected with its rival Tacoma.

Still objecting to these actions, Tacoma citizens were glad when, in 1883, Mr. Villard was fired by the Northern Pacific, replaced soon after by Tacoma's patron saint, George Wright. Mr. Wright wasted no time in stopping all railroad traffic over the "Orphan Line," as the rails past Auburn and Kent had become known. The Orphan Line's rails laid rusty for several years.

Then a leading Seattle lawyer, Judge Cornelius Hanford, changed the picture. Obtaining an injunction against Wright's railroad from the Washington Territorial Legislature decreeing that the Orphan Line's tracks be reopened, traffic resumed; slowed, however (as much as was legally possible) by Tacoma's Northern Pacific through scheduling tricks, such as forcing the Orphan Line's cargo (and sometimes passengers) to be delayed in Renton or elsewhere along the way through various sly excuses. In fact, it was not until 1893 that Seattle gained an equal footing with Tacoma. In that year locomotives of the Great Northern Railroad, a competitor of the Northern Pacific, rolled into Seattle's new railroad station. President of this railroad was John J. Hill, who soon put his rival, Mr. George Wright of the Northern Pacific, back in a shadow.

KINGSTON (H-8)

In May, 1841, when Commodore Wilkes of the U.S. Navy sailed in the 780-ton sloop of war, the USS *Vincennes,* past the site where Kingston now stands, no ferry boats connected Kingston with its eastward neighbor across Puget Sound (the city of Edmonds). The 41-year old Wilkes, his armada of ships having recently been sailing in the Fiji Islands, was coming here to remind the British (until now the complete rulers of the Puget Sound area) that until England and the United States came to some agreement in regard to ownership of the Pacific Northwest, the Americans had as much right to Puget Sound as did the British.

One mile before reaching the site where Kingston now stands, Commodore Wilkes had observed from the bridge of his ship what he believed to be apple trees blooming ashore, though actually they were dogwood blossoms. Accordingly, he named this landmark Apple Tree Point, although today it appears on the maps as Apple Cove Point. Seven miles before reaching this latter landmark, again from the bridge of Wilkes' sailing ship, some of the commodore's young navigators bestowed another of Kingston's neighboring landmarks, a most unusual one: Point No Point. They had been having trouble identifying the projections of land on the somewhat sketchy charts available to them (probably made back in 1792 by the Englishman George Vancouver) and, lacking a better identification, they placed this unusual historically-famous name on their chart.

Fourteen years later in January, 1855, Wilkes' Point No Point became the scene of a famous peace "powwow." At the request of Washington Territory's Isaac Stevens, recently-appointed governor of this new region of the world, twelve hundred or more Indians assembled here to listen to his blandishments. First, however, he presented the older Indians with blankets and tobacco, and for the younger ones beads and molasses were provided. The governor then harangued them with an hour-long speech, promising them fishing rights and certain other emoluments, for which they agreed to confine themselves onto lands set aside for their exclusive use. Then the Indian leaders stepped forward and placed their marks on the documents which the governor's assistants produced.

Governor Stevens is described at this time as "peppery, dynamic, frail in build." He was later killed in the Civil War while fighting for Union forces. The vessel in which Stevens and his retinue were sailing was a 97-foot sloop called the *Major Tomkins.* Derisively known as "the Major Pumpkins," it was reputedly so slow ". . . that somewhere along most of her trips she would meet herself coming back from an earlier one." From Point No Point, Stevens and his retinue then proceeded to Neah Bay to make similar arrangements with the Makah Indians.

Hansville, situated a mile west of Point No Point (nine miles north of Kingston) was named in honor of Hans Zachariason in 1873. The name Kingston was chosen in 1890 to designate a local real estate development laid out at this town. Originally Kingston was known as King's Town, King being the name of the developer.

KIRKLAND (H-9)

Hopes were high around Puget Sound in 1887 for gaining wealth from coal. Large quantities of this black mineral were being discovered east of Seattle at Newcastle, also north of Renton, near Cle Elum and Carbonado. The deepest coal mine in the United States had recently been dug at Black Diamond. A railroad carrying the coal from Wilkeson to Seattle delivered it into colliers to take it to San Francisco.

Great Western Iron and Steel Company, with assets of over a million dollars, was organized by Peter Kirk. He was a wealthy, and veteran ironmaster from Cumberland, England. On the east side of Lake Washington, just north of today's city of Bellevue, Mr. Kirk laid out streets for a planned city, which he called Kirkland, envisioning that it would soon become a veritable Pittsburgh. The events which followed, however, proved otherwise. The unlimited supply of iron ore which Mr. Kirk expected to find in the foothills leading to Snoqualmie Pass in the Cascade Mountains failed to materialize. Then suddenly, the Panic of 1893 hit the entire nation, and Mr. Kirk found his finances and himself engulfed in grief.

Soon afterward Mr. Kirk moved to the San Juan Islands, where he lived in retirement until his death. Although a small town developed around his planned city of Kirkland, it remained so for another five decades. Only recently has Kirkland developed into its present size.

KITSAP PENINSULA (I-7)

On some maps Kitsap Peninsula is aptly called the Great Peninsula, stretching as it does from Admiralty Inlet in the north all the way southward to lower Puget Sound, and from Hood Canal eastward to Bainbridge and Vashon Islands. This huge body of land as well as Kitsap County are named after an Indian leader named Kitsap or *k'sap* as the Indians pronounced the name.

There were two Indian leaders of Puget Sound named Kitsap. Older of the two was "Tom" Kitsap, remembered for saving the lives of three small white children in October, 1855, when hordes of Indians were attacking white homes in White River Valley, southeast of Seattle. The three children's parents had been massacred in the fighting. Old Chief Kitsap concealed the children beneath a bear skin rug in his canoe, then paddled them down the White River to Seattle, where the villagers thanked him for his kindness.

Probably, however, Kitsap County and Kitsap Peninsula are named after Tom Kitsap's son, called Kitsap the Younger, to distinguish him from the father from whom he inherited his tribal leadership. Second only to Chief Seattle in his influence among the Puget Sound tribes, Young Kitsap, unlike his father and Chief Seattle, chose to fight against the whites when war erupted. Consequently, Colonel George Wright, commander of the local military district at this time, placed Kitsap the Younger in the army jail at Steilacoom. Unlike a contemporary Indian leader named Leschi, who was similarly jailed at Steilacoom and sentenced to be hung, Kitsap the Younger was released.

Soon after his release (being a medicine man as well as a military leader) young Kitsap recalled that during his confinement in the Steilacoom jail, the whites had given him some red-colored medicine which had cured him of his ailment, probably a cold. Believing that the efficacy of this cure lay in the medicine's red color, Kitsap tried to treat several of his fellow Indians who were ill similarly. Lacking the medicine which the whites had given him, Kitsap substituted some red paint (which he happened to have acquired from the whites) until then intending to use it on his face for war paint. Mixing the red paint with water, Kitsap then administered it to his Indian patients. All of them died. Then, as was customary treatment for Indian medicine men who failed to effect a cure, the dead men's relatives fell on Kitsap and killed him.

L

LA CONNER (E-8)

The *l* and the *a* of this name are prefixes to Louise Anne Conner. Her husband, in establishing this town, fifty miles north of Seattle, chose its name in 1880.

Spanish sailors, led by Salvadore Fidalgo, were the first white men to view the site where La Conner now stands. They were sent here from Mexico by the Spanish viceroy to search for an opening eastward from these shores on Puget Sound, one which would enable ships to sail through America directly back to Spain without the hazards of Cape Horn. Fidalgo searched for this opening here in 1791. So strongly did the Spaniards believe in the existence of such a waterway, that in the year following Narvaez's probing these waters, the Spanish viceroy dispatched Salvadore Fidalgo to build a Spanish fort at the entrance to Puget Sound in order to prevent English ships (coming from the Atlantic through this waterway through the continent) from reaching the Pacific. The name of this officer today graces Fidalgo Island, located adjacent to La Conner to its northwest.

LACEY (K-7)

This city might be said to be a suburb of Olympia, for it lies scarcely five miles west of the Capitol City. In 1890, Lacey was laid out by a local real estate developer by the name of Mr. O. Lacey; hence the name. The history of Lacey, however, is derived primarily from its proximity to Nisqually Flats, that broad area which lies north of Lacey where the Nisqually River flows into lower Puget Sound.

Scarcely four miles from Lacey, in 1833, Nisqually House was erected, the first white habitation on Puget Sound. In the spring of 1841, there arrived at Nisqually House the virtual ruler at this time of all of Canada. Governor Sir George Simpson (1787–1867) had crossed the continent from Hudson's Bay in the record-breaking time of forty-seven days, during which by canoe and horseback he had driven his French-Canadian voyageurs to heroic effort. At Fort Vancouver, his initial destination, the inhabitantts of this Columbia River fur post received him with gun salutes and high ceremony. Despite his short stature, Simpson was a most impressive person, known by irreverent employees of his company as "god." The organization which he headed dated its origin in Canada to 1670, prompting such employees to remark that the company's initials of HBC stood for "Here Before Christ."

Simpson traveled from the company's elaborate headquarters on the Columbia River north to Nisqually House by horseback, a trip which took him three days. At Nisqually's dock on Nisqually Reach, the governor found awaiting him the company's recently-arrived paddle-wheel steamboat, named the *Beaver* (said to have been the first steamboat ever to sail the waters of the Pacific). The *Beaver* was about to take the governor to Alaska, there to meet the Russian governor at Sitka to discuss matters relating to British-Russian commerce along these Northwest coasts.

In the diary which Sir George always kept on such trips, he records the following description of the country in which today's city of Lacey then stood: ". . . being unwilling to commence the voyage on Sunday we remained here at Nisqually House . . . for six and thirty hours . . . the surrounding scenery is beautiful . . . with a variety of copses and oak, placid lakes and undulating plains of pasturage. The sound, Puget Sound, yields plenty of fish . . . salmon, rock cod, and halibut."

Since 1834, Nisqually had been a fur trading post to which the Indians brought their furs in exchange for petty trade items offered by the whites. However, by 1841, beaver pelt was becoming scarce, and plans by Simpson had already been put in motion to convert Nisqually House's operations from fur trading to agriculture. In the year following Simpson's visit, he officially decided to devote Nisqually House's efforts exclusively to growing farm products and to grazing livestock on the extensive plains extending from Nisqually House eastward to the Cascade Mountains. Here, under the new name of Puget Sound Agricultural Company, were soon being produced great quantities of beef and mutton as well as dairy products, which Simpson's Hudson's Bay Company began selling to the Alaskan market.

Despite this change, Nisqually House remained an anchor post for the string of fur posts which extended northward up the coastline to Sitka. In 1853, the twenty-four-year-old Boston writer, Theodore Winthrop (then engaged in a tour of the Northwest) in stopping at Nisqually House, was reminded in the post's appearance of the earlier stockades built in New England two hundred years prior to his visit here, also built to protect the whites against Indian attack. He records:

> Nisqually is a palisaded enclosure, two hundred feet square. Bartizan towers protect its corners. Within are blockhouses for goods and furs, and one-story cottages for residences . . . [and he continues] Rusty Indians were trading at the three b's . . . blankets beads and 'baccy. All the squaws purchasing today were hags beyond the age of coquetry in costume, yet they were buying beads and hanging them in . . . contrast about their wrinkling necks, and then glowering for admiration with dusky eyes. (Winthrop, Theodore, *Canoe and Saddle,* Portland, 1915)

LAKE UNION (H-8)

Today this small body of water is located in one of the busiest parts of the city of Seattle. However, when Thomas Mercer (1813–1896) built his log cabin on its shores in 1852, the lake was an isolated spot, its mirror-like surface reflecting the tall evergreen forest surrounding it. On its south shore, Mr. Mercer built a home for himself and his two small daughters. Two years prior to this the Mercer family departed Illinois over the Oregon Trail. Enroute, while passing through the hot dusty plains of southern Idaho, Tom's wife died of cholera, leaving him with these two small children to care for alone.

On the Fourth of July, 1854, Tom invited Seattle's residents to come and celebrate this holiday on the shores of his lake. Although no road had yet been laid through the woods leading from the village of two hundred to the south, called Seattle, Tom managed to clear enough of a path to allow his wagon to bring his guests to the scene of the picnic. He carried them here in the same wagon in which he had brought his family west over the Rocky Mountains.

The Indians of Puget Sound were particularly impressed with Tom's wagon. They called it a "land canoe," for it was the first time they had witnessed the invention of the wheel. Later the vehicle became known to them as a "chick-chick chick-chick," this name simulating the squeaky noise the vehicle's wheels made as it rolled over the rough terrain. The horses pulling Tom's wagon also amazed the Indians. Doubtless they had heard of these four-legged animals which the "horse Indians" rode in the regions east of the Cascade Mountains but most Puget Sound Indians had never ever seen horses before.

The picnic at Mercer's place proved to be a great success. Fireworks were followed by speeches. Seattle's founding fathers then discussed what name to choose for the twenty-mile-long body of water (today known as Lake Washington) which lay two miles eastward, known to the Indians as *hyas chuck* (big water). Reputedly Tom, himself, chose to name this lake after the father of our country. He is also reputed to have proposed the name Lake Union, for he correctly foresaw that a canal later would be dug to the east and to the west of Lake Union, thereby uniting Lake Washington with Puget Sound.

Soon after this famous picnic, Thomas Mercer was placed in charge of Seattle's first probate court, and thereafter he was called Judge Mercer. He should not be confused with his brother, twenty-five years younger than Tom, Asa Mercer by name, after whom Mercer Island in Lake Washington is named.

LA PUSH (G-1)

The people of the Northwest in early times were of varied nationalities—Hawaiian, Chinese, English, American, and Spanish being among them. Perhaps the most colorful of them were the French, most of them employed by the Hudson's Bay Company in paddling this organization's furs up and down the Columbia River, transporting supplies to inland fur posts, or delivering the furs to the coast for shipment overseas. The name of this town, located on the Washington Coast twenty-eight miles south of Cape Flattery, doubtlessly stems from the French *la bouche* (the mouth) which is descriptive of La Push's location where the Quillayute River flows into the Pacific Ocean.

When in July, 1787, Captain William Barkley sailed southward past the site in his 400-ton brigantine *Loudon* (also known as the *Imperial Eagle*) he had just made a momentous discovery. While enroute from the north down the coast, he skirted the shores of Vancouver Island (unaware that it was indeed an island) until he came upon the twenty-seven mile wide opening into Puget Sound and Georgia Strait, which today we call the Strait of Juan de Fuca. It was Captain Barkley who first recognized this opening to be the same waterway which, in 1592, the Greek navigator calling himself Juan de Fuca claimed to have discovered. Assuming, as do some historians, that Juan de Fuca never saw this opening, Captain Barkley was the discoverer of it.

Pretending that his was an Austrian vessel in order to evade the expensive trading license required of British sea captains in these waters, Captain Barkley was calling his ship the *Imperial Eagle* and flying the red and white flag of Austria. In March of this same year (1787) Captain Barkley anchored his ship at a place called Nootka on Vancouver Island, then used by all sea otter trading ships. Here he was greeted by a man clothed in greasy otter skins who, to his astonishment, introduced himself as Dr. John Mackey, late surgeon of his trading brig *Captain Cook*. Mackey had been living at Nootka amongst the Indians for the past twelve months, during which he had learned to speak the natives' language and to eat their native food. He had been left there in July, 1786, by one Captain Strange (skipper of the *Captain Cook*) with the intention of Mackey ingratiating himself with the Indians, so that upon his vessel's return from China with more trade goods, a rich supply of sea otter pelt would be waiting. Strange and his associates had failed to return, however, and Mackey was overjoyed to join the crew of Barkley's ship.

At the commencement of the *Loudon's* trip from England in October, 1786, Captain Barkley initially took his vessel to Ostend, Belgium, in order to re-register the vessel under the Austrian flag. Here he met and married a seventeen-year-old girl, daughter of Reverend John Trevor, whose Anglican church in Ostend was the scene of their wedding. The voyage from Ostend took the newlyweds initially to the Cape Verde Islands, then to Bahia in Brazil, and around the Horn to the Sandwich Islands. Here a young native girl named Winee so pleased Mrs. Barkley with her amiable manners that when the vessel sailed from here for the Northwest coasts, Winee accompanied them. Thus, when in June, 1787, they arrived at Nootka, then the headquarters for obtaining sea otter pelt, Mrs. Barkley became the first white woman of record to set foot in the Pacific Northwest and Winee certainly one of the first Hawaiians to reach these shores.

Soon after passing the site where today the town of La Push stands, Captain Barkley landed some of his sailors at the mouth of the Hoh River. Here, while attempting to exchange some copper sheets with the Hoh Indians for the Indians' sea otter pelts, several of the sailors were killed. The Barkleys then sailed in the *Loudon* (alias the *Imperial Eagle*) back to China, where at Canton the furs they had acquired since the previous June brought them the grand sum of twenty-nine thousand dollars (Spanish). Later the Barkleys returned to these coasts to engage in fur trading with less fortunate results.

LEAVENWORTH (I-13)

This mountain community can be reached from Seattle by traveling over Stevens Pass. It is located on the upper eastern slopes of the Cascade Range, nineteen miles northwest of Wenatchee, and was originally called Icicle after a local river of this name. The town's present name traces back to the year 1893, when the Northern Pacific was engaged in laying railroad tracks past here. At this time Charles Leavenworth was the official of this railroad who was in charge of the tracklaying, and it was he who chose the town's present name, thereby honoring a famous ancestor (reputedly his great uncle) Colonel Henry Leavenworth (1783–1834).

Colonel Leavenworth is remembered as the founder of Fort Leavenworth in Kansas, famous departing point for emigrants traveling into Apache Indian country along the Santa Fe Trail. Leavenworth was already a hero, thanks to his record in the War of 1812, when in 1823 a tribe of Indians known as the Arikaras began attacking American fur trappers as they ascended the Missouri by keel boat, poling supplies for William Ashley's fur trappers in the high Rockies. The Arikaras lived in several villages on the banks of the Missouri closeby today's North-South Dakota border, and they also were highjacking William Ashley's men while they were delivering furs downriver to St. Louis, thereby virtually ruining what would otherwise have been a highly profitable commerce.

Accordingly, Mr. William Ashley, then a leading St. Louis fur executive, concerned over the Arikara situation, demanded Colonel Leavenworth to send his U.S. troops to punish these Indians. Reluctant to accede to Ashley's request, since it was official U.S. policy to treat the Indians of the West as allies, Leavenworth nonetheless proceeded to the Arikara villages with two hundred fifty soldiers. Here, although aided by seven hundred Sioux Indians, enemies of the Arikaras, Leavenworth failed to clear the Missouri of their obstruction.

When news of the fiasco reached the east coast, some newspapers called it a disgrace while others praised Leavenworth for his humanity, characterizing Ashley's trappers as brutal exploiters. The episode had a happy sequence, however, when Ashley's men, still foiled in the use of the Missouri, blazed a land trail westward into the Rockies. Leading up the banks of Platte River into the presently-named regions of Wyoming, Utah, and Idaho, this same route was later followed by Oregon and California-bound emigrants.

The word icicle as applied to Icicle Creek (the stream which flows into the Wenatchee River at Leavenworth) is derived from the Indian word *na-sik-elt* meaning narrow canyon. "Place the letter *n* at the beginning of icicle and the letter *t* at its end, and you practically have the Indian word," records the Chief Topographer of the U.S. Geodetic Survey in this region for many years, Mr. Albert H. Sylvester.

LONG BEACH (N-3)

The city is named after Long Beach Peninsula and the twenty-mile stretch of sand which lies on this peninsula's west side. A tongue of land scarcely three miles wide, Long Beach Peninsula stretches north to Leadbetter Point, with its eastern shore bordered by Willapa Bay (whose entrance is between Leadbetter Point and Cape Shoalwater, ten miles across on the mainland).

The site where the city of Long Beach now stands was covered with deep forest in 1851, when a Virginian, Charles Russell, arrived at the Columbia River's entrance at present-day Ilwaco, seven miles south of Long Beach. Russell had come here to take up residence at Pacific City, as it was called by its promoter, a sleek-looking, fast talking ex-missionary named Elijah White. Reverend White's real estate develop-ment was a hoax, and Russel soon realized he was a victim. In order to recover the money he had lost in the venture, Russell hit upon the idea of harvesting oysters in nearby Willapa Bay. When shipped to California to hungry gold miners, they would, he believed, make someone's fortune. But Russell's love of adventure in real estate changed his mind, and again he reverted to this activity.

A group of Californians, in the meanwhile, had hit upon Russell's idea about Willapa Bay. They arrived here in their eighty-two-foot schooner, the *Robert Bruce,* and established a base at the mouth of the Willapa River on the bay's mainland side. The "Bruce Boys" (as they became known locally) prospered. They quickly accumulated a supply of oysters which netted them $20,000 that first year when sold in San Francisco. News spread along the coast of the opportunity for riches in Willapa Bay.

Among the next arrivals were Alonzo Clark and Robert Hamilton Espe, former lumbermen from the East. Thanks to the advice of a kindly local Indian, named Nahcati (after whom the town of Nahcotta, midway up Long Beach Peninsula today is named), Messrs. Clark and Espe learned that the oysters were as thick on Willapa Bay's peninsula side as they were on the mainland side where the Bruce boys were working. This led the pair to establish the site we now call Oysterville. By 1858, this enterprising team was shipping oysters from here to California at the rate of one hundred thousand baskets per year, thanks to their cleverly designed oyster-gathering boats, which enabled them to outstrip the Bruce Boys who operated from Indian canoes.

Initially, only an Indian trail connected Oysterville with the south, one which led through undergrowth and giant trees where bear, panther, and many other wild animals roamed. Mail was received only once a week at Oysterville, delivered by a mailman on horseback. By 1855, however, Oysterville had become a key point between Puget Sound and San Francisco. Here large sailing ships found it convenient to tie up at Oysterville's quarter mile long dock which projected into Willapa Bay, located closeby Leadbetter Point, where ships could easily enter the bay's waters through Leadbetter Bar. Also in 1855, Oysterville became a main stopover for stage coach travelers journeying between Olympia and the lower Columbia. Such travelers arrived at Oysterville by steamboat from the town of South Bend on the mainland, having come there from Puget Sound by way of Grays Harbor.

After a night's rest at Oysterville in one of its hotels, they were transported to the hard sandy beach on the peninsula's west side in "sand-dune buggies," each drawn by a single horse. Here they were met by a Concord coach, capable in peak traffic of carrying as many as twenty passengers, which took them south to Ilwaco. Drawn by as many as eight horses, the coach drivers often found themselves zigzagging their vehicles southward down the twenty-mile-long beach, in a manner calculated to take advantage of the harder sand provided by the ocean's line of waves. Particularly did the passengers riding on the coaches' tops enjoy this part of their journey. Sometimes, however, when the stagecoach became stuck in softer sand, passengers had to disembark, then assist the horses in pulling free.

By 1880, Oysterville possessed a population close to four hundred. Most of them, however, were transients. Being the seat of Pacific County, legislators frequented the town. The hotels were filled most of the time. Two saloons, two churches, seven stores, a schoolhouse, and a yacht were also included in the busy place. Oysterville was one of the wealthiest towns per capita in the Pacific Northwest.

By this time a narrow gauge railroad was being laid from Ilwaco north up the peninsula to Oysterville. When, however, the tracklayers reached the site of today's Nahcotta, just five miles short of Oysterville, the railroad's financial backers ran out of money. Oysterville by then had begun to suffer from the dwindling supply of oysters in the bay. Bruceport, where the Bruce Boys had laboured for so many years, had vanished. Railroads had begun shipping oysters to the West Coast from Atlantic seaports. Today Oysterville's commercial fortunes have completely vanished and it is almost a deserted village.

The Clamshell Railroad, as it was known, though possessing only two locomotives each weighing scarcely ten tons and running on tracks scarcely three feet wide, proved to be a welcome means by which the peninsula's residents enhanced their lives. Both of the railroad's engineers were beloved for their accommodating ways. Frequently they stopped to chat along the way and to pick up and deliver messages and groceries, causing their organization to be also known as the D. L. and W. translated "The Delay, Linger and Wait."

Traveling from Ilwaco either over the DL&W or by stage coach, commencing in the eighties came vacationers from south of the Columbia River, eager to spend summers on Long Beach's twenty-mile-long beach. The founder of Long Beach was Henry Tinker, around whose Long Beach Hotel, built about 1895, developed a village of summer cottages. By 1900, Oysterville's prosperity had definitely declined to the point that Long Beach had displaced it as the peninsula's leading community.

LONGVIEW (O-6)

Back in 1825, Dr. John McLoughlin, the handsome head of all fur trapping in the Pacific Northwest, erected a warehouse at the site where this city now stands. Here innumerable tons of furs, which had been brought by canoe from the interior regions of today's Washington, were delivered for storage. With the arrival of the annual ships of the Hudson's Bay Company from England and China, these furs were loaded aboard, then transported either around Cape Horn back to England or, by way of the Sandwich Islands, delivered to Macao in the Orient. During the period 1790–1810, millions of dollars-worth of beaver pelt alone were shipped to London from eastern Canada and from here at the mouth of the Columbia River.

Years passed, and in 1922, a Missouri capitalist named Robert Alexander Long (1850), already rich from lumbering off the forests north of here, decided to build from scratch a whole communnity where Longview now stands. Here the employees of his local lumber mills would have wider streets, newer homes, and superior recreational facilities than anywhere else in the country. It was one of the first so-called planned communities to be built in the United States. Modestly he called his new city Longview, the same name which he had already given to his horse-breeding farm back in Missouri, thereby reminding everyone of his benefactions. It is not true, therefore, that Longview derived its name from the long view to be seen from this city down the Columbia River.

Watching the construction of this upstart city in 1922, with some disdain tinged with jealousy, were the citizens of Kelso; the city which lies immediately opposite Longview across the Cowlitz River which flows into the Columbia River here. When the citizens of Longview, soon after their new city was completed, began boasting about their wider streets and superior facilities, Kelsoites responded quickly in the editorial page of their news sheet. All Longviewites, it was charged, were upstarts and had no sense of history.

Apparently forgotten by both sides in the quarreling was the fact that a town older than either of them once stood nearby, its name: Monticello. It was at Monticello that, in 1852, representatives assembled from communities all over Puget Sound to complain that the legislators of Oregon Territory (which then included the present state of Washington), operating from their territorial capitol in Salem, were not providing adequately for the increasing number of white families living north of the Columbia. Accordingly, at Monticello they framed a memorial to the U.S. Congress demanding that a new territory be established independent of then-existing Oregon Territory, that the citizens around Puget Sound might be better represented in the nation's capitol. The U.S. Congress, in response, then created the U.S. Territory of Washington. Although Monticello became this new territory's first capital, it was not for long. Within a year afterward, Monticello disappeared under a Columbia River flood, and the territorial capitol was moved to Olympia on Puget Sound.

Closeby today's Longview, twelve miles to the west, was a long-forgotten settlement called Oak Point, so named in October, 1792, after the British naval officer William Broughton discovered here ". . . a remarkable oak tree thirteen feet in girth." Lieutenant Broughton was ascending the Columbia River into waters never before seen by white men when he reached here. He was rowed by sailors of his ship, the armed tender *Chatham*, by small boat. The *Chatham* was anchored downstream of here in Baker Bay. Upstream of Longview, approximately opposite the town of Washougal, Washington, Broughton landed and held ceremony proclaiming all of the Pacific Northwest to belong to King George III of England.

Another Oak Point of historical interest is located opposite Longview, across the Columbia River on the Oregon side. Here was the site of the first American settlement in the Northwest, though a short-lived one. In May, 1810, Captain Nathan Winship in his sloop *Albatross* arrived here with twenty-five Kanaka laborers from the Sandwich Islands to establish a fur trading post. Due to the hostility of the local Indians, as well as to floodwaters which submerged his establishment, Winship was forced to abandon the place within a month. Upon returning in his ship the following year to make another attempt, Winship found that during his absence a rival fur post had been established at Astoria, too large for him to compete with. Accordingly, he sailed out of the Columbia River, never to return.

LOPEZ ISLAND (D-6)

Spaniards were the first white men to sail the San Juans, the archipelago of more than 400 islands which lie north of Seattle closeby Canada. This island, the third largest of them all, is named for Senor Lopez de Haro, first pilot of the Spanish warship *Concepcion*. In 1789, the viceroy of Spain hurriedly sent the *Concepcion*, sailed by Captain Francisco Eliza, north from lower California to Nootka (the Spanish naval base on the western shore of Vancouver Island) to make it clear to the Russians and the British that Spain was exclusively the owner of this then-new region of the world. Captain Eliza designated Lopez de Haro to accompany Manuel Quimper in a probe of the waters behind the Strait of Juan de Fuca to ascertain what lay behind this opening to the east. Sailing in a smaller vessel, the *Princesa Real*, the pair thus became the first white men to enter the waters of Puget Sound. From atop Mary's Hill in the city of Vancouver overlooking Pedder Bay, Senors Quimper and Lopez de Haro became the first white men to view the San Juan Islands in the distance. It was probably at this time that Quimper chose to designate the intervening channel separating them from these islands with the name *Canal de Lopez de Haro*. Two years later, in May, 1792, two more Spanish explorers, Captains Dionisio Galiano and Cayetano Valdes, while sailing in their respective ships named the *Sutil* and the *Mexicana,* chose again to honor First Pilot Lopez de Haro. They did so by emplacing his name upon Lopez Island, which lies south of Orcas Island and east of San Juan Island. The team of Galiano and Valdes were members of a Spanish governmental scientific expedition, sent to the Pacific Northwest by Viceroy Revillagigedo in Mexico City.

Carried by Galiano and Valdes on board their two ships were numerous scientific instruments. Landing on the south shore of today's Lopez Island, they proceeded to make astronomical observations and to thereby check their ships' chronometers. Unbeknownst to them, even as they were departing Lopez Island, two rival explorers were sailing closeby, scarcely a dozen miles to the north. They were two officers of the British Royal Navy, Captain George Vancouver and Lieutenant Commander William Broughton sailing in the warships *Discovery* and

Chatham. Off a shoal (today called Spanish Bank) Vancouver, sailing in one of his *Discovery's* small boats, was hailed by Senor Galiano aboard the *Sutil*. Galiano invited the Englishman to come aboard and have breakfast. On this occasion Vancouver learned that already the Spaniards had encountered and exchanged courtesies with his assistant, William Broughton, when the latter's ship, the *Chatham,* was off Point Roberts. During the breakfast Vancouver was chiefly impressed by the cramped quarters in which the Spaniards lived. He observed that the ship *Sutil* was of "scarcely forty-five tons burthen" (Vancouver's own ship *Discovery* enjoyed a 450-ton displacement).

In 1841, an American expedition led by Commodore Charles Wilkes of the USS *Vincennes,* 780 tons, explored the San Juan Islands, asserting claim to them on behalf of the United States. Spain by this time had dropped out of the competition for possession over the Pacific Northwest. England and the United States, while competitors for this region, agreed that both nations would share the region jointly, pending some later settlement. Wilkes renamed Lopez Island, calling it Chauncey's Island.

Commodore Isaac Chauncey, whom he thus honored, was a War of 1812 hero whose American ships seized control of the Great Lakes from the British, thereby preventing British troops in Canada from moving south to seize U.S. governmental headquarters in the nation's capital. In 1847, Captain Kellett (later Vice Admiral Sir Henry Kellett) of the British navy, surveying these waters for England, obliterated Wilkes' name from the island, perhaps recollecting the British defeat by Chauncey's Americans. Then he restored the Spanish name given by Senors Galiano and Valdes.

LYNDEN (B-8)

Lying almost on the Canada border, this town traces its beginning to the year 1858, when gold was discovered on nearby Fraser River. When in the spring of that year word leaked south to San Francisco that over a half million dollars in gold had recently been taken from the Fraser River's upper stretches, fifteen thousand Americans began pouring north to Bellingham Bay by sailing ship. From this point, twelve miles south of Lynden, they blazed a trail past Lynden to the Fraser River's lower stretch, then pushed up river all the way to Cariboo country, where that same year three and one-half million dollars in gold were obtained. Officially however, Lynden's history begins in the year 1870 when Phoebe Johnson, one of the town's first inhabitants, having read about a mythical place called Lynden in a novel she was enjoying, suggested this name for the new settlement, one which the rest of its inhabitants approved.

It was in June, 1808, that Simon Fraser (1776–1862) one of Canada's greatest explorers, traced down the banks of the upper Fraser River toward Georgia Strait, the river's entrance into salt water. Uppermost in his mind was the burning question of whether this river, down which for many weeks he had been labouring, was the long-sought Columbia River. He records that just north of Abbotsford (Lynden's closest Canadian neighbor to the north) he and his party of twenty-three were greeted by Cowichan Indians, brandishing war clubs and wearing coats of leather. As Fraser and his men approached their village, these Cowichans fired a volley of arrows at them. Fraser also reports that upon approaching salt water, their party saw in the several Indian villages encountered clear indication that white men had preceded them, as evidenced by a tea kettle and a Russian gun. Near tidewater, Fraser took astronomical sights which revealed the local latitude to be 49°, almost three degrees north of the latitude of the Columbia River's mouth. It was a great disappointment to him.

Contrary to the belief of many Americans, the Lewis and Clark explorers were not the first white men to cross the Rocky Mountains to the Pacific Ocean. This honor belongs to another great Canadian explorer, Alexander Mackenzie (1764–1820). Like the fellow-Canadian Simon Fraser who followed him in descending the Fraser River fifteen years later, Mr. Mackenzie hoped that in tracing downstream he was descending the Columbia River. Carrier Indians, when Mackenzie reached a point on the Fraser somewhere above today's town of Hope, warned him of the extremely rough waters which lay below (where much of the Fraser River's gold was later found). They guided Mr. Mackenzie across British Columbia's Coast Mountains to Bella Coola, a salt water port about two hundred eighty miles northwest of Canada's city of Vancouver. On a huge rock Mackenzie then painted the legend "Alexander Mackenzie from Canada by land, the twenty-second of July, one thousand seven hundred and ninety-three." It was at this time that Mackenzie learned from the Bella Coola Indians that another group of white men had reached here a few weeks before. Doubtless they were sailors of His Majesty's Ship *Discovery,* Captain George Vancouver of Norwich, England in command, then engaged in exploring these coastlines for his monarch, King George III.

M

MARYSVILLE (F-9)

As is well known, all of the Pacific Northwest belonged to the Indians before the arrival of white men. Marysville has the distinction of being situated adjacent to the extensive lands still owned by the Tulalip tribe. This land extends north from Everett's Port Gardner into the waters east of Camano Island. It was four miles west of Marysville, closeby the Tulalip Indians' home, that one of the first whites to challenge the Indians for possession of the Northwest arrived on 4 June 1792. This was Captain George Vancouver sailing in His Majesty's Ship *Discovery.* It being the birthday of England's monarch, King George III, he took this occasion to hold a ceremony on the shore of Tulalip Bay. Here Vancouver proclaimed that henceforth all lands of the Pacific Northwest belonged to England. Not far from here almost simultaneously, oddly enough, Spanish explorers were similarly holding a ceremony proclaiming their sovereignty over the Indians' native lands.

Marysville, located twenty-five miles north of Seattle, is separated from the city of Everett by Ebeye Slough (pronounced "slew"). A bridge over Ebeye Slough connects Marysville with Everett. Ebeye Slough represents an outlet of the Snohomish River which in turn stems from the Skykomish and the Snoqualmie Rivers. In 1892, sternwheel steamboats carried railroad workers from Ebeye Slough upstream all the way to the site on the Skykomish River where Sultan now stands. From here the workers laid railroad tracks eastward up the banks of the Skykomish, over Stevens Pass into Eastern Washington. Each night the workers returned by sternwheelers to Marysville.

Mr. Isaac Ebeye, after whom Ebeye Slough is named, is chiefly remembered as Puget Sound's first U.S. collector of customs. He was a founder of the city of Olympia, to which he is said to have given its present name. From his family's log cabin on Whidbey Island's southeastern shore, Mr. Ebeye loved the view of the snow-capped Olympic Mountains visible across Admiralty Inlet. Of these mountains he wrote: "Afar their crystal summits rise like gems against the sunset skies."

Mr. Ebeye started the so-called Pig War of Puget Sound when in 1854 he demanded of Governor James Douglas, ruler of the Crown Colony of British Columbia, that the British pay the U.S. government import fees for the privilege of introducing large flocks of sheep to graze on San Juan Island, which lies immediately east of today's city of Victoria, Canada. Governor Douglas flatly refused, stating that this island did not belong to the United States, but to England.

Mr. Ebeye met his death in 1857, age thirty-nine, when war-painted Haidah Indians traveling in two canoes beached their craft one midnight nearby Ebeye's cabin. Battering down the cabin's door they seized Mr. Ebeye, then killed and beheaded him. Mr. Ebeye, being in their eyes a "big chief," was chosen as their victim to avenge the death of one of their tribe's own "big chiefs" who recently had been killed by white men at Port Gamble, across Admiralty Inlet from Whidbey Island.

Marysville is named after the California city of this same name, two of the first settlers at Washington's Marysville having come here from the California town. The land on which Marysville stands belonged originally to an Irishman and Civil War veteran named J.P. Comeford. Before coming here to take his free claim of 640 acres, Mr. Comeford served in the Union army.

McGOWAN (N-3)

The famous one-eyed Indian chief named Comcomly (1760?–1830) lived closeby this village at the mouth of the Columbia, nine miles east of Cape Disappointment. He was rich and powerful and owned many slaves. Comcomly ruled over six tribes of the Chinook nation. They lived as far upriver on the Columbia as Celilo Falls (near today's city of The Dalles). Chief Comcomly was very much a part of the early white history of the lower Columbia. In 1805, Lewis and Clark visited this chieftain at his village after coming over here from Fort Clatsop on the Columbia's south side. The two explorers and their men were impatiently awaiting spring, when snows in the Rockies would be melted enough to permit them to return to St. Louis.

It was Comcomly, moreover, who in 1811 greeted Duncan McDougall and his Astorians when they arrived at the Columbia River's entrance, preparatory to erecting their fur trading post called Astoria. Soon after piloting McDougall's sailing ship *Tonquin* across the treacherous sandbar at the Columbia's mouth, Comcomly saved McDougall's life. The Scot nearly drowned attempting to cross from Bakers Bay to the river's south side, where the trading post was to be built. Heavy winds had overturned McDougall's canoe and he was about to perish when Comcomly suddenly appeared amidst the high waves and took the drowning Scotsman aboard his canoe.

Not long after building Astoria in July, 1813, McDougall married one of Comcomly's many daughters, Ilchee by name, in an elaborate ceremony which took place at Comcomly's "palace" atop Chinook Point, closeby today's town of McGowan. Ten years later, in 1823, Comcomly held a similar wedding ceremony in his elaborate cedar longhouse, this time giving another of his daughters, Princess Raven, in marriage to tall, handsome Archibald McDonald (1790–1853), founder of Fort Nisqually, the Hudson's Bay Company headquarters on Puget Sound. In her book titled *McDonald of Oregon,* its contents acquired by the author first-hand from the participants, Mrs. Eva Emery Dye describes the departure of Archibald and Comcomly's daughter, Princess Raven, on their honeymoon, as follows: ". . . from the water's edge to Comcomly's Great Lodge, three hundred yards away, a pathway was carpeted with the richest furs, enough for the carpet along the route for a wedding march." As the young couple walked this carpet of furs toward the boat landing, a guard of honor rolled it up behind them, then placed it upon the gunwales of Chief Comcomly's huge elaborately carved canoe-of-state which awaited the couple, his wedding gift to the bride and groom worth thousands of dollars.

Twenty miles upstream of McGowan is Pillar Rock, twenty-five feet high and ten feet square at the top, standing southeast of Grays Bay. The Lewis and Clark expedition paddled past this remarkable pinnacle in November of 1805, and were filled with excitement. It was a moment Captain Clark and his fellow-explorers had been awaiting ever since their departure from St. Louis a year and one-half prior to this. As he sighted this landmark, Captain Clark, as he notes in the journal he kept throughout the long trek, was moved to exclaim "Ocian [sic] in View! O! the Joy!" As he learned later, however, Clark had mistaken the twelve-mile width of the Columbia River just below Pillar Rock for the Pacific Ocean, the real ocean being still forty miles ahead.

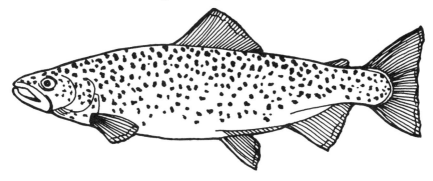

The community called McGowan takes its name after Patrick McGowan, who established a salmon hatchery at this site *circa* 1874. Pillar Rock was so named by Charles Wilkes, commander of the U.S. Navy expedition which explored the lower Columbia in 1841.

McNEIL ISLAND (J-7)

Best known as the site, at one time, of a U.S. penitentiary, this landmark in lower Puget Sound, eight miles southwest of Tacoma, bears the name of a Yankee named William McNeill (spelled with two *l*'s). Born in 1875, he sailed from Boston around the Horn to these Northwest coasts in the summer of 1851 in order to engage with the local Indians in trading for their furs. To induce them to part with their huge supply of pelt, worth large sums of money when transported to China, Captain McNeill had brought aboard his ship named the *Llama* a cargo of trade goods never before seen in this part of the world; namely: ". . . all sorts of inventions and contrivances," wrote the historian Hubert H. Humphrey in his *History of the Northwest Coasts,* ". . . calculated to win the Indians' covetous eyes." Carried on board McNeill's ship *Llama,* continues Bancroft, were ". . . wooden soldiers, jumping jacks, little toy wagons and whistles." He continues: "Funniest of all however were the squeaking cats and dogs which McNeill had to offer." Accustomed to receiving only bits of copper, nails, calice, or tobacco in exchange for their pelt, the Indians flocked to the American skipper's ship to exchange their mink, fox, beaver, and sea otter skins with McNeill, leaving the staid drab and dull British fur traders at Fort Vancouver at a tremendous disadvantage.

Until now Dr. John McLoughlin, head of the Hudson's Bay Company in the Northwest, had enjoyed a virtual monopoly over the region's fur trade, but now he became apprehensive. Shrewdly he offered to Yankee McNeill a tempting proposal. If McNeill would transfer his allegiance to McLoughlin's organization, the Hudson's Bay Company would pay this Bostonian a handsome price for his ship and cargo.

For the next three decades Captain McNeill, although he never became a British citizen, loyally served the Hudson's Bay Company. At the height of McNeill's career he commanded the HBC's glamorous paddle-wheel steamboat, a 101-foot-long craft named the *Beaver,* touted as the first steam-driven ship ever "to ripple the waters of the Pacific." Built in London and sailed around the Horn, the *Beaver,* when using its boilers, was capable of attaining the impressive speed of nine and three-quarters knots. By virtue of its paddle wheels, each ten feet in diameter, the vessel could maneuver into bays and inlets ordinary sailing vessels dared not enter. The vessel, moreover, used cordwood for fuel; a commodity available in unlimited supply along these Northwest coasts. Accordingly, the *Beaver's* crewmen were also lumbermen who frequently landed ashore to chop down trees.

From the outset, the *Beaver* attracted large numbers of coastal Indians, indeed they came from far inland bringing their furs with them in order to see this strange water contraption. Governor Sir George Simpson, the top man in the Hudson's Bay Company, made a trip with Captain McNeill aboard his *Beaver* in 1841. He recalls that by this time the Indians who greeted McNeill and his paddle-wheeler on his customary rounds had developed a real fondness for the brisk but kindly Yankee. As Sir George recalls in his book titled *A Journey Around the World* (London, 1847):

> Stationing himself at the steerage hatchway, Captain McNeill threw down each skin, as he examined it, with its price chalked on it—the equivalents being handed up from below by two or three men that were in charge of the store. The natives, now that they no longer dare to employ force against the whites, still occasionally resort to fraud, practising every trick and device to cheat their trader. One favourite artifice is to stretch the tails of land otters into those of sea otters . . . our traffic continued till the following noon; and meanwhile such of our men as were not occupied in trading . . . had been cutting wood, which the Indians conveyed on board in their canoes. The furs, amounting in value to about five hundred pounds sterling, consisted of martens, raccoons, beaver, bears, lynxes and both kinds of otter; while the equivalents were blankets, tobacco, vermillion, files, knives, a small quantity of cloth and only two guns, with a corresponding allowance of ammunition. Generally speaking, the natives were tiresome in their bargaining, and they were ever ready to suspend business for a moment in order to enjoy a passing joke. They appeared, however, to understand the precise length to which they might go in teasing Captain McNeill. They made sad work, by the bye, of his name; for, whenever his head showed itself above the bulwarks, young and old, male and female, vociferated from every canoe: Ma-ta-hell, Ma-ta-hell, Ma-ta-hell—a word which, with the comparative indistinctiveness of the first syllable, sounded very much like a request on their part that their trader might go down a great way beyond the engineer's furnace.

Captain McNeill retired from the Hudson's Bay Company in 1863 with the rank of chief factor. He lived out his remaining years on his 200-acre estate at McCauley Point overlooking Esquimault at the south end of Vancouver Island. Today the city of Victoria's McNeill Bay commemorates this former Yankee; also Port McNeill which lies fifty miles north of Vancouver Island's Kelsey Bay.

McNeil Island, here in Puget Sound, was so named by Charles Wilkes of the U.S. Navy in 1841. When, in 1844, it was widely feared throughout the Northwest that England and the United States were about to declare war upon each other over the question of which nation owned Puget Sound, McNeil Island was known to the British as Duntze Island. This name honored Captain John Duntze of the British Royal Navy who commanded HMS *Fisgard,* 42 guns. The *Fisgard* was anchored off McNeil Island to protect nearby Fort Nisqually, over which flew the Union Jack.

MERCER ISLAND (H-8)

There were two Mercer boys prominent in the history of Seattle. It is after the younger of the two that this island, located in lower Lake Washington, takes its name. Asa Shinn Mercer (1838–1917), the first white to claim a large parcel of land here, came west over the Oregon Trail in 1860, having recently graduated from Franklin College back in Columbus, Ohio. By virtue of this academic distinction (there were no college graduates for miles around) the whites then living in Washington Territory chose Asa to become president, at age twenty-three, of the territory's first college. Later it was to become the University of Washington, but at this time it was an humble school, the number of students being only seven. Situated in what is now the heart of Seattle, it faced the Olympic Mountains to the west, and overlooked Elliott Bay and Puget Sound.

Scandalous in the eyes of many was the idea Asa conceived soon after taking over this new job. He would, proposed Asa, travel back east to persuade a bevy of eligible females to return with him to marry the local males, Puget Sound then being a region where feminine company was scarce. Most Washington citizens, nonetheless, supported Asa in his unique idea. No governmental money, however, with which to implement Asa's plan, was forthcoming.

Raising his funds privately, Asa then traveled to Boston and successfully returned in 1864 with eleven young women carefully selected from Boston families, many of whose males had died in the Civil War. Again in 1866, Asa went east and returned with fifty more. In his book titled *Northwest Gateway* (Portland, 1941) Mr. Archie Binns describes the arrival on Elliott Bay of this second contingent of young ladies: ". . . the University bell rang and the town was on the wharf, dressed in its best to welcome the young women. Every man who could afford it bought a new suit of clothes and those who could not, new overalls." One early Seattleite described the awaiting males as ". . . looking like grizzlies . . . their hair slicked down like sea otters."

The key to Asa's success on this second trip east was a former northwesterner whom Asa met in the national capitol; his name: Ulysses S. Grant. Although not yet president of the United States, he was already high in governmental circles, still admired as a Civil War hero. Well did Grant remember his own lonely days as a shavetail army lieutenant in 1852–1853 while serving on the lower Columbia River at Fort Vancouver. Through Grant's influence, Mercer was able to purchase a surplus steamer in which the ladies journeyed around Cape Horn to San Francisco, then again by steamer to Seattle.

It is probable that the Indians who attacked Seattle from the east side of Lake Washington on the night of January 25th, 1856, stopped at Mercer Island preparatory to climbing Beacon Hill. We shall probably never know whether it was Yakima Indians from east of the Cascades, or local Indians led by Chief Leschi who originated this surprise attack on the then-small village of scarcely two hundred souls.

MOSES LAKE (J-17)

This eastern Washington city, located sixty miles southeast of Wenatchee, is named in honor of Chief Moses (1829–1899). He was one of the last Indian leaders to consent to his fellow tribesmen being relegated onto Indian reservations. As late as 1870, when U.S. census officials from Washington, D.C. attempted to take a count of his people, Moses refused them permission, declaring his tribe's government did not recognize the government of the United States.

Chief Moses' real name was *Que-tal-kim,* translated Half-Sun. Recalls Mr. Jack Splawn, one of eastern Washington's first white settlers:

> When I first saw Moses he was thirty-five-years old, and the finest looking Indian I have ever seen. Our friendship covered a period of thirty-five years . . . In point of intelligence he was the equal of any Indian in history . . . [he was] greater as a diplomat than as a warrior . . . To his great force of character . . . must be attributed his wonderful control over his Indian followers . . . Many a time have we matched horses and wagered all of our possessions on the result . . .

> The cheers went up . . . [among Moses people] just the same
> when I [a white man] won as when the chief's horse beat me
> . . . he was a tall commanding person with a massive frame
> . . . [he possessed] a large head set upon broad shoulders . . .
> he sat on his horse like a centaur. (Splawn, A. J. *Kamiakin,*
> *Last Hero of the Yakimas,* Portland, 1917)

The town of Othello, twenty miles south of Moses Lake, takes its name after the Shakespearean tragedy. A local tragedy occurred in 1880 when Edward O'Rourke, age fifteen, was pushed to his death by cattle off the 150-foot-high bluff six miles west of Othello, while night herding. Earliest pioneers of Othello were Giovani Para and his brother Barto, who came to America in 1909 from Italy. They settled at Othello in 1913.

MOUNT ADAMS (N-10)

Although 12,307 feet-high Mount Adams is the second highest of all Washington State's mountains, it receives relatively little attention. This is probably due to its remoteness from population centers; its nearest town, White Salmon, is little known to most citizens of the state.

Nor is it certain which of the two presidents named Adams in American history is the person for whom the mountain is named. This writer's belief is that it is named after the younger, President John Quincy Adams, rather than after his father, John, who was the second president of the United States. It was largely through the diplomatic efforts of John Quincy Adams that England's claims to the Pacific Northwest were negated.

First to utilize the name Mount Adams in this then-new region of the world, was Mr. Hall J. Kelley (1790–1874). The Boston schoolmaster quixotically harangued all Americans living along the east coast to move to the "Promised Land," which today we call the Northwest. This was in 1834, but Kelley applied the name Mount Adams to the peak which we now call Mount Hood, pride of all Portlandites since it is located near this Oregon city.

Generally it is believed that another early promoter of this region, Thomas J. Farnham (1804–1848) christened the present peak called Mount Adams. He was the leader of the Peoria Party, one of the first group of Americans to boldly migrate to Oregon, as the entire Northwest was first known. Despite the hazards of Indians, wild beasts, and the Rocky Mountains confronting them, Farnham and his followers left their homes in Peoria, Illinois. This enthusiastic group carried a huge banner reading "Oregon or the Grave." They boasted they would "twist the British lion's tail" upon reaching the Willamette Valley, where Dr. John McLoughlin of the Hudson's Bay Company represented England's rival claim to eventual sovereignty.

On their trip west, however, the Farnham party began fighting among themselves and split up. Farnham himself reached Fort Vancouver too bedraggled to engage in anglophobic combat, as he had boasted he would; indeed, he only remained on the lower Columbia less than a month before returning back east by ship and overland across Mexico.

Upon reaching the civilization centers of the east coast, however, Farnham became an important figure in arousing public interest in Oregon country. The book he wrote soon after his return became a best-seller of the day. Titled *Travels in the Great Western Prairies*, historians credit this book with having, to a considerable extent, prompted over fifty thousand Oregon Trail emigrants to pack all their worldly goods into covered wagons, then take the three-month-long trek to this new part of the world to establish new homes.

MOUNT BAKER (C-10)

On April 30, 1792 Captain George Vancouver, an English explorer, was entering Puget Sound in his 100-foot long, three-masted sailing ship named the *Discovery* when Lieutenant Baker, his officer-of-the-deck, pointed out to him a majestic snow-capped mountain in the distance ahead. This circumstance prompted Captain Vancouver to name this mountain after Baker.

Joseph Baker (1767–1817) was one of Vancouver's most able officers, a fine draftsman and the expedition's topographer as well. Also serving on board Vancouver's ship were two other officers of the British navy whose names also became affixed to Puget Sound landmarks; namely, Peter Puget the *Discovery's* third lieutenant and Joseph Whidbey, the vessel's sailing master. All three, just prior to joining Vancouver on the exploration to the Pacific Northwest, had served with him in the West Indies aboard His Majesty's Ship *Europa*. Thus the four of them were old shipmates, and doubtlessly proud to be a part of this expedition to these remote coasts (only the second such venture ever made by England, the first one having been made in 1776 by Captain James Cook).

Just prior to this sighting of what became known as Mount Baker, when their ship was still headed up the coast of Washington preparatory to entering Puget Sound, they chanced to meet at sea with Robert Gray, an American sea captain (soon to become famous for discovering the Columbia River and entering it for the first time). Captain Gray was the first white person these Englishmen had seen since arriving on the American coast.

It seems that Vancouver was unaware that Spanish explorers had preceded both Gray and himself in sailing inside the Strait of Juan de Fuca into Puget Sound. Two years prior, the Spanish explorer, Manuel Quimper, had accomplished this and anchored in his tiny Spanish vessel off Dungeness. Moreover, the following year another Spaniard, Francisco Eliza, entered the Strait of De Fuca, sailing even farther inside than did Quimper. Both of these Spaniards were sent here from lower California where Spain maintained a naval base. Already the Spaniards had established a naval base about 150 miles up the coast from the Strait of Juan De Fuca, called Nootka. There being no maps, the Spaniards thought Nootka was on the mainland, but as we know today, it lay on the west coast of Vancouver Island.

Even while Vancouver in the *Discovery* was entering Puget Sound in April, 1792, two more Spaniards were sailing in Puget Sound waters unbeknownst to him. They were Senors Galiano and Valdes, in their respective ships *Sutil* and *Mexicana*. Even as Vancouver was naming Mount Baker, the two Spaniards were christening this mountain with their name: *Gran Montana del Carmelo*. Soon afterward, the Spaniards saw flashes of fire erupting from the crater of Mount Baker. On June 22, 1792, Vancouver met with these Spaniards near today's Canadian city of Vancouver.

In later years, shipmates Joseph Baker and Peter Puget, the Vancouver expedition completed, continued their friendship. They and their families lived in Wales in subsequent years, as neighbors. It was at this time that Peter Puget christened his fifth son Joseph Baker Puget, while Baker named their recently-born child Peter Puget Baker. Lieutenant Baker, later Captain Baker, is remembered in history for the intricate Northwest maps he so skillfully made during his three year-long cruise aboard the *Discovery.*

During the winters, as a respite from the survey work on these Northwest coasts and in Alaska, the Vancouver expedition surveyed the coasts of the Sandwich Islands (the weather being more clement).

In 1795, the valiant group, after circumnavigating the globe, returned to England, having been away from their families for nearly five years. Before reaching the mouth of the Thames River, Vancouver was ordered to stop briefly at the mouth of Ireland's Shannon River. Here he found orders awaiting him from the admiralty to proceed overland to headquarters in London, war having just erupted between England and Holland. In complying, Captain Vancouver left command of his ship *Discovery* to Lieutenant Baker, who then sailed the ship from the Shannon River to Deptford on the Thames.

It was not Baker's last command. In later years, while captain of His Majesty's Ship *Pompey,* 74 guns, Baker had the bad luck of running the vessel aground. Although officially exonerated for the accident, it seems to have ended his chances for promotion. Baker died in 1817, age fifty, leaving nine children; the eldest, John Vashon Baker, attained the rank of admiral. Another son became General Sir William Baker. Baker's wife was the niece of the same Admiral James Vashon (1742–1827) after whom Vashon Island, in lower Puget Sound, is named.

MOUNT OLYMPUS (G-4)

This is the nearly 8,000 foot high snow-capped peak which rises so abruptly out of the Pacific Ocean at the entrance to Puget Sound. The Spanish naval officer Juan Perez (an ex-Spanish galleon skipper on the Manila run) first sighted it on August 10, 1774. Returning in a Spanish navy ship called the *Santiago* from a discouraging trip north in search of Russians, his crew was mostly disabled by scurvy. When he reached his home base, in Mexico, he was reprimanded for his failure to reach Alaska, Russia's main base in the New World. Capitain Perez called Mount Olympus by the name *Sierra de Santa Rosalia,* a name chosen (as was the Spanish custom) commemorating the church saint of the day, as specified in the church calendar carried aboard all ships of the Spanish navy.

Captain John Meares, an English fur trader, was next to sight this peak. It was he who named it Mount Olympus, doubtlessly after Mount Olympus in Greece, home of Greek gods. The date of his christening was July 4th, 1788. Meares, a British naval officer on half pay at this time was seeking riches by trading worthless gewgaws with the Indians along Washington's coast for the abundant supply of sea otter pelt, which they came carrying in their canoes to trade with him. He was returning to a base up the coast from here called Nootka (located on what is known today as Vancouver Island). Earlier in this same year, Meares had arriived at Nootka from China carrying on board his small ship, the *Felice Adventurer,* forty Chinese laborers and the parts of a ship which Meares planned for them to assemble ashore. When Meares returned to Nootka, soon after naming Mount Olympus, he found the craft successfully assembled there, and launched it soon after, the first sailing ship ever constructed in the Pacific Northwest.

It was from Shelton, Washington, located on lower Puget Sound, in 1897 that mountaineers first began climbing into the Olympic Mountains' unexplored heights. Mount Ellinore was the first of the peaks to be climbed, then in 1900, Mount Olympus itself.

Within days after Meares returned to Nootka, a Spaniard named Estevan Martiniez arrived at this base in a Spanish warship. Seizing Meares land, house, and his recently-launched *Northwest America,* Martinez hoisted the Spanish colors here and demanded all English captains entering Nootka's harbor to first obtain his permission. This prompted Meares to go back to England, where he complained to the British Parliament over the Spanish behavior. Also he pamphleteered the English public over the incident, further arousing anti-Spanish feelings. The British fleet was mobilized and William Pitt, then England's prime minister, threatened war against Spain. However, the diplomatic skills of Lord Saint Helens (after whom Washington's Mount Saint Helens is named) served to prevent this outbreak. By a Treaty of Nootka between the two nations, Spain agreed to make restitution to John Meares for Martinez's seizure.

The seized land which Meares had purchased at Nootka from Chief Maquinna, reportedly for two pistols, suddenly (according to Meares) became worth astronomical amounts of money, as did the sea otter pelts which Martinez had seized, as well as Meares' house. Initially he demanded 653,433 Spanish dollars in compensation. As finally decided by the treaty-makers, Meares received an estimated $180,000 (U.S. money). Meares then wrote a livid account of the Nootka Affair, a best seller of the day. To cap his good fortune, he was then reinstated to active duty in the British navy, his new rank two steps above the one he held previous to entering the fur trade.

So rugged and wild are the interior regions of the Olympic Mountains, and so close in altitude are its three tallest peaks, that confusion still exists with regard to just who were the first climbers to reach the top of Mount Olympus itself. Benjamin Franklin Shaw, the bold Indian fighter and indispensable aide to Washington's first governor, Isaac Stevens, was believed by some early white settlers around Puget Sound to have ascended Mount Olympus in 1854. It is more likely, however, that it was not until September, 1890, that Mount Olympus' summit was reached, accomplished by a team named Bretherton, Lisely, and Danton.

MOUNT RAINIER (K-10)

Peter Rainier (1741–1808) after whom this highest of the many snow-capped peaks in the Pacific Northwest is named, was a commoner by birth, his grandparents being Huguenots named Regnier. As a youth of fifteen, eager to join the British navy, he found it necessary to begin as an able-bodied seaman instead of as a midshipman, as was the custom for youth of more important parentage.

Rainier's first sea duty took him to the East Indies aboard His Majesty's Ship *Oxford.* England at this time was competing with the French and Dutch around Trincomalee (Ceylon) and the East Indies in exploiting these areas' great natural wealth. When in 1760 the size of the British navy was reduced, young Rainier, age nineteen, was paid off. He then became a civilian working for the East India Company in Madras, India. After passing admiralty examinations in about 1769, Rainier rejoined the British navy, this time with the rank of lieutenant. At age thirty-three we find him serving aboard HMS *Maidstone,* this time on the West Indies station in the Caribbean. Commander of the *Maidstone* at this time was Captain (later Admiral) Alan Gardner, whose name today graces the city of Everett's harbor which is called Port Gardner. In 1777, age thirty-six, Rainier assumed command of HMS *Ostrich* in the West Indies. This was during the American Revolution when the waters of the West Indies were being sailed by numerous American privateers seeking to carry supplies from these islands to their beleaguered Thirteen Colonies.

On July 8, 1778, Rainier, still in command of the *Ostrich,* successfully engaged in battle with one of these American privateers, named the *Polly,* which at the time was flying the flag of the sovereign state of South Carolina. In the fierce battle which ensued he was hit by an American cannonball. Despite his wounds, Rainier refused to go below decks to have his wounds treated, and as an upshot of his courageous handling of his ship under these adverse circumstances, he captured the American vessel. As a result of this success, Rainier in 1779 found himself in command of one of England's first class ships-of-the line, His Majesty's Ship *Buford,* 64 guns. However, with the end of the American Revolution, at age thirty-nine, Rainier found himself again placed on inactive status, this time on half pay. Recalled to active duty in 1788, Rainier was given command of HMS *Monarch* operating in the English Channel. Then, at age fifty-three, in command of HMS *Suffolk,* 74 guns, he sailed back to his youthful haunts in the East Indies. Here he remained for the rest of his naval career, achieving before his retirement, the position of commander-in-chief of the British fleet there.

After retirement to civilian life, Admiral Rainier served for many years in the British Parliament. He died in 1806, age sixty-five. Under the provisions of his will, Rainier left one-tenth of his estate to the British government. It was a sizeable one, since while on the East Indies station, Rainier, as was the custom and as was fully authorized, acquired wealth derived from raids upon East Indian civilians. The admiral left to the Britich government an amount which represented 250,000 pounds, requesting that this money be used to diminish England's ever-growing national debt.

Said one of Rainier's sarcastic contemporaries of this unusual action: "Rainier's bequest was like a drop of water in the ocean whereon it had been gained, and was received without thanks, for none could be grateful for that which, being spread over so large a surface, was unfelt and unseen." The writer continues: "With the highest respect for the memory of this excellent officer I should humbly suggest that if in the future any of our admirals should happen to have more money than they require they would think of the widows of their brother officers."

Most of the first Americans to settle the Pacific Northwest had fresh recollections of the American Revolution, and were therefore inclined to be anti-British in their sentiments. In having their tallest mountain named after a "British butcher," as some called Admiral Rainier (remembering his defeat of the *Polly*), many were unhappy, so much so that a movement was started to rename this mountain after what was alleged to be its original Indian name of *Tahoma.* For years this proposal was widely supported, even reaching the halls of Congress for its approval before it was finally rejected.

In naming this mountain after Admiral Rainier in May, 1792, Captain George Vancouver, commander of His Majesty's Ship *Discovery,* refers to him as "my friend." Probably Vancouver and Rainier first knew each other when both were serving under Admiral Gardner in the West Indies. Records for 1788 indicate that George Vancouver was serving there aboard HMS *Fame* at the same time that Lieutenant Commander Rainier, also in the West Indies, was commanding HMS *Astrea.*

MOUNT SAINT HELENS (O-9)

This volcanic snow-cone, situated in southwest Washington, fifty miles northeast of Portland, erupted as recently as March, 1988. It is named for Baron St. Helens, Mr. Alleyne Fitzherbert (1753–1839). He was England's ambassador to Spain in 1790, when news of the Nootka Affair reached London, prompting England to prepare for war.

Today Nootka is a deserted place on Vancouver Island, but at this time it was the center of the Northwest's fur trade, its harbor, Friendly Cove, visited by fur trading ships from all over the world. The year prior to this (1789) Spain's ruler in the New World, Viceroy Manuel Flores in Mexico City, became alarmed at the threat to Spain's possession over these Northwest coasts being exerted by the Russians in Alaska, and feared a Russian takeover of Nootka. So he dispatched two Spanish warships north from Spain's naval base near Acapulco. In charge of one of them was Estevan Martinez, with orders to build fortifications at Nootka and deal prudently but firmly with any foreigners entering the harbor. However, Martinez was not a prudent man. Chief among his encounters with visiting "foreign" ships occurred with the arrival of two British ships, the *Argonaut* and the *Princess Royal,* their respective commanders James Colnett and Thomas Hudson. At a dinner which Martinez gave for Colnett, the captain took exception to the Spanish governor's assertion that Spain owned the harbor. In the confrontation which ensued, Martinez allegedly pointed a pistol at the Englishman who in turn drew his sword.

Unfortunately, the *Argonaut* was anchored immediately below the guns of the governor's house, thereby enabling Martinez to seize Colnett's ship. Hauling down the Union Jack and hoisting Spain's red and yellow colors, Martinez then placed a Spanish prize crew aboard the English vessel, and with Captain Colnett a prisoner aboard his own ship, the *Argonaut* was sailed south to San Blas. When news of this startling development reached London, both England and Spain were shocked. Weakened by the French Revolution, when England mobilized her fleet, Spain backed down. Under the terms of a treaty, one in which Baron St. Helens played an important role, Nootka itself would be shared by both nations. Accordingly, Vancouver was dispatched in 1791 from England to meet at Nootka with Spain's representative, Senor Bodega y Quadra; their mission was to agree upon the details of Nootka's joint occupation.

In October, 1792, while sailing in his flagship *Discovery* southward from Nootka toward Monterey, having failed in his negotiations with Quadra, Captain Vancouver sighted this majestic peak, one hundred miles away from the bridge of his ship. It was at this time that Mount Saint Helens received its name.

N

NACHES PASS (J-11)

In the summer of 1853, the Yakima Indians were fast becoming angry. White men were trespassing on their lands. A wagon road was about to be laid from Walla Walla over Naches Pass in the high Cascade Range into Puget Sound. They also were hearing about the approach of "iron horses," strange contraptions bigger and faster than buffaloes which snorted fire and smoke. Tracks for these strange contraptions were being laid. They would go through Yakima lands, thence over the mountains into Puget Sound country.

In August, confirmation of this rumor came with the appearance among the Yakimas of Captain George B. McClellan (later General McClellan, of Civil War fame) accompanied by sixty-six U.S. army troops; also seventy-three horses and mules. They were greeted (upon reaching the approximate site where the city of Yakima now stands) by handsome Chief Kamiakin, then the leader of the Yakima nation. In response to McClellan's inquiries, Kamiakin convinced him that snows were too deep in winter to lay railroad tracks over the opening through the high Cascades lying westward, called Naches Pass. Upon learning that McClellan would lead his surveyors north along the east side of the mountains seeking another possible opening, Chief Kamiakin promptly dispatched Indian runners to precede McClellan's surveyors, warning the tribesmen to the north that they must similarly convince this American leader of the impossibility of laying such tracks. Carefully concealed to the whites was the low opening through these mountains, which we know today as Snoqualmie Pass, whose gradients on either side of the opening could readily be used by the snorting steam locomotives which were about to arrive from the East.

Two months later, emigrants from the Oregon Trail appeared in Yakima country, traveling in strange contraptions which the Indians dubbed land canoes, never having seen wheeled vehicles before. It was the Biles-Longmire party of one hundred seventy men, women, and children, headed for Puget Sound where they hoped to establish new homes. Traveling in thirty-six covered wagons and accompanied by large numbers of cattle (animals which the Yakimas had never seen before), more than one hundred of these Indians followed them as they progressed up the banks of the Yakima River. "Chick-chick-shuile-kai-kash" was the name they initially gave to the strange vehicles in which these strange people were traveling, this name simulating the monotonous grinding and squeaking sound the covered wagons made as they crept along.

In ascending the Naches River toward Naches Pass, the emigrants were forced to cross this stream fifty-eight times, so twisting was its course. Moreover, when they reached Naches Pass—with the 14,000-foot-high Mount Rainier looming overhead—they learned that the worst part of their journey, the descent, was yet to come. At one point, as they traveled down the precipitous western slopes, their wagons had to be lowered over cliffs by ropes fastened to their vehicles' axles, whose other ends were secured to trees. Much of the time they were forced to continue descending the steep, untracked slopes with locked wheels. The Greenwater River, down which they next traced, like the Naches, was so twisting that it had to be crossed sixteen times; and the succeeding White River, an additional six times, before they finally reached Fort Steilacoom. No lives were lost, but several of the wagons were broken into pieces while being lowered over the cliffs when the leather ropes (obtained by splicing strips of hide from some of their slaughtered oxen) broke.

The whites had known of Naches Pass since 1840. In the summer of that year Pierre Pambrum (1792–1841), the chief trader at Fort Walla Walla, and his young friend, Cornelius Rogers, had explored it from the eastern side. They were followed the next year by Lieutenant Robert Johnson, U.S. Navy, and members of the Wilkes Exploring Expedition, two of whose ships were anchored at this time in Puget Sound (having recently arrived here from the South Seas). Although a highly capable officer, Lieutenant Johnson appears to have taken his new role as a mountain explorer too lightly, indulging in alcoholic refreshment as he rode horseback into the snow-capped heights from Tacoma's Commencement Bay. Particularly did he offend the five scientists who comprised the remainder of his group. Soon after surmounting Naches Pass, Johnson fell into the Naches River, not only nearly drowning himself, but also ruining some of the scientists' instruments. As they traced up the left bank of the Columbia River, the group believed they were running out of food only to find, upon reaching Fort Okanogan (then a British fur post) that Lieutenant Johnson had forgotten a supply of delicacies which their pack animals had been carrying since the start of the trip. They proceeded eastward from here, inspecting the depths of Grand Coulee before reaching Fort Colville, another trading post of the Hudson's Bay Company. Thence they traveled to two American missionary stations, Chamokane and Lapwai, before reaching Pierre Pambrum's fur post at the mouth of the Walla Walla. All then returned safely over the Cascades to Nisqually, having completed a journey of over a thousand miles in about six weeks. Lieutenant Johnson, upon boarding Wilkes' flagship, found himself disciplined by confinement to his cabin for several days.

NEAH BAY (E-2)

This historic spot lies five miles east of Cape Flattery, just inside the south entrance to the Strait of Juan de Fuca. Neah Bay takes its name after a local Makah chieftain named Deeah. The first white man to discover Neah Bay was Robert Gray, the Rhode Island sea captain who, while sailing in his ship *Lady Washington,* stopped here to swap his beads, buttons, and cheap rings with the local Indians in exchange for their sea otter pelt. This was the same captain Gray who, on a second trip to the Northwest in 1792, sailing in the *Columbia-Rediviva,* discovered and entered the Columbia River for the first time. Gray, at the time he stopped here, was operating his ship from a base one hundred fifty miles north of here, called Nootka. When he returned to Nootka, soon after visiting Neah Bay, he found that a Spaniard named Estevan Martinez (with the help of Spanish warships and soldiers) had seized Nootka, and was commencing to establish a Spanish naval base there. Later that year (1789) the erratic Martinez seized two British fur trading ships at Nootka. He then dispatched these vessels south, under the command of Spanish crews, to San Blas, Spain's naval base in lower California.

In July, 1790, about a year after Gray's visit to Neah Bay, a Spanish ship arrived at Neah Bay named the *Princesa Real,* another of the ships the mad Martinez had seized at Nootka (this vessel under its British commander was called the *Princess Royal*). A new Spanish governor at Nootka, Francisco Eliza, had ordered Manuel Quimper, an ensign in the Spanish navy, to sail the *Princesa Real* south from Nootka to ascertain the extent of the sea-opening visible behind the Juan De Fuca Strait's entrance. Ensign Quimper (by small boat and in his ship) managed to probe north into Georgia Strait, and prior to his arrival at Neah Bay, Quimper probed into the waters of Puget Sound eastward as far as Whidbey Island before deciding to exit these waters.

At Neah Bay, Quimper landed some sailors to wash clothes in a local river. In so doing, one sailor was killed by a Makah Indian, and another suffered the loss of his sabre before returning aboard. Despite this bad start, Quimper and his *Princesa Real* remained at Neah Bay for eleven days. So friendly did he and his sailors become with the Makahs, in fact, that on the eve of their departure to return to Nootka, Chief Tatoosh presented them with salmon "of 100 pounds or more in weight."

Two years later, on 29 May 1792, there arrived at Neah Bay an expedition from San Blas in Mexico, led by Salvadore Fidalgo. Since Quimper's previous visit two years prior to this, there had been a realignment of powers in Europe. Spain was no longer in the ascendancy and England was gaining greater strength. By the treaty following the near-war between England and Spain over Governor Martinez's seizure of British ships at Nootka, it was agreed by the two nations that England as well as Spain owned Nootka, and that the Northwest coasts, hitherto claimed exclusively by Spain, must now be shared with England. Accordingly, the Spanish king had decided to establish an exclusively Spanish military base at the site of Neah Bay. The site, they believed, was a very strategic place, for from this point Spain might control entrance into the mysterious waters lying behind here, which the Spanish believed led through the American continent to the Atlantic Ocean.

Accompanying Fidago aboard his ship *Princesa Real* were seventy seamen, thirteen Catalonian soldiers, a chaplain, and a surgeon. Ashore the group erected a fort surrounded by palisaded walls to protect from attack. The soldiers were alerted to the possibility, not only of Indian attack, but also of attack by foreign ships arriving here from the Atlantic Ocean, having crossed over the top of America to capture the post. Russians in Alaska were still feared and it was known that a British warship, His Majesty's Ship *Discovery* commanded by Captain Vancouver, would soon arrive in these waters to assert England's rival claims to Puget Sound.

Fidalgo's new base was christened Fort Gaona, and the harbor which today is called Neah Bay was christened *Bahia de Gaona,* for a Spanish admiral, Manuel Nunez Gaona. Completing this Spanish fort were a bakery, blacksmith shop, dispensary, and farm buildings. The fortunes of the base soon waned, and it became evident that the bay was too exposed to ocean winds to be a satisfactory anchorage. In July, one of Fidalgo's subordinates, Antonio Serantes, was found murdered in the woods near the fort, apparently by the local Makahs. Investigation revealed he had been having a romantic affair with a Makah female. The excessively severe and hasty manner in which Governor Fidalgo took revenge for Serante's death brought down upon him the wrath of his superiors at Nootka. The incident also marked the beginning of the end of Neah Bay as a Spanish fort, even though Fort Gaona had been operating only five months. Abandoning the buildings they had so laboriously erected, the Spaniards retreated southward down the coastline, hoping to establish a base on the Columbia River. Spain by now had lost the support of France, heretofore her ally. Both Spain and England, for the time being, were preoccupied with affairs in Europe.

Thereafter, Neah Bay received various names. Fur traders visiting here called it Poverty Cove. Then for a time it was called Scarborough Cove, after James Scarborough, a fur trader and captain of the British ship *Cadboro* (this name was proposed by Wilkes in 1841). Finally it received its present name in 1847, given by Lieutenant Commander Henry Kellett of the British Royal Navy.

NISQUALLY (K-7)

This small town on the shores of lower Puget Sound is located nine miles from Olympia to the southwest. Largely forgotten now is historic Nisqually House which was built here in 1832. This fur post was the first white man's structure to be erected in Puget Sound country.

The man who built Nisqually House was white-haired, handsome John McLoughlin, known to his fur trappers as "King of the Columbia." From Fort Vancouver, his impressive headquarters to the south of Nisqually House, McLoughlin ruled with an iron hand over a fur trapping domain which included all lands west of the Rocky Mountains, lying between Russian Alaska in the north and Spanish California in the south. The trade goods necessary for carrying on this vast fur trade arrived at Fort Vancouver aboard supply ships from London, but in unloading at Fort Vancouver, too often these ships went aground, their precious cargo a total loss.

To prevent this, Dr. McLoughlin chose Nisqually House as a superior place to unload this cargo. Here at the dock, within yards of Nisqually House, these vessels could arrive without risk of going aground. The trade goods, after being offloaded at Nisqually House, could be reshipped north from here by a fleet of smaller sailing ships, who would carry the cargo to the chain of fur posts which McLoughlin was extending north to Alaska. Furs at this time were in great demand, not only in Europe but also in China. Beaver hats were worn by all stylish men; particularly in China were fur coats in high demand.

The man to whom McLoughlin assigned the task of building Nisqually House was Angus McDonald (1790–1853), known to the Indians as "The Black Eagle." He is remembered as a tall Scotsman, fond of chanting the Gaelic songs of his native Scotland. Accompanying McDonald north from Fort Vancouver was twenty-one-year-old Fraser Tolmie, a fellow Scot recently arrived from Glasgow. There he had attended the university and became a doctor. He was hired by the HBC as their surgeon. McDonald and Tolmie were accompanied by crews of French-Canadian and Hawaiian laborers, driving six oxen before them. From Fort Vancouver this group descended the right bank of the Columbia to the mouth of Cowlitz River, up which they traveled until reaching the Chehalis Plains. From here they marched overland to lower Puget Sound, finally reaching the mouth of the Nisqually River. The trip required fourteen days.

Curious Indians gathered to watch as they felled giant trees and cleared land on a small hill overlooking Nisqually Reach. The Indians watched in wonder as the oxen, animals which they had never seen before, dragged the logs to the site where Fort Nisqually was to be built. Wooden pegs were used in constructing the fort.

"Nisqually is a palisaded enclosure two hundred feet square", recorded Theodore Winthrop describing this trading post. "Bartisan towers protect its corners reminding me of the stockades built in New England two hundred years earlier . . . Within are blockhouses for goods and furs and also one storied cottages for residences." A huge gate at the front of the palisade was seldom opened, the transactions with the Indians being carried on through apertures. A dock was built, to which London supply ships and coastal delivery vessels could tie up in loading and unloading their cargo. Winthrop describes the merchandise store inside the palisade to which the Indians, in later years, were allowed to come: "Rusty Indians were trading at the three b's—blankets, beads, and 'baccy. All the squaws purchasing today were hags beyond the age of coquetry."

From the very beginning, Nisqually House was a magnet to the Indians. Archibald, the Black Eagle, had married an Indian woman, and his part-Indian son, Ranald, lived with Dr. McLoughlin at Fort Vancouver, tutored by a white school teacher, to become a great man some day. Also the Indians took a liking to the twenty-one-year-old Dr. Tolmie, particularly when they learned he was able to cure their ills. Tolmie, too, was definitely interested in the Indians, their customs, and languages. He also was a botanist and, as it soon developed, an ardent mountain climber. It was soon after his arrival at Fort Nisqually that he became the first white man to ascend into the slopes of snow-capped Mount Rainier, whose 14,000 foot high snow-cap loomed closeby to the east.

The following are extracts from the *Journal of Occurrences*, as the daily record of events at Fort Nisqually was known:

> Today the Indians assembled in front of the house to the number of seventy or eighty, male and female. With Brown as interpreter, who spoke in Chinook, Heron and I explained the Creation of the World, the reason why Christian and Jews abstained from work on Sunday . . . and we had gotten as far as the Deluge in sacred history when we were requested to stop, as the Indians could not comprehend things clearly.

By October, 1834, Indians from east of the Cascade Range were coming here to visit. A race track had been built just outside the palisade, and Klickitat and Yakima warriors began racing their horses here. The following is the entry in the *Journal of Occurrences* for Sunday, the twenty-fourth:

> A great day for the Indians who assembled here. Mr. Heron . . . [by now promoted to Trader-in-Chief, Archibald McDonald having been transferred to Fort Langley to the north of here] made a speech in the Flathead language which was understood by our Chief Frenchman who became linguist for the rest. There were about two hundred and fifty men, women, boys and girls in the dance which followed . . .

everyone peaceable. The Indians belong to eight different
tribes.

Meanwhile the Indians were bringing to the fort large amounts of fur to
trade. As recorded in the *Journal of Occurrences*, the following
summarizes the types and numbers of furs acquired at Nisqually House
between March, 1834, and January, 1835: "Large black bears, 33; small
black bears, 13; large beaver, 1,038; small beaver, 412; mink, 80; sea
otter, 1; land otter, 340; raccoon, 190; elk skin, 2; muskrat, 700."

By 1839 the supply of furs in the entire Pacific Northwest was
beginning to decline, and the Hudson's Bay Company was apprehensive
over dwindling profits. To remedy this they began grazing cattle and
sheep on the vast prairie lands east of the fur post. These lands were
extensive, stretching as they did all the way to the mountains. Russians
in Alaska were eager for supplies and soon sailing ships began carrying
the beef and mutton, which his farm activity produced, to Sitka. Added
to the concerns, not only of the Hudson's Bay Company but also of the
British government as well, were the hundreds of Americans by now
arriving over the Oregon Trail to take out land in Willamette Valley.
Pointing out to his superiors in London the seriousness of this ever-
increasing migration, Governor Simpson, the Hudson Bay Company's
ruler in America, began to recognize the probability that these Oregon
Trail emigrants would also invade the regions north of the Columbia. In
order to compete with this, steps by the British government were taken
to attract British settlers also to come to the northwest to settle. To
those willing to do so a house, barn, fifteen cows, one bull, fifty sheep,
and an ox and horse were promised by the HBC. The attempt to so lure
these settlers, however had its drawbacks. One-half of the crops such
Britishers raised would belong to the HBC. Worst of all, and unlike the
American emigrants, the British ones were not given title to the land
they farmed.

When the Boundary Treaty of 1846 decreed that the United States
owned all lands south of the forty-ninth parallel, the days of Fort
Nisqually under the Union Jack became numbered. Notwithstanding
this treaty, British farming operations under the Puget Sound

Agricultural Company were allowed to continue; that is, until 1868. In this latter year, in return for U.S. payment of $200,000, all land and remaining British property here on the Nisqually plains then became a possession of the United States.

There were numerous ex-fur trappers who were placed in charge of this operation, among these: William Kittson, who learned his skills under the great Peter Skene Ogden. Due to careless surveying here in Puget Sound, Ketron Island, located closeby Nisqually, was misnamed. It was intended to be called Kittson Island after this man. Mr. Alexander Caulfield Anderson, another British officer-in-charge at Nisqually during its days of prosperity under the Union Jack, is today commemorated by the name Anderson Island which lies just offshore of Old Nisqually House's original site. The last of such officers, William Fraser Tolmie who presided over the demise of Old Fort Nisqually, was the same Tolmie who, with Archibald McDonald, founded it.

NORTH BEND (I-10)

This name refers to the location of this river town which is twenty-two miles east of Seattle. It is situated on the north bend of the Snoqualmie River. The river derives its name from the Snoqualmie tribe of Indians who lived in great numbers on the banks of the stream. The word *snoqualmie* translates "moon people," for the Snoqualmies believed that their ancestors came from the moon. An important leader of the Snoqualmies was Chief Patkanim.

In his younger years Patkanim vowed that he would drive every paleface from Puget Sound country. He believed the best way to accomplish this involved capturing Fort Nisqually which was located at the southern end of Puget Sound. It was a strongly defended British fur post, surrounded by a twenty-foot-high barricade atop which guns were emplaced at each corner. In May, 1848, Chief Patkanim led his Snoqualmie warriors south from where North Bend now stands to make an attack upon Fort Nisqually. Feigning a preliminary attack upon some Nisqually Indians living closeby the fort, Patkanim used the attendant confusion to place his main body of Snoqualmie warriors at Fort Nisqually's rear. Anticipating correctly that the Hudson Bay Company's people inside Fort Nisqually would open their big gate to the fort in front in order to shelter the neighboring Nisquallies during the feigned attack by his Snoqualmies upon them, Patkanim's main body of warriors in the rear of the fort meanwhile made preparations for scaling the fort's walls there.

Execution of this clever plan commenced with Patkanim's personal appearance at the big gate at the fort's front side where, through this gate's peephole, he informed the white guard within that he wished entry in order to talk peace. By accident at this instant, a gun went off prematurely, fired accidentally by one of Patkanim's warriors at the fort's rear. This alerted the Britishers inside the fort, who quickly sensed Patkanim's real intentions. Swivel guns from atop the fort's barricade were fired upon the Indians below, and the frustrated Snoqualmies were quickly subdued, not, however, before a white man, Leander C. Wallace of nearby Anderson Island who chanced to be walking by the fort at this time, was accidentally killed.

Puget Sound country at this time was still a part of the U.S. Territory of Oregon, and was governed accordingly by Joseph Lane whose capitol headquarters were at Oregon City on the Willamette River, south of the Columbia. Upon hearing of Chief Patkanim's sneak attack, he dispatched his Indian agent, Mr. J. Quinn Thornton, north to the scene with orders to punish the Indian offenders with the U.S. troops which accompanied him. Instead of carrying out these orders, Thornton attempted to persuade the Snoqualmies to surrender those Indians of their tribe who launched the attack, offering a reward of eighty blankets if they would do so. Angrily declaring that Thornton's orders were to punish, not to bribe the Snoqualmies, Governor Lane himself then marched with more troops to the scene. At Fort Nisqually he held a trial which resulted in two of six alleged offenders being executed by hanging.

Professing complete innocence of all that had transpired, Chief Patkanim himself was left unscathed. Not long afterward, the wily chieftain changed his allegiance; in the Indian wars of 1856 which followed, Patkanim assisted the whites in spying upon his fellow Indians.

OKANOGAN (E-16)

This name has a lilting ring to it, and is pronounced by Americans living south of the Canadian border like the word toboggan although north of this international line it becomes Okan-a-gan with the broad *a* pronunciation. Okanogan (the town) lies forty miles south of the

Canada border and sixty-five miles northeast of Wenatchee. The word is doubtless Indian in origin although its translation is obscure. One early Irishman living in The Okanogan, as the general area is usually referred to, swore that the word was originally O'Kanagan, and that he was a judge who lived on 89-mile-long Okanogan Lake.

The town of Okanogan was established in 1868 under the name of Alma. In 1905 it was renamed Pogue after the town's first doctor. It received its present name in 1907. Located thirty miles southeast of Okanogan was the settlement of Kartar, so named after the Kartar people, a sub-tribe of the Okanogan tribe. At Kartar is still to be found a marker on which is inscribed "Coxey George, 1850–1922, 72 years" marking the resting place of George Lahome, or Loup Loup George. Widely revered among the Indians of the Okanogan, he was famous for the numerous thoroughbred horses and fine cattle which he owned.

Traveling north up the banks of Okanogan River past the present-day city of Okanogan in 1835, came the great Peter Skene Ogden (1794–1854) at the end of a horse brigade. Dressed in a black broadcloth frock coat and wearing a beaver hat, he was mounted on the lead horse with about two hundred of these animals following in column, each carrying two 100-pound packs of supplies slung from opposite sides of their backs. Ogden was the son of a Canadian Chief Justice whose forbears came from New Jersey. He had already won his reputation as one of the West's greatest explorers. He was now headed north, having recently been promoted to become chief factor of Fort St. James, located about four hundred fifty miles northwest of the Okanogan, at this time the capital of the New Caledonia fur trade.

Twenty days prior to Ogden and his horse brigade's passing the site where Okanogan now stands, in the summer of 1835, they had departed Fort Vancouver on the lower Columbia River in ten boats loaded with the same trade goods their animals were now carrying. About sixty French Canadians rowed them upstream. When they finally reached Fort Okanogan at the confluence of the Okanogan River with the Columbia, sixty or more horses were awaiting, and as the French-Canadians unloaded the boats their contents were reloaded onto the backs of these animals. Another six weeks of travel overland past the shores of Okanogan Lake and the forks of the Thompson brought them to Fort Alexandria, where today the city of Williams Lake stands. Here the goods were reloaded onto Fraser River boats. After two weeks pushing up the Fraser River and thence the Stuart River, Ogden and his brigade reached Fort St. James on Stuart Lake.

For many years Mr. Ogden and his Indian wife Julia and their six children lived at Fort St. James like royalty, waited upon hand and foot by the post's servants. Food, however, at times became scarce, sometimes reducing all the fort's occupants to a diet of salmon and water. Each spring Ogden loaded the annual catch of furs on boats, then commenced the delivery down the Stuart River to the Fraser, thence down this stream to Fort Alexandria (where Williams Lake now stands). Here the precious cargo was offloaded from the boats onto the backs of horses, two hundred or more of the animals then forming a column with Ogden at the head progressing southward. As they passed Okanogan Lake the column of these animals, each carrying two 100-pound packs of furs slung from opposite sides of their back, stretched out for over a mile. It is estimated that the annual value of the furs Ogden was thus delivering averaged at least $250,000 annually in terms of modern values. After passing down the Okanogan River past the site where the city of Okanogan now stands, the pelts were loaded aboard a fleet of the twenty-five-foot rugged Columbia River boats awaiting where the town of Brewster now stands. From here they sped with the current down the Columbia until at The Dalles a portage was necessary. Finally at Fort Vancouver, opposite today's city of Portland, they were loaded aboard the annual sailing ship recently arrived from England. Sailed back around Cape Horn to England, they were in London made into beaver hats (then worn all over Europe), also men's and women's coats.

Mr. Ogden first achieved fame when Governor Simpson of the Hudson Bay Company chose him to lead, in the fall of 1824, a fur brigade of fifty-eight men, women, and children from Flathead Post, in present Western Montana, southward following the crest of the Continental Divide into Snake Country (today called Southern Idaho); a region then almost totally unexplored. Accompanied by 268 horses, 324 traps, and 22 portable leathern lodges, the unusual group constituted a moving village. Throughout the winter of 1824–1825 they were constantly on the move, living off the land and setting traps beneath icy streams. All the while they were dodging Snake and Blackfoot Indians who attempted to steal their animals. Unexpectedly, while so engaged, Ogden and his followers found rival American "mountain men" also seeking beaver pelt in the region. Throughout that winter the two rival groups shadowed each other, each hoping to discover from the other the best places to find beaver. On May 22, 1825, the two groups narrowly missed coming to blows, so fierce was the rivalry. The

Americans on this occasion warned the Britishers they were trapping on U.S. soil. Ogden stoutly denied this, reminding the Yankees that the region known as the Northwest was, by treaty, equally shared by both nations pending a final settlement. For his refusal to be intimidated by the larger American group, Ogden earned the praise of Governor Simpson. Mr. Ogden led four such expeditions into regions of today's American West, during which he discovered California's Mount Shasta, and Nevada's Humboldt River. In the winter of 1829–1830, he even led his trappers all the way south, through today's California, to the Gulf of lower California before returning north to Fort Vancouver.

OLYMPIA (K-7)

This is the southernmost of the cities located on the shores of Puget Sound. Today it is the State of Washington's capital. Founder of Olympia was Mr. Levi Lathrop Smith. He was born in New York State's Mohawk Valley. Initially Smith studied for the Presbyterian ministry. He then migrated west to Wisconsin. Here he became infatuated with a local Indian girl, a Catholic. Unhappy in these circumstances, Smith then traveled west over the Rockies to Puget Sound to make a new start.

The two acres of land which Mr. Smith claimed here is today situated on the city of Olympia's Main Street, between Second and Third Avenue. To the Indians whom Smith encountered here, the site was known as *stu-chu-sand,* translated "Place of the Bear." It was in deep forest. Here Smith felled trees and built a cabin sixteen feet square made of cedar planking. This planking was cut from a sawmill which already existed one mile southward of his cabin, at Tumwater Falls (where the city of Tumwater now stands). A giant Kentuckian, Michael Troutman Simmons (1814–1867), had settled at Tumwater Falls the year prior to Smith's building of his cabin at *stu-chu-sand.* Simmons' sawmill was powered by the big drop in the Deschutes River called Tumwater Falls.

Except for Simmons and his workmen at Tumwater Falls, Smith was the only American then living on Puget Sound. Ten miles northeast of here however, back in 1833, the British Hudson's Bay Company built a fur trading post called Fort Nisqually. England at this time still claimed ownership over all of Puget Sound country, and they opposed the American settlement where Olympia now stands. This however did not prevent them from assisting both Levi Smith and Mike Simmons in getting settled. Thanks to their help, Levi began raising pigs on his land;

also hens, a cock, a cat, and a dog. Soon he had acquired a yoke of oxen and a team of horses.

When news of the Anglo-American Boundary Commission's decision of 1846, placing Puget sound on the American side of the international border, reached Puget Sound in early 1847, more Americans began pouring into this new region to take up homes, and Levi Smith became their leader. By 1848 the number of these Americans increased to almost four hundred. They elected Mr. Smith in this year to be their representative in attending the first meeting of a recently formed U.S. Territorial Legislature, held that year in Oregon City. Tragically, while traveling there, Levi Smith died—drowned in a canoe accident.

In his will Levi bequeathed his cabin and property at *stu-ch-sand* to a friend, Mr. Edmund Sylvester, a native of Calais, Maine. Sylvester then moved from his home on nearby Chamber's Prairie to live in his deceased friend's log cabin. Sylvester had begun laying out streets here, envisioning a seaport arising locally along these shores of Eld Inlet. He had even given to the future city the name Smithfield, in honor of his deceased friend. Then gold was discovered in California. Upon receiving this news Sylvester rushed south to seek his fortune. Not long after he was so successful in this effort that he was able to purchase in San Francisco a sailing ship named the *Orbit*. In this tiny vessel Sylvester sailed back to Smithfield full of hopes to make his Smithfield the leading city in the Northwest.

By now, the Kentuckian Michael Simmons had prospered enough to build a grist mill as well as the saw mill at Tumwater Falls. Impatient to find still more prosperity, big Mike then moved to Smithfield and erected here a merchandise store, the first one to open on Puget Sound. Several thousand Americans were by now living at Olympia and a new U.S. Territory of Washington had recently been established with Smithfield as the site of its capitol. In anticipation of this, Sylvester by now had decided that a grander name than Smithfield was needed for his future city. It was he who in all likelihood changed the name of the town from Smithfield to Olympia, this latter name chosen in view of the impressive snow-capped Olympic Mountains visible from here northwestward.

The first governor of Washington Territory, Governor Isaac Stevens (1818–1862) was no ordinary individual. Short-statured, an ex-U.S. Army engineer who turned politician after the Mexican War, he was a person of positive ideas and great energy. The idea of settling Indians on reservations in order to bring them under control, for which Stevens is criticized popularly today, did not originate with him as is widely believed. Indeed in the eastern United States such practices had been used as early as 1786. When Stevens arrived on the lower Columbia in October, 1786, after a five month trip on horseback over the Rockies, anxious to see the recently established capitol where he would soon govern his new territory, he decided to ride alone ahead of his entourage. It rained throughout the journey north up the banks of the Cowlitz. As Stevens was entering the town of Olympia, wet, tired, and unshaven after his long journey, he encountered one of the town's inhabitants of whom he asked where to obtain some food, for he had not eaten since early morning. He was directed to a rickety structure, Olympia's only hotel. Here Stevens was told they could not feed him, for they were preparing a banquet to be held that evening for a new Territorial Governor. The amused Stevens then introduced himself, much to the embarrassment of his hosts.

From the outset of Stevens' regime as the new governor, he antagonized his British neighbors at nearby Fort Nisqually. When, in the fall of 1855, a rash of local Indian uprisings plagued Puget Sound's American settlers, Stevens organized a volunteer militia. Experienced as he was in fighting, by virtue of earlier experience in the U.S. Army, Stevens made himself commander of this group of Indian fighters.

The focal point of the trouble, it seemed to Stevens, were Indians living a few miles east of Fort Nisqually on Muck Creek. Here, it so happened, lived several retired Hudson Bay Company fur trappers of French-Canadian extraction, former employees at Fort Nisqually. They lived on Muck Creek with their Indian wives. Suspecting these "squaw men," as they were disrespectfully known, of assisting the Puget Sound Indians in their attacks upon the local American whites, Stevens arrested several of them and placed them in jail at a U.S. Army post, called Fort Stellacoom, recently established.

Loud protests ensued, not only from the British at Fort Nisqually— enraged at this summary treatment of their former employees—but also from an unexpected source; namely: Edward Lander, the governor's new appointee as Chief Justice of Washington Territory's recently-formed Supreme Court. Sworn to uphold his new duties regardless of his indebtedness to Stevens for his high status, Justice Landers was not bothered by the fact that he also served under Colonel Isaac Stevens as a company commander in Stevens' volunteer militia. A series of clever moves on the part of Stevens versus Lander ensued. When Lander asserted that the governor's retention of British civilians on a U.S.

military reservation to be illegal, Stevens responded by declaring all of Pierce County, the site of Fort Steilacoom, under martial law. When Landers persisted in demanding the prisoners be removed to civil jurisdiction, Stevens had the Supreme Court Justice arrested. Popular demand, however, caused Stevens to release him. Lander then shifted his legal base of operations to adjoining Thurston County. He resumed there his demand that the governor release the prisoners to civil custody. Stevens responded by placing Thurston County, too, under martial law. Lander then fined Governor Stevens fifty dollars for contempt of court. Stevens paid the fine; then, as military governor of Thurston County he ordered the fine remitted—to himself.

The battle of Stevens versus Lander shook not only the citizens of Washington Territory, it resounded back to the national capitol. Governor Stevens was then reprimanded by the U.S. Congress for his role in the incident. By 1857, however, Stevens' popularity had returned and Washingtonians elected the peppery governor as their first Territorial Delegate to the U.S. Congress.

ORCAS ISLAND (C-6)

This is but one of the more than four hundred islands known today as the San Juans which lie northward of Puget Sound. In May, 1791, when the Spaniard Pantoja y Arriago discovered Orcas Island, he and his sailors who were rowing and sailing his longboat felt quite insecure, for hideously-painted Indian warriors journeying in elaborately-carved war canoes were also cruising these waters, showing their distaste for these palefaces' intrusion into their waters. In fact, about the same time Pantoja sighted Orcas Island, his co-explorer, Jose Verdia, traveling in

another longboat rowed by Spanish sailors, was forced to turn back from his attempt to proceed northward, and retreat to these explorers' base southwestward, today called Esquimault Harbor.

It was a time when there were no maps of these waters; indeed no maps of North America. Some believe that Pantoja, in naming this island "Orcas" did so having in mind a recently-appointed viceroy of New Spain who had recently arrived in Mexico City. One of this dignitary's many names was "Horcasitees" (although he was generally known under the name "Revillagigedo"). It is this writer's belief, however, that Pantoja did so because of the numerous killer whales which cavorted about his longboat. *Orcas* was a Spanish word translated "killer whale."

Orcas Island lies closeby today's Canadian border. It is located twenty-three miles northeast of Victoria. At the base from which Pantoja and Verdia rowed and sailed into these islands. now called the San Juans, lay at anchor their mother-ship, *San Carlos* commanded by Senor Francisco Eliza.

Later that May, Senor Eliza, in the *San Carlos* departed Esquimault and, after sailing inside the Strait of Juan de Fuca, anchored in the harbor now called Port Discovery, which lies adjacent to Port Townsend. Although another Spaniard, Manuel Quimper, had preceded Eliza into these waters behind the De Fuca Strait (the first white man ever to do so), Senor Quimper had not sailed as far inside as did Senor Eliza. From Port Discovery Senor Eliza dispatched Jose Narvaez in his smaller ship, the *Santa Saturnina,* to further probe into the innumerable islands of San Juan Archipelago. Narvaez too, like Verdia before him, found his ship's progress barred by Indians in their heavily painted war canoes, each carrying as many as fifty warriors. However, after firing his ship's cannon over these Indians' heads, they fled; and Narvaez was able to continue his exploration.

Narvaez and the men of his *Santa Saturnina* were probably the first white men to view today's Lopez Island. In their ship they continued sailing north past the site where Blaine, Washington, is situated, closeby the U.S.-Canada border. On the delta lands visible to the north, Narvaez detected the presence of the Fraser River's mouth. Here he met Indians who told him of white men who came from east of the mountains; they rode strange four-legged animals, and possessed beads, copper, and bits of iron. Narvaez continued sailing north along Georgia Strait's eastern shoreline and reached present Texada Island. He then crossed Georgia Strait and turned southward, skirting Vancouver Island's eastern shore and discovering Nanaimo Harbor before returning to Port Discovery. The following year two more Spanish explorers from Nootka (Spain's headquarters on Vancouver Island), Cayetano Valdes and Dionisio Galiano sailing in the *Mexicana* and the *Sutil* also explored the San Juans.

Sucia and Matia islands, which lie closeby Orcas Island to the north, were probably also named by Pantoja. In Spanish the word *sucia* means "dirty," descriptive of the bad weather encountered. *Matia* or *mata* was probably given here by Pantoja to describe the terrain of this island; the word *mata* in Spanish being translated "bush" or "bushy." Nearby Patos Island received its name from Galiano in 1792, so named after the ducks he saw here (in Spanish *patos* means "duck"). Francisco Eliza's name for the extensive waters north of Orcas Island (now called Georgia Strait) was *Gran Canal de Nuestra Senora del Rosario la Marinera,* chosen in conformance with Spanish explorers' custom of naming their discoveries after saints or other religious personages.

A portion of this long name now designates the small settlement situated on the eastern shore of Orcas Island's East Sound, namely: Rosario. This name was chosen by a wealthy Seattle shipbuilder named Robert Moran. When he came to Orcas Island in 1904, his doctors had advised him that he had only six months more to live. In fact, however, he was to live at Rosario another four decades. From Rosario, Moran soon began enlarging his land holdings on Orcas Island, purchasing even the tallest mountain here, today called Mount Constitution. Most of his land holdings he bequeathed to the State of Washington, including Mount Constitution, and today Moran State Park surrounding this 2500 foot eminence commemorates him. Moran also erected a mansion at Rosario which is still one of the show pieces of the San Juan Islands.

Mount Constitution received its name in 1841 from the U.S. Navy's Commodore Charles Wilkes, then in command of ships surveying Puget Sound. Keenly aware at this time of the danger of Puget Sound to England, Wilkes proceeded to replace the Spanish names earlier given here with American ones. Pointedly, the ones which he chose in the San Juans commemorated U.S. naval victories over England gained in the recent War of 1812. Wilkes renamed Orcas Island, calling it Hull's Island after Commodore Isaac Hull (1773–1843) who in August, 1812, while commanding the USS *Constitution,* fought the celebrated battle with the British frigate *Guerriere* commanded by one of England's then-prominent warriors, James R. Dacres. Hull's victory over Dacres on this occasion created high exaltation of the American navy throughout the then-struggling United States. Captain Dacres' defeat, moreover, caused great annoyance in the then-preeminent British navy which, during the two decades previous to this, had won all of their numerous sea battles against such European powers as France, Spain, and Russia.

Jones Island, which lies off Deer Harbor on Orcas Island's West Sound, is named for still another U.S. naval hero admired by Wilkes: Jacob Jones (1768–1850). The famous battle which Jones fought in his USS *Wasp* against the British took place in the West Indies in October, 1812. Opposing Jones' ship was His Majesty's Ship *Frolic*. The battle was probably the bloodiest of all the sea battles fought in the War of 1812. A storm having for days preceded the fracas, the sea was rough and the waves were so high that, as the two vessels squared off, both ships found difficulty in firing their broadsides due to excessive rolling. Frequently the guns fired their cannons over the masts of the opposing vessel, but Captain Jones' superior training of his American sailors in preparation for this contingency then came into play. Of the British vessel's complement of one hundred and seven, ninety suffered death or serious wounds. The *Wasp's* casualties numbered five dead and five wounded.

P

PADILLA BAY (D-8)

Few Puget Sounders realize that Spain, not England, first claimed possession over their region. Evidence of this fact is in the name of this body of water, situated three miles east of Anacortes (sixty miles north of Seattle). Padilla Bay received its name from a young Spanish naval officer, Ensign Jose Narvaez, who, while sailing in his tiny schooner named the *Santa Saturnina*, discovered this body of water in June, 1791. Senor Narvaez, was honoring a recently-appointed ruler over America, Padilla Revillagigedo who replaced Antonio Flores as viceroy of New Spain in Mexico City. This predecessor of Revillagigedo had offended England when one of his subordinates, Estevan Martinez, governor of a Spanish base at Nootka (located on what we now call Vancouver Island) seized two British sailing ships which were engaged in coastal fur trading with the Indians. Governor Martinez made the two English skippers prisoners. Then he sailed them aboard their own ships, commanded by Spaniards, southward from Nootka down the coast to Mexico where Spain maintained a naval base. When the British Parliament heard of this they forced the mobilization of England's fleet. War with Spain was imminent, but then through diplomacy a Treaty of Nootka was reached by the two nations.

As a result of this incident at Nootka, Governor Antonio Flores was replaced by Padilla Revillagigedo. Ensign Narvaez was on his second trip north from Mexico at the time he named Padilla Bay. He was probing the uncharted complicated shoreline in hopes of discovering what the nations of Europe believed to exist in these latitudes: an opening in the coastline which would lead into the Atlantic Ocean. Known to the Spanish as the Strait of Anian, it was known to the English as the Northwest Passage.

PALOUSE (K-24)

"Appaloosa," the name of the spotted horses so common in the west today, doubtlessly finds its origin in this name. It was in the Palouse Hills that this breed developed. The Washington town of this name lies on the Idaho border, thirty-five miles north of Clarkston in the southeastern part of the state. Palouse is also the name of the region called Palouse Country, its rolling hills fanning from where the city of Spokane stands today southward to the Snake River. The Palouse Indians, in addition to their fame for the horses they bred, are remembered for their independence even from other tribes in their attitudes toward the whites.

Through these Palouse hills in ancient times led a famous trail, which ran from the mouth of the Palouse River on the Snake northward toward Spokane along the river's banks. The first white man to travel this trail was the trapper David Thompson in June, 1811, returning northward to Spokane House, a British fur trading post which he had recently erected. Thompson had just made his famous canoe trip on the Columbia River from its source in the Canadian Rockies downstream to the river's entrance into the Pacific Ocean, a distance of over 1200 miles. He was the first white man to do so. When he had reached the Pacific, the previous April, Thompson found that competing American fur trappers, today remembered as Astorians, had recently built a rival fur post there (where the city of Astoria now stands). Rivalry between England and the United States was thus being evidenced at this early date in the presence of these opposing organizations; John J. Astor's Pacific Fur Company and David Thompson's British organization, The Honourable North West Company of Montreal. Later this rivalry would erupt between the governments of England and the United States over the question of which nation would ultimately gain control.

The rivalry increased in the spring of the following year (1812). An Astorian named John Clarke (1781–1858)—a former North Wester, lured to work for Astor through higher pay—journeyed from Astoria by canoe up the Columbia, and Snake Rivers, this Old Indian highway through the Palouse Hills. There he built the American fur post called Fort Spokane, situated within a few hundred yards of Thompson's Spokane House. Here the two rival fur posts presented a unique sight (eight miles north of Spokane Falls); the Union Jack flying over Thompson's post, the Stars and Stripes waving over Clarke's Fort Spokane.

A vain and pompous man, Mr. Clarke was returning down the banks of the Palouse River in the spring of 1813, when he camped one night at the juncture of the Palouse with the Snake River, four miles west of today's town of Starbuck. While making camp for the night, Clarke displayed two silver goblets, which he always carried on the trail to impress the natives. When he arose the following morning to continue downstream, Clarke discovered that these two much-prized objects had disappeared. After failing to elicit information as to the goblets' whereabouts from the Palouse, Clarke erected a guillotine with three teepee poles. Then singling-out a member of the tribe whom he suspected of the theft, Clarke hung the poor man. It was a form of punishment never before witnessed by these Indians. News of the cruel act spread throughout the Northwest, and set back Indian-white relations for years thereafter.

The origin of the word *palouse* is a mystery. Lewis and Clark records of 1805 show the name to be a tribal designation, which they spelled *palloatpallah*. According to Mr. Alvin M. Josephy's book *The Nez Perce Indians* (New Haven, 1965) the expression *pello-ut pelus* in the Nez Perce tongue designated people along that portion of the lower Snake River where the Palouse lived.

Closeby Palouse Falls, seven miles westward, is the settlement called Kahlotus, commonly said to mean "hole in the ground", descriptive of the town's unique setting. In this writer's opinion however, the name is that of a Chief Kahlotus whom historians record as the only representative of the Palouse tribe who was so gullible as to place his mark upon Governor Isaac Stevens' so-called "peace treaty," the negotiations for which were held at Walla Walla in the summer of 1855.

PASCO (N-18)

Meriwether Lewis and William Clark, while enroute crossing the Rocky Mountains to the Pacific in 1805, were the first white men to reach the site where this city now stands, at the confluence of the Northwest's two greatest rivers, the Columbia and the Snake. They and their party of thirty-two (counting the lone female in their party, Sacajawea) approached the "Great Forks," as the Indians called the site, from the east, traveling in six leaky canoes hollowed from ponderosa pine on the Clearwater River, down which they had drifted into the Snake. Included in their party, too, were Sacajawea's baby boy, nicknamed Pomp, and a huge Newfoundland dog named Seammon, whom Captain Lewis acquired back in St. Lewis on the eve of their departure. As they approached the site of today's Pasco—they had been on the road for almost a year and one-half—they were excited at their first glimpse of the "River of the West" and eager to reach the final goal of their trip; the Pacific Ocean. Although they had no maps, they had learned from the Indians that the Pacific was not too far downstream. The date was October 16th, 1805. Watching the strange fleet descending the Snake toward the Great Forks were hundreds of Indians, most of them on horseback. For six days they had been struggling down the Snake since leaving the mouth of the Clearwater (where the city of Lewiston now stands). Steering their frail craft over rapids and through currents so swift that their canoes frequently overturned, they finally reached the site where Pasco now stands. Records Captain Clark: ". . . a Chief came at the head of about 200 Indians singing and beeting their drums Stick and keeping time to the musik they formed half a circle around us and Sung for some time Gave the principal chief a Meadel of Small size . . . and to the Chief who came down from the upper villages a Small Medal & Handkerchief."

The next white man to visit the site of present-day Pasco was David Thompson (1770–1857), a Canadian and one of the world's greatest geographers. Even today, geographers are amazed at the accuracy of Thompson's maps. Indirectly (through these maps having been sent to London, then to America) President Thomas Jefferson may have been influenced by Thompson when he began preparations to send the Lewis and Clark Expedition into the Rockies in 1804.

Thompson was married to an Indian woman who, with their small children, accompanied him on the trail. Each night before retiring, Thompson recorded by campfire light the results of celestial observations taken with his crude octant. The Indians, who regarded such proceedings as they would a religious ceremony, called him *Koo-Koo-Sint,* translated "The Man Who Watches the Stars." On his famous trip down the Columbia in the summer of 1811, Thompson traveled in a canoe which he had hollowed from a giant cedar, felled at Kettle Falls upstream of here. When he reached the future site of Pasco, Thompson beached his canoe. At the juncture of the two rivers he erected a tall pole, and scrawled in large letters on a sheet of paper affixed to the top:

> Know hereby that this country is claimed by Great Britain . . . and that the N.W. Company of merchants [this was the title of the fur organization of which he was a Partner from Canada] . . . do hereby intend to erect a factory [or trading post] in this place for the commerce of the country around. signed D. Thompson, Junction of the Shawpatin River this was the Indian name for the Snake with the Columbia, July 8th, 1811.

Six days later, Thompson (having resumed travel downstream) reached the Columbia's mouth to find the American flag flying over a recently-constructed fur post called Fort Astoria, operated by rivals of his Montreal Company. If his purpose in coming here was to precede these Americans so as to claim the spot for England, Thompson had lost. If, however, he had simply descended the Columbia to its mouth to reconnoiter the river's feasibility for delivering his company's interior furs to a Pacific outlet (instead of eastward across Canada to Hudson Bay), his trip was a success. Perhaps we shall never know. Through the foolscap notice he emplaced atop the pole at Pasco, Thompson appears to have been warning the Yankees that his North West Company of Montreal owned all rights to trap inland of the site, and that this inland territory belonged to the English Crown.

John Commingers Ainsworth (1822–1893), the founder of Pasco, was born of impoverished parents in Ohio. Left an orphan at the age of thirteen, he drifted westward to become first a deck hand, then a pilot on board Mississippi River steamboats. Aboard one of the sternwheelers that Ainsworth commanded was a hired crewman named Samuel Clemens, later known as Mark Twain, whose writings about the steamboat days on the Mississippi have become world famous.

Discovery of gold brought Ainsworth to California in 1850, then to the Columbia River soon after. Here he designed and built the first sternwheeler to grace the waters of this river. He was also the first steamboat skipper to risk piloting his sternwheeler through the Cascades; in those times a white water stretch in the Columbia through which a passage, even by conventional boat, was considered impossible. Operating a fleet of eighteen steamboats during the gold rush days, when tens of thousands of prospectors poured into Idaho, Ainsworth became extremely wealthy.

The river boat town of Ainsworth, named in his honor, stood immediately south of today's Pasco, across the Snake River. In the 1860s, thousands of gold prospectors arrived at Ainsworth Junction, as it was known, swarming ashore from the elaborate "palace boats" operated by Ainsworth. Ashore they were greeted by swindlers, card sharps, confidence men, and ladies of the night. Fist fights, gun fights, and even hangings were not unknown and, as described by one contemporary, ". . . something happened every minute . . . and not always good." To one eastern newsman who was sent west to cover the town, Ainsworth was ". . . a den of iniquity . . . a town of dust and sand, the latter ankle deep . . . the streets paved with old playing cards and broken whiskey bottles."

After a night of carousal at Ainsworth, the prospectors again boarded one of Ainsworth's sternwheelers then proceeded up the Snake to Lewiston. There, equipped with pickaxes, mules, and as much bacon and flour as could be carried, they headed into the rough Idaho wilderness to such spots as Orofino, Baboon Gulch, Elk City, and Florence.

By 1879 the gold rush days had subsided. The following year a bridge was built across the Snake to the site of today's Pasco. Ainsworth's citizens flocked across it en masse with all their possessions, eager to take up residence near railroad tracks being laid along the Snake River's north side. Still known as Ainsworth, the future Pasco prospered—as did all communities to which tracks for the Iron Horse were laid.

The name Pasco is probably a abbreviation for the name "Pacific Steamship Company." This was an organization owned by the wealthy Mr. Ainsworth. About 1883, before a railroad bridge was built across the Columbia (connecting Pasco with railroad tracks leading over the Cascade Range to Puget Sound), large steel barges were used to transport the Northern Pacific's railroad cars across the water here. Since the barges were operated by the Pacific Steamship Company, the bills of lading pasted on the outside of each freight car were stamped "VIA PASCO" in huge, conspicuous letters. From this beginning, use of the word "Pasco" spread. The departure of passenger trains from the budding town's depot were announced by the train master's loud voice: "All aboard, all aboard, passengers now departing for points west via Pasco;" thus the town gradually gained its present name.

POINT GRENVILLE (I-12)

The first white men to discover this promontory, located on the Washington coast about thirty miles north of Grays Harbor, were Spaniards sailing north up the coastline. The year was 1775, one year before a struggling little country called the United States would establish itself as an independent nation on the east coast of North America; but here on the continent's western shore, no attention would be given to this event. From his headquarters in Mexico City, the Spanish viceroy, Antonio Flores, instead was worried about the Russians in Alaska (whom he feared were pushing southward down these coasts, challenging the Spanish king's claim to ownership of all the west coasts of America). So he had sent ships north from lower California to investigate.

On July 13th, 1875, when Bruno Heceta in his eighty-two-foot sailing ship *Santiago* and Bodega y Quadra in his thirty-six-foot *Sonora* reached this coast, the crews of both vessels were ill from scurvy. They had been struggling northward from Spain's naval base at San Blas in lower California since the previous March. Morale aboard the two ships was low and Senor Heceta, commander of the two ships, was inclined toward abandoning their mission and turning back. Senor Quadra, however, favored continuing on.

As they approached this promontory, today called Point Grenville, the weather was stormy. In view of the big waves breaking offshore, Senor Quadra in his smaller vessel, led the approach toward land. Quadra anchored immediately north of Point Grenville near the mouth of Quinault River. Sending one of his officers by small boat to the larger ship *Santiago,* Quadra advised his superior to anchor well offshore. Thus the two vessels lay at anchor on the night of the thirteenth, about three miles apart. At six o'clock A.M. on the fourteenth, seven crewmen of the smaller ship *Sonora* landed ashore to fill their vessel's casks with fresh water from the mouth of the Quinault River. They were the first whites to set foot in Washington State.

Simultaneously, Commander Heceta from his ship *Santiago* was rowed ashore. He was accompanied by his second-in-command, Juan Perez, a priest and twenty armed soldiers. From wood found onshore, a huge cross was built and erected at the site. Then a solemn ceremony was held. In a loud voice, Senor Heceta declared that henceforth all surrounding regions belonged to King Carlos IV of Spain. The soldiers fired a volley of guns, then a bottle was buried in the ground containing a paper which recorded this ceremony and the date on which it was held.

Even while this was transpiring, sad events were taking place to the north. Sailors from Quadra's ship were massacred as they were filling their casks with fresh water, ambushed by Indians hiding in the grass nearby. It was against this background that Senor Heceta chose to call the present Point Grenville by the Spanish name of *Punta de los Martires,* translated "Point of Martyrs."

The departure from Point of Martyrs was a sad one. The two ships continued northward until they reached the waters of Clayoquot Sound on Vancouver Island. Here Captain Heceta, inasmuch as more than half of his crew were overcome by scurvy, turned his *Santiago* back south, unable to continue. Senor Bodega y Quadra and his sailors aboard the *Sonora* continued alone to Alaska, there to carry out the Spanish viceroy's orders to spy on the Russians.

While returning southward to San Blas, Senor Heceta in the *Santiago* passed the mouth of what clearly appeared to be a great river, today known as the Columbia. So ill were his sailors, records Heceta, he dared not enter it, lest his crew be unable to sail out again. But for their illness, Senor Bodega y Quadra of Spain, not Robert Gray of Rhode Island, would have attained the honor of first entering this 1200-mile-long stream.

Seventeen years after the above events, there arrived on these coasts a British explorer named George Vancouver. He had come here from England to assert that the Northwest belonged not to the Spanish, but to his sovereign, King George III. Almost exactly one year prior to arriving here, Vancouver and his expedition of two ships had departed England. From there they sailed around Cape of Good Hope to Australia's south coast, thence to New Zealand, Tahiti, and the Sandwich Islands before making a landfall on the coasts south of here. It had been Lord Grenville (of the King's Cabinet) who personally helped Vancouver in equipping for the voyage. Furthermore, Grenville had been an advocate of sending this expedition to these waters.

In 1790, two years prior to Vancouver's arrival, Spanish naval officers at Nootka (a harbor up the coast from today's Point Grenville about two hundred fifty miles) had seized several British ships engaged on these coasts as fur traders. After this seizure, Lord Grenville had been outspoken, advocating that England declare war upon Spain. Fortunately, diplomacy prevailed in the two nations drawing up a so-called Treaty of Nootka, under whose provisions both nations agreed to share Northwest sovereignty. Vancouver's chief mission was to meet at Nootka with a Spanish counterpart to arrange the details of sharing the region.

It was against the above background that on April 27th, 1792, Captain Vancouver, sailing up the coast past this promontory, decided to call it Point Grenville. For those wishing to read more about the events as related above, the book *Flood Tide of Empire* (New Haven, 1973) by Warren L. Cook, is recommended.

POINT VANCOUVER (Q-8)

Captain George Vancouver, after whom this landmark (located on the north bank of the Columbia near Washougal) is named, was a very serious man. Throughout his adult life he was driven by great ambition, doubtlessly to emulate the role model of the British naval officer under whom he had served for many years, Captain James Cook (still remembered in naval history as England's greatest navigator). Though he never attained Cook's heights of fame, Vancouver nonetheless is admired for his nautical skills.

Beginning in 1792, he explored the Northwest coasts from Oregon to Russian Alaska, spending over two years in this task, briefly gaining respite from the effort each winter by surveying the Hawaiian Islands. On Vancouver's last trip to these islands, he and his two ships, *Discovery* and *Chatham,* stopped enroute in Spanish California (off today's Santa Barbara) where the explorer took on board six cows, a bull, and some sheep. He then sailed with these animals to Kealakakua Bay on the west side of Hawaii's biggest island, Hawaii. Upon anchoring there, Vancouver presented the animals as a gift to Chief Kamehameha, king of the island. They were the first such animals he and his people had ever seen. Kamehameha was delighted, and he and Vancouver became fast friends.

Early the following spring upon the eve of Vancouver's departure, the king gave Vancouver and his sailors a farewell party. After much native singing and dancing, followed by spear-throwing and a mock battle by Kamehameha's warriors, the Hawaiian king presented to Vancouver a superb cloak made of bird feathers, brilliant in yellow, with the request that upon the explorer's return to England he present the cloak to His Majesty King George III of England. On the following, morning moreover, just before Vancouver and his ships weighed anchor, Kamehameha paid a final visit to Vancouver's flagship, the *Discovery.* There, at his request, a formal ceremony was held on the quarterdeck during which King Kamehameha formally ceded the Hawaiian Islands to England, asking that henceforth the English rule over his people.

PORT ANGELES (F-5)

This name is an abbreviation of the original Spanish one given on August 2, 1791, by Francisco Eliza. He called it *Puerto de Nuestra Senora de Los Angeles* (Port of our Lady of Angels). Carried on board all Spanish ships at this time was a Church calendar listing a saint for each day of the year, one to which, by Spanish naval regulations, the captain and crew were to pray at the start of each day. Clearly this calendar specified the Lady of Angels for this date.

Since February of that year Senor Eliza in his ship, *San Carlos,* accompanied by Jose Maria Narvaez in his ship, *Santa Saturnina,* had been exploring the inland sea inside the Strait of Juan de Fuca. For centuries a waterway leading through America into the Atlantic Ocean had been rumored to exist in these waters. Lying on the southern shore of the Strait of Juan de Fuca, fifty miles east of Cape Flattery, Port Angeles was the last stop Eliza made ashore before returning to the Spanish fort called Nootka on Vancouver Island. This fort has long since vanished, but at that time Nootka was the capitol of the Pacific Northwest.

The founder of today's city of Port Angeles was Victor Smith of Cleveland, Ohio. He was a wealthy newspaperman who aspired to public office. Having contributed large sums of money to elect Abraham Lincoln to be President of the United States, Smith demanded reward. Through Lincoln's Secretary of the Treasury, Salmon P. Chase who was a close friend, Smith received an appointment to become the collector of revenue for Puget Sound. The route which Smith took was indicative of the remoteness of this new part of the United States. By sailing ship he traveled to Panama. Thence he rode by horseback across the isthmus to the Pacific. Another long sea voyage transpired traveling up the west coast before he reached his new home grounds, Puget Sound.

Smith took a particular dislike to the custom house which had already been built as his headquarters. The structure itself, he felt, was inadequate for a man of his importance. Moreover, the town in which it was located, Port Townsend, displeased him. Particularly did he dislike the people of this town, who considered him a snob. Pompous and erratic, Smith then cast about for a new site for his customs house. He was not long in finding it. Soon he began concocting reasons for moving his customs house to a site overlooking the harbor which Francisco Eliza had discovered seventy-one years previous. Awed by its beautiful location overlooking the Strait of Juan de Fuca with the snow-capped Olympics for its backdrop, Smith was determined to move his customs house here.

The commencement of the Civil War brought news to Puget Sound that a Confederate warship was sailing up the west coast; its mission: to enter Puget Sound and bombard its settlements. Arguing that this new site would be a superior one compared to Port Townsend (located further inside the De Fuca Strait) from which to defend Puget Sound residents from the Confederate attack, Smith moved with his family from Port Townsend to Port Angeles. However, the citizens of Puget Sound refused to allow his customs house to be moved with him.

In 1862 Smith returned to the national capitol to arrange with his friend Secretary of the Treasury, Salmon P. Chase, that the latter issue an order to move Puget Sound's U.S. Customs to his pet site. When Puget Sounders, particularly Port Townsendites, heard of the impending transfer they were furious. They defied the Secretary of the Treasury, and placed the custom house at Port Townsend under lock and key. They refused to allow Smith to remove his official files from the building. Smith retaliated by warning them if they continued to defy him, dire consequences would follow. As part of his job as collector, Smith had beeen assigned a U.S. revenue cutter, equipped with several guns. When relations with the people of Port Townsend deteriorated, Smith announced he would bombard their town. This threat, however, failed to produce surrender. Smith then moved his gunboat closeby the town. The localites at this point allowed Smith to rescue his official papers, alleging however, that when they had been in control of the documents they had found in them clear evidence that his official funds were short by $15,000. The feud continued.

When news of the hubbub reached the national capitol, President Lincoln ordered Smith to resign. Thanks to his continued friendship with Secretary Chase however, Smith was soon appointed to another federal position on the west coast, this one more lucrative. As special treasury agent for the entire west coast with headquarters in San Francisco, Smith prospered. In 1864 however, while returning from another trip east to Washington, he was shipwrecked off the coast of Georgia. The disaster attracted national attention, for allegedly about $3,000,000 in gold bullion, destined for the west coast, sank with the ship. Shortly afterward, having reached San Francisco following the shipwreck by crossing overland, Smith was again enroute by sailing ship north from San Francisco to Puget Sound, when the vessel struck an uncharted reef. Along with 300 other passengers, Smith was drowned.

On one of his trips from Port Angeles back to the national capital, Mr. Smith arranged, through Secretary Chase, for the U.S. Congress to pass legislation setting aside 3,500 acres of land at his pet town ". . . for the defense of the Northwest against invasion by a foreign power." He also persuaded Congress to designate Port Angeles as an alternate seat of the U.S. Government in the event Washington, D.C. were captured. For many years the townsfolk of Port Angeles suffered commercially. The new city was a natural outlet for shipping the vast lumber supplies available inland in the Olympic Mountains but, being on government property, such activity was not allowed. It was a wealthy logger, Michael Earle, who in 1914 finally arranged to have Port Angeles' U.S. Government claims removed. From the lumber mill which was then built here, the "City of Angels," as it is known today, obtained its start.

Ediz Hook, the sandspit which forms Port Angeles harbor, was so named in 1847 by Lieutenant Commander Henry Kellett of the British Royal Navy. The word *ediz* is probably a corruption of the Indian word *yennis* which was the name of a Clallam Indian village which once stood upon the site of today's city. About 1850, Ediz Hook was briefly called "false dungeness," a reference to a similar projection of land called Dungeness Spit which lies closeby Port Angeles to the east.

PORT GAMBLE (G-7)

This town lies five miles northwest of Kingston on Kitsap Peninsula. It traces its name to the nearby harbor of Port Gamble, at whose west entrance it is located. The harbor received its name in 1841 from a U.S. naval officer named Charles Wilkes, who was surveying the shoreline of Puget Sound. He named Port Gamble Harbor after Lieutenant Robert Gamble, a hero of the War of 1812; in which the infant American navy found itself fighting the English navy, then the most powerful in the world.

Lieutenant Gamble was serving aboard Commodore John Rodger's flagship USS *President,* 44 guns, on June 23, 1812, when it was chasing a British ship HMS *Belvidera* of smaller size, hoping to capture it. The pursuit began off Nantucket Shoals and as the USS *President* gradually closed within gunshot of the *Belvidera,* Commodore Rodgers ordered Lieutenant Gamble to fire the starboard forward gun of the *President* at the English warship. Gamble's shot scored a direct hit on the *Belvidera,* as did two more rounds. Then on the next round, Lieutenant Gamble's gun blew up, killing several sailors in Gamble's battery, wounding

Commodore Rodgers himself, and also Lieutenant Gamble. These shots were the first fired against the British in the War of 1812. For Gamble's heroism he was decorated for bravery.

The town of Port Gamble was originally named *Teekalet,* an Indian word translated "brightness of the noonday sun." Allegedly this phrase was a reference to the "splendor of the sands in Port Gamble Harbor at noon on sunny days." The name was first applied to the site in 1853 when lumbermen from Maine arrived here: Josiah P. Keller and Messrs. Pope and Talbott. The sawmill they erected that year is still in operation.

About this time Haidah Indians from British Columbia began invading Puget Sound waters in their huge canoes, each one carrying fifty or more warriors. Cruising the coastlines, they engaged in terrifying white settlers in their homes. Shortly after, the local tribes around Puget Sound became hostile also, causing fears on the part of the whites that these two Indian forces might unite in a widespread attack upon them. For the defense of these whites, in case such fears eventualized, the U.S. Navy hurriedly dispatched the battleship USS *Decatur.* It arrived in time to save the then-struggling settlement called Seattle in January, 1856, from Indian seizure. As the Indian trouble increased, however, the USS *Massachusetts* also was dispatched to the scene.

In November, 1856, Port Gamble became the scene of another memorable, though one-sided battle; this one between seven large canoes full of Haidah Indians from the Queen Charlotte Islands and the USS *Massachusetts.* The *Massachusetts* surprised the Haidahs while they were encamped on Port Gamble Harbor's eastern shore (opposite the present town). This vessel had recently driven off these same Indians, who were on a rampage against white settlers at nearby Port Townsend.

When he steamed from Port Townsend over to Port Gamble, the commanding officer of the *Massachusetts,* Captain Swarthout, found Haidah war canoes, their occupants painted hideously in war colors, beached on the harbor's east side. Under a flag of truce, crewman of the *Massachusetts* rowed across from their vessel, anchored at the bay's entrance, to warn the Haidahs to depart. This warning, however, appeared to increase the Indians' hostility. Captain Swarthout then landed a howitzer cannon on the beach adjacent to the Haidah's encampment. Despite firing this weapon over the heads of these Indians, they refused to leave, responding defiantly with bows and arrows. Twenty seven of the group of Haidahs who then paddled out to the ship to attack it died. Twenty-one were wounded. The total Haidah force was estimated at one hundred and seventeen. It was during this foray that one of the sailors aboard the *Massachusetts* was killed by an Indian arrow which penetrated his chest. His grave marker, situated in the little cemetery on the hill adjacent to Port Gamble, is still there. It reads "Gustave Englebrecht—Germany—Coxswain U.S.N. Indian War—November 21, 1856—In Line of Duty."

To guard against further such attacks, Fort Townsend, under the charge of Major G.O. Haller, was erected; also Fort Bellingham, commanded by Captain George E. Pickett (the same Pickett who as a Confederate general attained fame in the Battle of Gettysburg fighting for the Confederacy) was built. The Port Gamble battle with the Haidahs did not end their rampages on Puget Sound. On the night of August 11 the following year, Colonel Isaac N. Ebeye, one of the first white settlers on Whidbey Island, and his wife were entertaining guests at dinner when a knock was heard at their log cabin door. Haidahs greeted the colonel when he opened it and forced their way inside. The Indians allowed the guests, Ebeye's wife, and children to escape but they killed Ebeye and beheaded him.

PORT LUDLOW (G-7)

Located fourteen miles south of Port Townsend, this town began in 1853 when Cyrus Walker of Maine, then the leading lumberman of the Pacific Northwest, built a mansion named Admiralty Hall on a hill here overlooking Port Ludlow's commodious harbor and Hood Canal. It was an elaborate New England-style structure of many rooms complete with a "widow's walk" at its top—in which ladies were supposed to anxiously gaze out to sea awaiting their loved ones' arrival after months of separation. Extensive lawns and elaborate gardens, planted with shrubs brought here via Cape Horn from Mr. Walker's state of Maine, grew in front of the mansion sloping down to the water. At the pier sailing ships of Mr. Walker's fleet—which numbered over eighty ships—tied up here after many months carrying Pacific Northwest lumber to ports all over the world. In front of the mansion a brass cannon, which had been fired in anger during the recent War of 1812, was now fired to greet the ships as they approached their home port. Upon docking, the captains of the vessels and their ladies (who frequently accompanied them on their voyages) were received at Walker's house atop the hill with formality. A large staff of servants waited upon them at the elaborate welcome dinner. Hospitality was lavish. Dressed in the bustled style of the day, the parasol-carrying ladies joined the gentlemen in an exciting game of croquet following dinner, on the croquet-grounds amidst the gardens. Top hats were worn by the males, with frock coats and ascot ties. Occasionally Mr. Walker himself joined in the frivolity, dressed in his usual dark broadcloth. But the days of Port Ludlow's prosperity came to an end. By 1900 Walker's empire had vanished.

The name Port Ludlow was bestowed by the American naval officer Charles Wilkes, who in the summer of 1841 entered Puget Sound waters in his two warships to remind British fur men at Nisqually that the United States, too, might some day come to Puget Sound. Wilkes, in choosing the name Port Ludlow, commemorated a famous battle fought by the then-struggling American navy against the British navy in the War of 1812. Augustus Ludlow was one of the American heroes in this conflict.

The scene of the battle was not far out to sea from Boston Harbor. For days the commander of a British ship, Captain Phillip Broke, had been sailing His Majesty's frigate *Shannon* off Boston Harbor daring the American vessel, *Chesapeake,* James Lawrence in command, to come out and fight. Reluctant to do so until he had trained his American recruits, newcomers to life at sea and the ways of shipboard life, Captain Lawrence could stand the taunts no more, and exited with his "green" sailors. As the two ships approached, Lawrence surprised his British opponent by failing to maneuver his *Chesapeake* to rake the *Shannon's* stern, as was the usual opening move, with his broadside guns. Instead he forthrightly sailed his Yankee warship alongside the British vessel. Lawrence's order to his crew to board the English ship failed because his Vermont bugler was too frightened to blow the call signalling it.

Aboard the British vessel, the surprised Captain Broke then ordered his sailors to board the *Chesapeake.* Quickly they gained possession of the American ship's main deck. Bullets flew, sabres were swung, cannonballs crashed.

Aboard the *Shannon* Captain Broke was severely wounded, slashed across the head by a cutlass. Captain Lawrence was killed, struck by a musket ball fired from the *Shannon's* rigging. As the valiant American commander expired, he uttered the now-famous order to his men: "Don't give up the ship. Fight her 'til she sinks."

Victoriously Captain Broke escorted his defeated American prize-of-

war to Halifax, then England's main base in North America. The dead
Captain Lawrence as well as the wounded First Lieutenant Ludlow
were still aboard. Upon his ship's arrival at the Nova Scotia seaport,
however, Ludlow had also died.

PORT TOWNSEND (F-7)

It is still a mystery why the Spaniards, the first white men to discover
Puget Sound, failed to detect the presence of Admiralty Inlet, that
passageway lying immediately east of Port Townsend through which
ships sail into lower Puget Sound. From 1789 to 1792 they sailed their
ships, examining seemingly every nook and cranny of the waters lying
north of Admiralty Inlet, yet during this time all of them, from Quimper
to Valdes and Galiano, missed discovering that portion of Puget Sound
which today is best known to the rest of the world.

The first white man to view the site where Port Townsend now
stands was Juan Carrasco. In the summer of 1790, Carrasco sent his
sailors north from Port Townsend to explore the myriad islands of the
San Juans. The following year, Senor Francisco Eliza, anchored his
warship *San Carlos* in Discovery Bay which lies to Port Townsend's
west. Like Carrasco, Eliza sent small boats exploring northward into the
San Juans, apparently believing that Admiralty Inlet, lying just east of
Port Townsend was not a thoroughfare for ships. In fact, he named it
Boca (Bay) *de Caamano,* honoring a fellow Spanish explorer. Today
much shipping passes through Admiralty Inlet headed for Puget
Sound's most important cities, Seattle and Tacoma.

It remained for Captain George Vancouver—then thirty-five years old
and commander of a very important expedition to these coasts—in
May, 1792, to anchor his ninety-nine-foot-long brigantine in Port
Discovery and to sail the waters of lower Puget Sound. In arriving here,
Vancouver had reached the goal of his year-long trip from England, to
search for the discovery of a rumored waterway leading through
America into the Atlantic.

One year prior to this, he had been chosen for the high honor of
leading this expedition by England's most prestigious naval body, The
Board of Admiralty. After naming Admiralty Inlet after them, Vancouver
named Port Townsend after one of this board's most important
members, the Marquis Lord Townshend (1724–1807). Back in 1759, this
soldier fought in the seige of Quebec in eastern Canada under General
Wolfe. When, during the seige, Wolfe died, Lord Townshend succeeded
him to the command of the British armies attacking the French-held

city. Upon the fall of Quebec to England, moreover, it was Lord Townshend who received the surrender of the French armies.

In 1851 there appeared on the hill overlooking Port Townsend four Americans seeking free land on which to build their homes, all of them God-fearing individuals. Two from New England, like many other Yankees of that day, hoped, upon claiming the 640 acres of free land provided for them under the recently-passed Donation Land Laws, to subdivide it into a budding city. Unimpressed with the landsites they had seen south of the Columbia River, they had come here seeking their fortune. Giving to their future city the same name Captain Vancouver had bestowed on the harbor which lay adjacent, they proceeded, however, to drop the *h* in Lord Townshend's name—most Americans at this time being devout Anglophobes. Being serious-minded individuals all, the settlement they formed here was initially a pretty blue-nosed place. However, being the first harbor at which sailing vessels soon began dropping anchor after long months at sea, Port Townsend soon blossomed with brawling saloons, despite their founders—one saloon for every seventy residents, it was alleged.

Then in 1853, Mr. J. Ross Browne, the U.S. Treasury Department's chief for the Pacific Coast arrived here to inspect his recently-established U.S. Customs house. A seeker after publicity and a would-be writer, Browne returned to San Francisco from the trip and published the following in San Francisco's *Chronicle:* "Port Townsend . . . is filled with beachcombers seated on greasy benches around greasy tables playing poker with greasy decks of cards . . . imbibing from the same bottle . . . a good many lying on the sun fast asleep." As to his own U.S. Customs employees, he proceeded to characterize them as ". . . uselessly engaged in chasing wild Indians and porpoises." While Browne had written the article in an attempt at humor, the team of Plummer, Batchelder, Hastings, and Pettygrove were quick to respond, their articles written as open letters to the *Chronicle* deriding Brown's errors. Being an aspiring author, Browne continued the attack, writing further a book titled *Crusoe's Island* published by Harpers in 1864, in which he also wrote of this town. The feud having reached the national capitol, Port Townsend became the best-known seaport north of San Francisco.

From the outset Port Townsendites enjoyed good relations with the local Indians, some two hundred of whom lived on the beach nearby. Unable to pronounce their jaw-breaking names, the whites took to calling them by such appellations as Jenny Lind, King George, Prince of

Wales, etc. By far the best-liked and most helpful of these Indians was Chetzamokah, known to the whites as the Duke of York. In 1852 he traveled south to San Francisco at the invitation of one of the numerous sailing ship captains who visited Port Townsend. There he was awed by the thousands of palefaces he saw and by the hundreds of "skookum canim copa maxt stick" (giant canoes with two masts) to be seen in the bay. Chetzamokah found himself befriended by a young white about his own age, James G. Swan (1818–1900), later to become Port Townsend's most distinguished citizen. Together Swan and Chetzamokah toured the streets of San Francisco visiting Seal Rock, Golden Gate, Telegraph Hill, and all the other attractions. When Chetzamokah returned to Port Townsend, he did not forget his white friend. In the book titled *The Northwest Coast, or Three Years Residence in Washington Territory* (New York, 1857) Swan wrote of his friendship with Chetzamokah, recalling that not long after the Indian's departure he received from Chetzamokah—delivered aboard a sailing ship which arrived at the San Francisco docks—a beautiful canoe, elaborately carved, sent from Port Townsend in appreciation for Swan's kindness and hospitality.

James Swan was born in Medford, Massachusetts in 1818. He inherited his restless disposition from a sea captain father. When Swan was seven years old, his father disappeared with a cargo of palm oil, ivory, and gold dust while sailing his brigantine *Hope Still* off the coast of west Africa. While Swan, still a small boy, was being educated back in Boston by his widowed mother, he recalled sitting around the kitchen listening to his mother's brother, also a sailor. This uncle regaled young Swan with stories of a visit he made in 1818 to the northwest coast of America.

Doubtless, it was this memory which took Swan to the mouth of the Columbia River. Here he established himself in the oyster business on nearby Shoalwater Bay, today called Willapa Bay. Swan soon lost interest in this commercial activity, however, as he became absorbed in the local Indians, their customs, legends, music, and manners. Thanks to the lingual skills he soon acquired, Swan was selected by recently-appointed Isaac Stevens, governor of Washington Territory, to accompany him on peace treaty conferences with the Indians. When in 1857, Stevens became Washington Territory's delegate to the U.S. Congress, Swan accompanied him to the nation's capitol as his private secretary. It was while here that Swan became affiliated with the Smithsonian Institute, where his experience and talent as an ethnologist were quickly realized. On his return to Puget Sound, Swan became a collector of Indian artifacts for the Smithsonian.

Swan's permanent residence in Port Townsend began *circa* 1858. By this time, sailing ships were being replaced by steamships, some big enough to make Port Townsend Bay seem cramped quarters in which to anchor. With their speed, steamships did not mind the added distance involved in proceeding past Port Townsend down Admiralty Inlet to Seattle, its location closer to the mainland shipments from the east for transportation overseas. The heyday of Port Townsend as a commercial harbor was declining. Already, however, its prosperity had become evident in the several mansions which had been built overlooking its bay. Today the city, while a thriving one, is a museum of the past, as well.

As a permanent resident of Port Townsend, Swan became engaged in admiralty law, for which he had been trained in his youth back east. He also served as a steamship ticket agent at Port Townsend and as a probate judge. As the Northern Pacific slowly built its transcontinental railroad tracks toward Puget Sound, the citizens of Port Townsend dreamed of their town becoming its western terminus. As yet unaware of the town's impending decline, they chose Mr. Swan to be their public relations agent. Swan waxed eloquent, depicting Port Townsend as the "Gateway to the Orient" and as the "City of Destiny." It was all in vain. The Panic of 1893 signalled the end both to Port Townsend's prosperity and that of Swan. The man who recently had been presented by Port Townsend's admiring citizens with a golden cane, which he sported at the head of parades down Port Townsend's Main Street, now became an abject figure. In 1900 he passed away at age eighty-two, having been in poverty for several years.

Like its neighbor Bremerton to the south, Port Townsend prospered in its early days from the presence of the military in its vicinity. It was a day when the employment of big guns at strategically-placed points along coastal harbors was believed to protect the entire region from enemy attack. Fort Townsend, the first U.S. Army post in the vicinity was erected overlooking Port Townsend Harbor in 1858. At Point Wilson, northernmost point in today's city, the army mounted two twelve-inch disappearing guns at a cost of over a million dollars. In 1896, the Spanish-American War having erupted and the War Department fearing an attack from Manila-based Spanish warships on Puget Sound, the army built Fort Flagler on nearby Marrowstone Island; Fort Casey across Admiralty Inlet on Whidbey Island; and Fort

Worden, adjacent to Port Townsend. Meanwhile, the original Fort Townsend, the first of such establishments overlooking the harbor, had long since closed—Army inspectors disgusted by the excessive luxury and leisure enjoyed by its soldiers.

Point Wilson, the northernmost part of this city, was named in 1792 by Vancouver after an unidentified friend in England. Point Hudson, which lies at the easternmost part of the city, is named for William L. Hudson, skipper of explorer Charles Wilkes' second largest ship, the USS *Peacock.* While Commodore Wilkes in his own ship, the *Vincennes,* surveyed Puget Sound waters through the summer of 1841, he waited anxiously for news of Captain Hudson and his USS *Peacock.* Prior to arriving on Puget Sound, Wilkes had been exploring the Pacific islands. When he came to Hawaii, he detached Hudson and the *Peacock* to conduct unfinished survey work among islands to the south while he in the *Vincennes* sailed to the Pacific Northwest. Soon after Wilkes named this point after Captain Hudson, he learned that Hudson and his *Peacock* had gone aground while attempting to enter the mouth of the Columbia River. The 650-ton vessel was a total loss, although no lives were lost.

Today Port Townsend (though still a papermill town with farming and fishing also a part) is being touted for its beautiful nineteenth-century mansions, its San Francisco-like streets, and views; indeed one publication lists Port Townsend as one of the most desirable places at which to retire in all of the United States.

POULSBO (H-7)

The founder of this Kitsap Peninsula city, located six miles south of Kingston, was Jorgen Eliason. He arrived here in 1893 in a small boat containing all his worldly possessions, having rowed across Puget Sound from Seattle. Other persons of Scandinavian descent were living on Dogfish Bay, as Liberty Bay was originally known, who, like Mr. Eliason, were able to claim free land. Under the provisions of the Homestead Law, each male over twenty-one was granted 160 acres. If the male so claiming was married, the law allowed him to claim another 160 acres. This latter provision caused every unmarried female around Puget Sound to become instantly popular. But in Eliason's case, either he was unable to find a mate or else he was content with the smaller acreage. Originally the name of the town was *Paulsbe,* in Norwegian translated "Paul's Place." Reputedly Mr. Eliason chose this name after his native home in Norway.

At the turn of the century, Liberty Bay residents were overjoyed when steamboats began arriving here to relieve their isolation from the outside world. Literally hundreds of such craft plied the waters of Puget Sound. Poulsbo's citizens, by this means, could reach the town of Seattle in only about three hours, with eleven stops at similarly small, isolated settlements along the way. With the building of a bridge across Agate Passage soon afterward, together with the advent of "horseless carriages," Poulsbo's connections with the outside world seemed perfect.

PRESCOTT (N-21)

The first recorded white men to view the site where Prescott stands, eighteen miles north of Walla Walla, were the members of the Lewis and Clark party. They reached here on May 1, 1806. They were headed back east to St. Louis, having achieved their goal the previous fall of reaching the Pacific Ocean. They had spent a dreary winter there living in log cabins, and for the past weeks had been struggling by canoe and on foot up the Columbia River. When they encamped here they discovered (in unpacking their gear for the night) that they had lost three steel traps which were of considerable value, since the party of over thirty were becoming short on food supplies. While they were preparing for their evening meal three Indians reached their camp, having been trailing them for some time. They were recognized as Indians encountered at their previous night's camp. To the explorers' delight, they had brought with them thhe three lost traps, discovered by the Indians shortly after they had departed. Records Captain Clark:

> This act of integrity was the more pleasing because it corresponded perfectly with the general behavior of the Wollahwollahs among whom we had carelessly previously lost several knives, which they returned as soon as found. We may indeed justly affirm that of all the Indians whom we have met since leaving the United States . . . the Wollahwollahs are indeed the most hospitable, honest and sincere. (LV, 345)

From 1856 to 1859, the famous missionary Henry Spalding lived where Prescott now stands. Reverend Spalding came west with Marcus Whitman in 1836, their newlywed wives becoming the first white women to cross the Rockies. When Cayuse Indians killed the Whitmans in 1847, Spalding and his family were forced to flee to the safety of Willamette Valley. Here Spalding directed a church of white settlers until the death of his wife Eliza, in 1851. Thereafter his fortunes waned. When he arrived at the present-day site of Prescott he was completely impoverished and largely discredited by his fellow whites due to his fanatic hatred for Catholic missionaries operating in the area. Spalding's stay at Prescott ended in 1859 when the U.S. government appointed him Indian agent at his former mission station at Lapwai, the area having been made an Indian reservation. Before his death, at age seventy-one, Spalding experienced more success in reviving the Indians' interest in his earlier teachings.

When in 1882, the residents of Prescott chose their name, they were hoping a transcontinental railroad (of whom C.H. Prescott was a high local official) would lay railroad tracks through here.

PRIEST RAPIDS (M-15)

Today at this site on the Columbia River, twenty miles east of Yakima, is located a giant hydroelectric project. Past here in early times the Columbia flowed with terrific turbulence, though now its waters are restrained by Priest River Dam.

In the spring of 1811, the first white men to ascend the Columbia River traveled through here in two leaky canoes they had hollowed out of trees downstream. They were American trappers proceeding inland from the recently-established fur post at Astoria, where the Columbia flows into the Pacific. While his trappers were portaging their canoes around this obstruction, David Stuart, head of this American group, met an Indian dressed in elaborately-colored costume. His name was *Ha-que-la,* and he indicated he was a priest. The Indian proceeded to entertain Stuart with a succession of weird incantations and convolutions appearing to be religious in tone. Upon the conclusion of this, Stuart reached into his pocket for the gold watch he carried. He discovered it was no longer there, and realized it had been stolen. Hearing the watch ticking, Stuart quickly detected the source of the noise beneath Ha-que-la's priestly robes. In no way, Stuart writes, was the Indian embarrassed when his theft became obvious.

Stuart and his men resumed their progress up the river, portaging and paddling until they came to the mouth of the Okanogan River, where the city of Brewster now stands. Here they erected a trading post, the first American one east of the Cascades, to compete with a British one recently established not far to the east called Spokane House.

Priest Rapids, as the falls became known, was the site in the 1850s of an Indian village where a real Indian priest lived. His name was

Smohalla, and he is remembered as the founder of the famous Indian religion known as the Dreamer Cult. In his book titled *The Ghost Dance Religion,* James Nooney describes the beliefs of the members of Smohalla's Dreamer Cult:

> Those who cut up the lands or sign papers for lands will be defrauded of their rights and will be punished by God's anger . . . you ask me to plough the ground! Shall I take a knife and tear my mother's bosom? Then will I die, she will not take me to her bosom to rest. You ask me to dig for a stone! Shall I dig under her skin for her bones? Then when I die I cannot enter her body to be born again. You ask me to cut grass and make hay and sell it and be rich like white men? But how dare you cut off my mother's hair!

PUGET SOUND (H-8)

This name, as intended by the English explorer George Vancouver in 1792, covered only a small portion of the inland sea which today goes by this name. Vancouver's purpose in sailing his ship *Discovery* inside the Strait of Juan de Fuca to these waters was to find a water passage through the American continent, then believed to exist, called the Northwest Passage. A reward of 20,000 pounds awaited Vancouver and the crews of his two ships should they find the passage. The English explorer believed this was to be found behind the as-yet unexplored waters inside the De Fuca Strait. Initially Vancouver probed southward into waters he named Hood Canal hoping to find it, but without success. On May 19, 1792, Vancouver's one hundred-foot-long three-masted sailing ship and its one hundred thirty-five-man crew dropped anchor at the southern tip of Bainbridge Island (opposite Seattle). They were the first white men to invade the waters of lower Puget Sound.

At four o'clock the following morning Lieutenant Puget, the *Discovery's* second lieutenant, and Sailing Master Joseph Whidbey descendeed the *Discovery's* ladder into their two respective boats. Rowed "by sixteen sailors" southward down the west side of Vashon Island, they commenced their historic trip. It was a beautiful morning and they witnessed, as they rowed south, a beautiful sunrise over 14,000-foot-high, snow-capped Mount Rainier which loomed to the east. Their orders were to follow the shoreline, wherever it led, keeping it on their starboard hand and charting as they progressed. Anyone familiar with the intricacies of this shoreline can appreciate the arduous task which confronted them. As they progressed the tide was ebbing strongly.

By the time Peter Puget and his explorers reached the Tacoma Narrows they began encountering Indians, many of whom were warlike in appearance. The males wore red and black ochre on their faces and carried bows and arrows. Both sexes wore few clothes, with beads and ornaments suspended from their ears and noses. The Indians appeared to be in awe of the explorers.

On the second day, one of the largest groups yet encountered (near the site of today's Home, Washington) appeared threatening. Led by a one-eyed warrior, their bows and arrows menacingly drawn, they approached Puget's party close enough that he found it necessary to fire a shot from the swivel gun mounted in his boat, over their heads. Surprisingly, the Indians appeared not to associate the loud noise of the gun to the lethal nature of white men's weaponry. Their only response was to make noises imitating those of the gun, in a seemingly deprecating manner. It was characteristic of the clever cool-headedness of young Puget that he devised a way to show his party's friendliness. Lashing small gifts to pieces of driftwood he floated them toward the Indians who received them, apparently impressed. At the same time, however, he ordered Thomas Manby, a young midshipman of his party, to fire his double-barreled shotgun at a crow, bringing it down and illustrating to the Indians that the gun's noise meant possible death for them.

Thereafter, encounters with the Indians were more friendly. Canoes carrying several Indians came to offer the whites food. Beads, bits of iron and copper offered by Puget and his men in trade yielded several bear skins. On Eld Inlet, adjacent to the site of today's Olympia, the Indians even held a party for Puget and his followers, welcoming these strangers by dressing in special costumes, their hair covered with the down of birds, and the females (as waggishly reported by Peter Puget) were lavishly decorated, "their paint only differing in the colours but not in the quantity, used on the faces of our own countrywomen."

Meanwhile, Captain Vancouver, himself, had been leading a similar exploring party southward from the *Discovery* following the land "on the port hand" of Puget Sound. This took them down the water passage east of Vashon Island. When the two groups met, they returned to the *Discovery* together. Captain Vancouver records: "Thus by our joint efforts we had completely explored every turning point of this extensive inlet; and to commemorate Mr. Puget's exertions, the south extremity of it I named Puget's Sound." Doubtless, despite this recognition, Peter Puget was keenly disappointed that his quest for the Northwest Passage in these waters had ended in failure.

This was not the first time Vancouver had entrusted Puget with special assignments which the young officer carried out with skill. Just three weeks prior to the encounter at Eld Inlet, Vancouver and his expedition were sailing northward up the Washington coastline, groping for the entrance to Puget Sound. Vancouver was concerned that he might miss the opening, known as the Strait of Juan de Fuca, because of his experience fourteen years before. He was, at the time, a twenty-year-old lieutenant, serving under Captain Cook aboard HMS *Resolute*. Cook's party had missed finding the De Fuca Strait, and Vancouver did not want to make the same mistake. The explorer was delighted therefore at this point to sight a ship, and he records:

> . . . at 4 o'clock a sail was discovered to the westward standing in shore. This was a great novelty, not having seen any vessel but our consort H.M.S. *Chatham* during the last eight months. She soon hoisted the American colors, and fired a gun to leeward. At six we spoke her. She proved to be the *Columbia,* commanded by Mr. Robert Gray, belonging to Boston, whence she had been absent nine months. Having little doubt of his being the same person who had formerly commended the sloop *Washington,* I desired he would bring to, and sent Mr. Puget . . . on board to acquire such information as might be serviceable to our operations.

Peter Puget soon returned, not only with the glad news that the Strait of Juan de Fuca's entrance lay just sixty miles ahead to the north, but he also brought with him Captain Gray himself. He had persuaded the Yankee skipper to return with him so that Vancouver might inquire personally concerning the waters he was about to explore.

The previous spring (April, 1791) Vancouver and his two ships, *Discovery* and *Chatham,* had sailed from England knowing that he would meet with Spaniards sailing these Northwest coastlines. Vancouver hoped, however, that the Spanish would not have ventured into the then-mysterious waters inside the Strait of Juan de Fuca. His orders, upon departing England, were not only to search for the Northwest Passage but also to meet with a naval officer representing Spain at Nootka, a naval base on Vancouver Island, concerning an imbroglio which had occurred in 1789 between the two nations there.

Later in 1791, Peter Puget became commander of Vancouver's second ship, HMS *Chatham,* and for the remainder of the four-year-long expedition, was Captain Vancouver's mainstay in the expedition's conduct.

Peter Puget was born in London, England, in November, 1765. His forbears were French Huguenots who fled to England in the seventeenth century. Joining the British navy when he was twelve, soon Puget saw action against the French both at St. Kitts and St. Lucia in the West Indies. When in 1789, the British admiralty was preparing an expedition to the South Seas, Puget was ordered to the ship *Discovery*. Then the mobilization of the English fleet as a result of the tiff at Nootka, Puget found himself serving under Captain Vancouver, headed for the Northwest coasts.

Following the disbandment of the Vancouver Expedition in 1795, Peter Puget was promoted to the command of a convoy of English ships loaded with gunpowder, with orders to proceed to Gibraltar to bring relief to this English fortress. It was while returning from Gibraltar to England, his ships loaded with British women and children being evacuated from The Rock, that Puget was tricked by a seemingly-harmless French vessel into attempting to capture it. The vessel proved, to Puget's dismay, to be a French warship, its forty guns well disguised. Puget and his convoy of women and children were captured and taken to France.

It was an act which, for a time, cast a shadow over Puget's hitherto excellent reputation, causing him to be dubbed as an officer of "audacious recklessness." It was, nevertheless, this same reputation which subsequently caused Puget to be promoted by the British admiralty over the heads of his contemporary officers to command a succession of England's finest warships. Among these were HMS *Fondroyant*, 68 guns; *Temeraire*, 87 guns; and *Barfleur*, 95 guns.

In 1807, Captain Puget commanded HMS *Goliath* in the most famous action of his career, a punitive attack on the city of Copenhagen designed to dissuade Denmark from surrendering its fleet to Napoleon. As a result of this action Peter Puget was decorated for gallantry. Thereafter he is remembered for the succession of proposals he sent to the British admiralty toward gaining military advantage over England's European adversaries. Among the more notable of these was his advocacy of the use of fire boats for attacking and bottling up the French fleet in the Harbor of Brest.

Peter Puget's last years in the Royal Navy were spent in Madras and Trincomalee, where he was Naval High Commissioner. In 1819, he was made a Companion of the Order of the Bath; and in 1821, promoted to Admiral of the Blue. Married to Hannah Elrington in 1797, Admiral and Mrs. Puget had eleven children, seven boys and four girls. He died at Wooley, England, on 31 October, 1822, age fifty-seven.

PULLMAN (L-24)

This eastern Washington town, located fifty miles south of Spokane, is the home of Washington State University. In 1885, it sprang to life when railroad tracks were laid here, thereby insuring its prosperity. Until now a sleepy place called Three Forks, the village now felt the need for a more imposing name. Often lucky townsfolk such as those of Three Forks found that if they renamed their town for one of the railroad officials, the latter would respond with monetary reward. Accordingly, the citizens of Three Forks renamed their town after the most prominent of all the railroad executives in the entire nation, George Pullman (1831–1897). Mr. Pullman had recently invented, and was gaining great wealth from the manufacture of, a new kind of railroad vehicle known as a Pullman car. These contraptions on wheels, pulled by snorting steam engines, were indeed exciting—enabling travelers to live, sleep, and dine in luxury for days at a time, all the while traveling at breathless speeds even as high as twenty miles an hour. Soon they became the rage of the wealthy. European nobility began visiting the West. In their private Pullman cars, they traveled for weeks, sipping champagne as painted Indians galloped alongside their car windows and rear observation platforms. Occasionally they would stop their train to shoot deer, elk, or quail and if a buffalo were sighted, a feast ensued. At night Western songs were sung by the light of kerosene lamps swinging overhead, a small organ setting the tunes. As described by Irving Stone's book *Men To Match My Mountains,* bustled ladies retired at night, the prospect of sleeping in their Pullman cars with strange men causing them to retire fully dressed "armed with lethal hatpins."

Fifteen miles due west of Pullman on the Snake River was a now-forgotten settlement called Almota. This name is derived from the Nez Perce word *almotine* translated "moonlight fishing," a reference to the Indians' practice of spearing salmon on moonlit nights as the fish swam up the Snake during spring and fall salmon runs. The town of Almota was an important one in the 1860s when travel up the Columbia and Snake rivers by steamboat was the principal way prospectors reached the gold fields above Lewiston on the Clearwater River. The first of such craft to stop regularly at Almota was a sternwheeler, the *Colonel George Wright,* named for a U.S. Army officer who had recently quelled the Indians in the Pullman area. The steamer *George Wright* was commanded by Captain Leonard White, then regarded as the best of the Snake River pilots in avoiding treacherous spots along this stream and in ascending the riffles in it the most skillfully. On her maiden trip in 1861, the *George Wright* so frightened the Indians as they gazed from the river bank at this "fire boat" belching clouds of smoke and sparks, that they fled hastily into the Palouse Hills.

Another largely-forgotten site on the banks of the Snake River called Wawawai, fifteen miles west of Pullman, marks the birthplace of a Nez Perce Indian named *Tuekakas,* known to the whites as Old Joseph. He is remembered for the great hospitality he showed Benjamin de Bonneville. The thirty-eight-year-old U.S. Army officer was sent to spy on British strength in the Northwest, arrived at Old Joseph's winter home in the Blue Mountains in 1834. Captain Bonneville regarded the Wallowa Indians, of which Old Joseph was head, as "the gentlest and least barbarous peoples of these remote wildernesses," wrote Washington Irving in his classic book *Astoria.* Old Joseph loved these strange palefaces, and even became a convert to Christianity under the influence of missionary Henry Spalding, with whom he used to go swimming in Wallowa Lake. By 1869 however, Old Joseph, almost blind, was forced to admit that many of the whites he admired "spoke with forked tongues." By this time white ranchers were grazing their cattle on Old Joseph's ancestral lands without his permission. Exhorting his son Young Joseph to never surrender these lands to the whites, Old Joseph passed away in the summer of 1871, age eighty-three.

PUYALLUP (J-8)

Pronounced pyoo-AL-up, this city, located ten miles southeast of Tacoma, bears the name of an Indian tribe numbering about eight hundred when the first whites arrived here. Founder of the town was

Ezra Meeker (1830–1928). A colorful figure, Meeker came to the Northwest in 1852 driving a team of oxen. He was accompanied over the Rockies by two thousand fellow emigrants. Many years later when he was seventy years old (by now a wealthy man) Mr. Meeker retraced his route west; again driving a team of oxen, but this time alone. Then, eighteen years later, when he was ninety-one years of age (four years before his death) Mr. Meeker again retraced the Oregon Trail, this time making headlines throughout the East's newspapers; for he did so at this advanced age in a biplane, flying in an open cockpit.

Meeker became wealthy through growing hops on the land around Puyallup. Used in the making of beer, hops produced by Meeker gained a great market in England. In his book titled *My Pioneer Past* (Seattle, 1905) Meeker describes the reaction by one of his acquaintances in London to the name of Meeker's home town: ". . . I say, old boy, I can't remember that blarsted name—what is it again?"

In 1855, not only the Puyallup Indians but virtually all of the tribes both in eastern and western Washington went on the warpath against the whites. White men searching for gold angered the Indians by trespassing on Indian lands without their permission. In September, the Yakima Indians killed Mr. A.J. Bolon, a U.S. Indian agent, as he rode eastward through Yakima country to warn Washington Territory's governor, Isaac Stevens, of the trouble. The deputy governor, boyish-looking Charles Mason, a recent graduate of Brown College in Rhode Island, was serving as acting governor in Steven's absence.

Mason held a peace powwow with the local Indians in White River Valley near Puyallup. He came away completely deceived by what the Indians told him. There would no longer be any attacks upon the white settlers around Puget Sound, he was told. So Mason advised his constituents that the trouble was over. Lulled by this false sense of security, the whites became even more complacent when soon afterward, the U.S. navy sent a warship to anchor off the village of Seattle. The outlying settlers, until now huddled together in hastily constructed blockhouses, returned to their homes.

Less then a month later however, on October 28, 1855, seven white men were found massacred in White River Valley. The only warning of the concerted Indian attack which followed was given by a friendly Indian named Tom Kitsap, today remembered as Kitsap the Elder to distinguish him from his son (Kitsap County today bears the younger man's name). Frantically the whites in outlying areas fled their homes with all their belongings. Some went to Fort Nisqually where the

British could protect them. Others fled to the U.S. Army post at Steilacoom. Ezra Meeker, in his *Reminiscences,* describes the scene which greeted these fugitives upon their arrival at the American fort:

> A sorry mess this, of women and children crying, some brutes of men cursing and swearing, oxen and cows bellowing, sheep bleating, dogs howling, children lost from their parents, wives from husbands, no order; in a word, the utmost disorder.

Q

QUINAULT RIVER (I-3)

Spaniards were the first white men to visit the coast of Washington State where this stream flows into the Pacific, off the steep slopes of the Olympic Mountains. They were sailors of the Spanish Royal Navy, whose base lay far down the American west coast near Acapulco. It had taken them months to struggle in their small, fragile ships this far north. There being no maps in their day, they scarcely knew how far north of here they would find them, but they had come trying to ascertain how far south the Russians, then enemies of Spain, had moved from Alaska.

On the morning of July 14, 1776, the same year in which the United States was gaining independence from England, Senor Bodega y Quadra, skipper of the *Sonora* (a tiny craft less than forty feet long) decided to land members of his crew at the Quinault River's mouth to fill his vessel's water casks with fresh water. Although the previous evening when Quadra first anchored his ship in these waters the Indians who came in their canoes to greet them seemed friendly (even presenting gifts of whale meat, salmon, and wild onions), Senor Quadra had nevertheless taken the precaution of providing each man with a musket and a cutlass. Quadra watched them row ashore in their small boat reaching the river's mouth despite intervening shoals.

Suddenly, through his spyglass, he saw great numbers of Indians leap from the bushes at the river's mouth and attack his sailors. Helplessly he watched as the Indians hacked his sailors to death, their bodies making the water red with blood. When Senor Quadra reported the tragedy to his senior, Captain Bruno Heceta (who in the larger of their two ships, the *Santiago,* had spent the night farther from shore to the south), Heceta decided that both vessels should vacate the area. The two ships resumed sailing northward up the coast, carrying out the orders of the viceroy of New Spain, whose headquarters were in Mexico City.

Somewhere near presently-named Clayoquot Island on the west coast of Vancouver Island, Senor Heceta with the eighty-four men of his larger ship decided to return to lower California, most of the crew too ill of scurvy to continue the search.

The brave Senor Quadra and his sailors, however, continued on. It was six weeks later, while retreating southward down the Washington coastline, having failed to find any sign of Russian settlement to the north, that Captain Quadra, in the *Santiago,* came upon an island lying offshore close to the Quinault River's mouth where he had lost several of his crew. Today this island is called Destruction Island, a name given it in 1787 by the British sea captain William Barkley, sailing the *Imperial Eagle.* However the original name, given by Senor Quadra, was *Isla de Dolores* (Island of Tears), commemorating the sailors who lost their lives here. Captain Barkley, too, suffered the loss of several of his sailors at the hands of local Indians at the mouth of the Hoh River, which lies but a few miles up the coast from the Quinault River's mouth.

R

RENTON (I-9)

This city lies adjacent to Seattle to its southeast. When William Renton (1818–1891) after whom it is named, was a small boy of eleven he went to sea serving on board square-rigged sailing ships from his native home in Nova Scotia. By the time Renton was twenty-three and married, he commanded his schooner. Together he and his bride sailed in the vessel to Europe on a trading voyage. Next they sailed around Cape Horn to San Francisco, then a booming gold rush town. Selling here both their ship and cargo, they then purchased the hulk of a vessel tied up to one of San Francisco's docks in which they operated a store.

Tiring of this, they traveled by sailing ship to Puget Sound where, with the money they had thus far been able to amass, they built and operated lumber mills; first at Seattle's Alki Point, then at Port Orchard.

Finally they established a sawmill at Port Blakely on Bainbridge Island. Here in 1857, a boiler explosion caused Renton to become partially blind, a condition which resulted in total blindness when he reached age fifty-six. The Port Blakely Mill prospered, and by the time of Renton's death was the largest sawmill in the world. Cutting over twenty million board feet of lumber annually, the mill's goods were sent from Port Blakely by sailing ship to ports all over the world.

A public-spirited man, Captain Renton took part in many local activities directed toward improving the Puget Sound region. Coal mines which he owned in Cedar Valley, southeast of today's city of Renton, prompted him to build railroad tracks from these mines to Seattle, in order that the coal could be transported by sailing ship to San Francisco. Mr. Renton planned to connect this railroad by tracks eastward over the Cascade Range to Walla Walla. Here he wanted to connect his railroad with the Union Pacific, whose transcontinental tracks from the East were fast approaching. Had the Renton-to-Walla Walla project materialized, Seattle might have become the first leading city on Puget Sound. Instead the citizens of early Seattle had to suffer the agony of watching the nearby city of Tacoma become the terminus of Puget Sound's first transcontinental tracks. Nonetheless, Mr. Renton's coal mines were the chief economic mainstay of the Tacoma-Seattle area for over fifty years.

When he died at age seventy-three, Mr. Renton was widely mourned—not only by workers of his mill and the citizens of the Puget Sound region generally, but also by the large numbers of local Indians who remembered him as a fair man. Renton was a millionaire at the time of his death.

The town was named in Mr. Renton's honor in 1876. The site where Renton stands was known to the Indians as *Moxlapush.*

ROCHE HARBOR (D-6)

Richard Roche was the name of the British naval officer after whom this body of water, located at the north end of San Juan Island, takes its name. The Hudson's Bay Company was operating a salmon curing station at Roche Harbor in 1845 when Midshipman Roche, then serving aboard HMS *Herald,* first arrived here. In later years Roche served on the Boundary Commission, whose task was to decide whether San Juan Island was to become a part of England or a part of the United States. He is also famous for the trip he took in 1852 into the Arctic in search of Sir John Franklin who, with his two ships, the *Frebus* and the *Terror,* along with 129 officers and men, disappeared in the Arctic regions while attempting to discover a northwest passage. On this unsuccessful search Roche traveled by dog sled for seventy-eight days, covering nearly 800 miles of frigid wasteland before abandoning his effort.

In 1886 (all of the San Juan Islands, by then flying the American flag), Roche Harbor became the home of John S. McMillen, a shrewd politician and businessman. He came here to exploit the large quantities of lime available for export. Lime, then universally required as a building material, enabled McMillen to build a mansion here at Roche Harbor, which for years was one of the show cases of the Pacific Northwest. Through McMillen's control of the local newspaper, he became an influential politician state-wide. At Roche Harbor he then built Hotel de Haro, touted as the most luxurious hotel north of San Francisco. McMillen's luxurious mansion here was called Afterglow, this name derived from his family's fondness for watching from its porticoes the sunsets over Canada's Gulf Islands. Today all that is left of the grandeur of his home is a family mausoleum marked by seven thirty-feet-high granite columns.

Spieden Island, which lies closeby Roche Harbor to the north, is named for William Spieden, one of the members of the Wilkes Expedition which surveyed the Northwest in 1841. Mr. Spieden was ship's purser aboard Wilkes' second largest ship, the *Peacock,* when it ran aground entering the Columbia River that summer. The *Peacock* being a total wreck, Captain William Hudson mustered the survivors on shore nearby, relieved to find there had not been any deaths as a result of the tragedy. Spieden, the ships purser, was responsible for paying the crew. When it was decided to raise the sailors' morale by paying them at this time, Speiden set himself up in an abandoned chicken-house on shore near the wrecked ship and began paying portions of the crew each morning for several days while they were awaiting rescue. This led to the crew's joke, which soon circulated and lasted for some time, that it was Chief Spieden's duty to crow to the roosters each morning at dawn.

Also related to the Expedition of 1841 is Henry Island, which lies adjacent to Roche Harbor forming the harbor's western shore. It is named after a midshipman named Henry who, prior to Wilkes' surveying of Puget Sound, had met his death in the Fiji Islands.

When Wilkes and his two ships first arrived in these islands, he and his men were slow to believe reports that some of the Fijians were cannibals. All doubt was removed, however, when some of the natives came one morning in their canoes alongside the *Vincennes,* munching on some human skulls and a thigh bone.

One morning later, while a group of sailors were surveying the island called Malolo, Fijians suddenly appeared out of the bush. As the boat in which the midshipman was traveling pushed up on the beach, the natives jumped into the craft and clubbed the young lad to death. Midshipman Henry was the Commodore's sister's only child, whom she entrusted to her brother's care during the four-year-long trip. Henry's death left Wilkes grief-stricken. Henry's full name was Wilkes Henry.

S

SAN JUAN ISLANDS (D-6)

On May 20, 1790, two Spaniards, Manuel Quimper and Lopez de Haro climbed Mary's Hill at the southern tip of Vancouver Island where the city of Victoria now stands. Gazing off to the east they became the first white men to view San Juan Island and the more than one hundred fifty islands lying beyond. It was the practice at this time for Spanish naval ships to carry a church calendar on board, designating for each day a saint to whom the crew was to pray daily.

Thus, the custom came about that Spanish explorers, such as these two, named the landmarks which they discovered after the saint for the particular date on which their discovery was made. Thus did the name "San Juan Islands" come into being.

At this time four nations were competing for sovereignty over these northwest coasts: Russia, Spain, England, and the United States (then a very new nation). By the turn of the century however, only England and the United States were in contention. In 1846, these two nations reached an agreement on how to divide the region. All lands north of the forty-ninth parallel of latitude belonged to England, while all lands south of this dividing line became American. This solution seemed quite simple except when the line was extended into these San Juan Islands. If continued westward through them it would cause England the loss of her choicest city, Victoria, located at the southern tip of Vancouver Island. So the boundary commissioners decreed that the forty-ninth parallel be diverted south upon reaching the San Juans enough, before turning westward, that Vancouver Island in toto might continue to fly the Union Jack. The question was, at what point would this international line jog southward? If it were done adjacent to the Washington mainland, then all of the San Juan Islands would belong to England. If it were done adjacent to Vancovuer Island, then all of these islands would belong to the United States. The problem remained unresolved for decades.

Meanwhile, England's all-important Hudson's Bay Company, whose headquarters were on Vancouver Island (closeby San Juan Island itself, the westernmost of the group of islands), decided to act anyway, disregarding the question of which nation owned San Juan Island. In 1850, the company established a salmon-curing station on San Juan Island's northern shore. Three years later the HBC commenced grazing thirteen hundred sheep on San Juan Island, calling it "Bellevue Island" after their local Bellevue Farm. At this point Washington Territory's recently-appointed Governor, Isaac Stevens, declared the San Juan Islands, and San Juan Island in particular, to be within American jurisdiction, not British. He dispatched Colonel Isaac Ebeye, the U.S. collector of customs for Puget Sound, to visit Bellevue Farm. Ebeye happened to arrive on the island on the same day Governor James Douglas, England's officer-in-charge of the entire Crown Colony of British Columbia, was also visiting here. Ebeye told Governor Douglas the British sheep he had introduced here were liable to seizure for having been brought here without U.S. permission.

The problem was exacerbated with the arrival on San Juan Island of American homesteaders. Recently they had been seeking gold on the Fraser and Thompson rivers of British Columbia. Now they had come here to take out free land under the U.S. Donation Land Law. One such person was Lyman Cutler, of Ohio. He staked out his free land claim right in the middle of some of Bellevue Farm's choicest property. Erecting a fence around the claim, the American commenced growing potatoes. Somehow British pigs, also grown on Bellevue Farm, managed to penetrate Cutler's fence one morning. Asleep in the log cabin he had built, Cutler and his wife, an Indian girl, woke up to the sound of these pigs rousting in their potato patch. Angrily rushing out of the cabin, Cutler shot one pig dead, but not before the swine had eaten most of his potatoes. Thereafter feelings ran high on San Juan Island between its British and American inhabitants. Governor Douglas fined Cutler one hundred dollars. Advised of this, Paul Hubbs, having replaced Ebeye as U.S. collector of customs, embarked from the island by rowboat for the mainland. He complained of the fine to Lieutenant George Pickett, U.S. Army, who from Fort Bellingham was protecting the local whites from Indian attack. Several days later Lieutenant Pickett told Hubb's story to blustering General William Harney, who chanced to be visiting Fort Bellingham on an inspection trip. Harney was commander of all U.S. Army troops in the Northwest at this time. The general wasted no time in responding to the situation. He immediately ordered Pickett to proceed with sixty of his Fort Bellingham soldiers to occupy and seize San Juan Island.

Lieutenant Pickett landed his men on Griffin Bay, on San Juan Island's southern shore, then hoisted the Stars and Stripes over his encampment. Furious upon learning of Pickett's act, Governor Douglas in Victoria responded by ordering three British warships, anchored in Esquimault, England's naval base adjacent Victoria, to proceed to the scene. On board these vessels were two thousand British soldiers. Upon reaching Griffin Bay, Captain Geoffrey Phipps, in command of the British troops, prepared to land his overwhelming military force and fight Pickett's handful of men. With the same defiance he later was to display in the Battle of Gettysburg as a Confederate General, Lieutenant Pickett advised Captain Phipps that he was ready for action. "Whether you land five or fifty thousand men," he declared, "I will open fire."

Fortunately at this crucial point, the British naval commander of the ships transporting the troops, Captain Phipps Hornby, possessed a cooler head. Captain Hornby's superior, Admiral Baynes, commander-in-chief of the Pacific Fleet, was away from his Esquimault headquarters engaged in inspecting British ships in the Hawaiian Islands. All the more credit is due, therefore, to Captain Hornby for the cool decision he now made on his own. Refraining from calling Lieutenant Pickett's bluff, and restraining the desire of Captain Phipps to land his troops, Captain Hornby ordered that no action be taken pending the return of the admiral, his superior.

Doubtless Hornby was relieved, as was Lieutenant Pickett, when after a week of tense suspense, with the opposing forces still poised across Griffin Bay ready for action, Admiral Bayne arrived on August 10 at Esquimault. Quickly apprising himself of the situation, he completely approved of his subordinate's restraint. Declaring that it would be stupid to lose lives over a pig, Baynes added that he would rather shed tears than blood. The San Juan dispute was not resolved until October, 1872, when, asked by England and the United States to arbitrate the dispute, Emperor William I of Germany decided that little San Juan Island, indeed the San Juan Islands in their entirety, belonged to the United States, not England.

Rivalry between England and the United States for possession of these islands had evidenced itself long before the Pig War. In 1841, the U.S. government sent Commodore Charles Wilkes and two navy ships to survey the San Juan Islands. Their primary purpose in doing so was to warn England that someday these islands, indeed all of Puget Sound, would become a part of the United States.

At this time, however, the sovereignty of the region was in doubt. England was claiming that all lands north of the Columbia River belonged to Queen Victoria. Keenly aware of this situation, and with the memory fresh in his mind of the recent War of 1812, Wilkes proceeded to erase the older Spanish names given in these waters and substituted place-names related to American naval heroes. San Juan Islands was renamed Rodger's Island, honoring John Rodgers (1771–1838), who ended the practice of pirates and rulers of Tripoli of seizing American seamen from their merchant ships in the Mediterranean.

Many of Wilkes' names, interestingly enough, were in turn obliterated by a naval officer and surveyor of these waters in 1845, Captain Henry Kellett of the British Royal Navy.

SEATTLE (H-8)

Chief Sealth (1767?–1866) was a leader of the Duwamish Indians, on whose lands this city now stands. On November 13, 1851, the founding fathers of this Puget Sound metropolis landed at Alki Point, now a part of West Seattle. There were twenty-four in their group, twelve of them under the age of ten. The previous spring they had departed Cherry Grove back in Illinois in four covered wagons, their leader: Arthur Denny. Joining at Independence, Missouri, the Oregon Trail emigration of that year, which numbered over 2,000 men, women and children, they began the long trek across the plains over the Rockies to Willamette Valley in Oregon.

While traveling up the banks of Burnt River in eastern Oregon, someone told them of a newer region of the Northwest which was about to open up, until now known simply as Puget Sound country. For years occupied solely by the Hudson's Bay Company fur trappers, Americans had succeeded recently in also invading this new Indian territory.

Upon the Denny party reaching the lower Columbia, they decided to dispatch David Denny and two others to hike up the Cowlitz River to investigate. "We have examined the valley of the Duwamish river and find it a fine country. There is plenty of room for one thousand settlers. Come at once," was the message they sent back.

The eight-day voyage from Portland to Puget Sound aboard the tiny sailing schooner *Exact*, Captain Isaiah Folger of Nantucket in command, was a stormy one, and all became seasick. The situation, moreover, which confronted them upon their landing at Alki Point was a surprising one. As recalled in later years by Arthur Denny:

> Alki Point had not . . . [until now] been a general camping ground for the Indians . . . but soon after we landed they began to congregate here, and continued coming until we had over a thousand of them in our midst . . . Most of them built their homes near to ours, even on the ground we had cleared. Although they seemed very friendly we did not feel safe for fear of offending them. (Arthur Denny, *Pioneer Days on Puget Sound*, Seattle, 1917)

By far, the most impressive of all the Indians who camped that winter among the whites was Chief Seattle, his name pronounced with a guttural sound resembling Scaldh or Sea-at-thl. In the book *Four Wagons West* (Portland, 1931), Mrs. R.F. Watt describes the old Indian "about 65 years old and walking with a cane, broad-shouldered, deep-chested and with a voice like a trumpet which he frequently used, exhorting his fellow-Indians to behave in a mannerly fashion lest they frighten away these newcomers."

As a youth of about six, Chief Seattle remembered watching "the great canoe with giant white wings," referring to Captain George Vancouver's ninety-nine foot long three-masted brig which entered Puget Sound in the summer of 1792. Vancouver anchored the vessel off Blake Island, immediately across Puget Sound from today's city. Blake Island was Chief Seattle's birthplace, and where he was raised. Perhaps young Seattle accompanied his father, Chief Schweabe and other Indians when, with Vancouver's encouragement, they paddled their canoes to visit the strange giant canoe. In his journal, Captain Vancouver describes what transpired.

> . . . they approached cautiously . . . to within about two hundred yards of our ship HMS Discovery . . . there resting on their paddles a conference was held . . . followed by a song sung by one of the men who at stated intervals was joined in chorus by several others, whilst some in each canoe kept time with the handles of their paddles by striking them against the gunwale or side of their canoes forming a sort of accompaniment which though expressed by simple notes only, was by no means destitute of an agreeable effect. (*Vancouver's Discovery of Puget Sound,* E.S. Meany ed., Portland, 1942)

Chief Schweabe and his young son may have been among those who attended the picnic which Vancouver gave for the Indians several days later, on the shores of Commencement Bay where the city of Tacoma now stands.

"New York" was the first name with which Seattle's founding fathers ambitiously dubbed their new settlement. But as the winter wore on they began to have doubts about the site's suitability, due to the strong northwest winds which blew constantly. Soon they began adding the word *alki,* an Indian word translated "maybe" or "bye and bye", to "New York". In the spring they moved from here (at today's West Seattle, where only the name Alki Point now survives) to a site farther east and across the water. There they were more protected from the weather. This spot was initially dubbed Duwampsh after the Duwampsh band of Indians living here, but by then Chief Sealth had become recognized by everyone as their friend and helper. So they decided to change the name Duwampsh to its present one, honoring the Indian who was so hospitable to them.

The founding fathers of Seattle were not the first whites whom Chief Seattle had known. Since 1833, the British had been residing at Nisqually House, a trading post a few miles to the south. Here Puget Sound Indians, young Seattle among them, brought their furs in exchange for beads, calico, and other luxuries offered by these British white men. On at least one occasion young Seattle offended these white fur traders; in fact at one time they forebade Seattle to enter the British post ever again. Two years later, however, Seattle attended a nearby school operated by a Catholic missionary, Father Modeste Demers. Soon Seattle became a convert to Catholicism, was baptized, and given the Christian name of Noah.

Isaac Stevens (1818–1862), the first governor of Washington Territory, was not the sole originator of the Indian Wars which swept the Pacific Northwest in the 1850s, but certainly the so-called "peace treaties" which he persuaded the Indian chiefs to sign served to ignite the resentment that arose when the Indian leaders realized the mistake they had made in signing them. Apparently it was the presence of the USS *Decatur* in Seattle's harbor, called Elliott Bay, which caused the Indians to choose this future city as their target. The warship had been dispatched from Hawaii to protect the whites from Haidah Indians who were raiding white settlements around Puget Sound from their war canoes.

Soon after its arrival on Puget Sound, the *Decatur* ran aground closeby Bainbridge Island. Laid up for repairs at Henry Yesler's Wharf in Seattle, then a struggling little community of scarcely two hundred souls, the naval vessel may have presented to the Indians too tempting a target to resist. Certainly they would have liked to capture the gunpowder stored in the *Decatur's* magazines. According to at least one source, it was the Indians' plan to attack both Seattle and the nearby U.S. Army Fort Steilacoom simultaneously. It is believed that the attackers, mostly Yakima Indians from east of the Cascade Mountains, failing to gain whole-hearted support from the local Indians, delayed too long.

Surprised to find the warship no longer dismantled, they were terrified upon finally launching their attack on the morning of 26 January, 1856. The USS *Decatur* responded by lobbing her slow-detonating shells from her anchorage off Yesler's wharf over the heads of Seattle's white residents into the forests of Capitol, First, and Beacon Hills. Here the Indian attackers had been waiting stealthily to commence their depredations all night but had not yet attacked.

The fact that the *Decatur's* shells would land, then detonate afterward, seems to have terrified the would-be conquerors of the white village. Before retreating, however, the Indians set fire to several white homes situated around the periphery of the small settlement. As viewed from the deck of the *Decatur,* all of Seattle appeared to be on fire. By the time the U.S. Marine detachment had landed from the warship, the Yakimas, if indeed they were members of this tribe, had retreated to their canoes on Lake Washington's west bank. From here they retired across this lake to areas where Bellevue and Renton now stand. The fracas ended with the loss of only two whites. It was estimated that twenty-eight of the Indian attackers died.

Seattle's promise as a future city improved markedly in 1861 when the Territorial Legislature chose to locate the Pacific Northwest's first state-supported educational institution here. The land on which to build it was donated by Arthur Denny. Local citizens donated their

labor in erecting the first buildings. Situated in the area where Seattle's tallest skyscrapers now stand, the future university consisted of three small frame structures surrounded by a white picket fence, its most distinguished feature being the view of the waters of Puget Sound backed by the snow-capped Olympic Range in the distance. The largest of the buildings was topped by a belfry, containing a bell which had been sailed here around Cape Horn, used not only to call students to class but also, during foggy weather, to guide ships into Elliott Bay. Appointed as head of the school was twenty-two-year-old Asa Mercer, a recent graduate of Ohio's Franklin College. Asa's duties included serving not only as university president, but also as the sole teacher, janitor, and handyman. To overcome the total lack of students, President Mercer paddled a canoe around Puget Sound enlisting them, promising free tuition in return for chopping wood for the school's single classroom stove. Little was it then suspected that, soon after the school was moved to its present location on Portage Bay and Lake Washington, it would grow to become one of the finest educational institutions in the nation.

The struggling status of the University of Washington, even as late as 1892, is illustrated by the following conversation which occurred during a visit East by the University of Washington's Professor O.B. Johnson, during which he called on the President of Harvard University, Dr. Charles William Eliot.

> Eliot to Johnson: "What chair do you occupy?" Johnson to Eliot: "I don't know what chair, but I teach mathematics, physics, zoology, botany, physiology, astronomy, mathematics and . . .". Eliot to Johnson, interrupting: "Oh, yes, I see, you don't occupy a chair, you occupy a settee."

All Seattleites turned green with envy in 1872, when the upstart settlement of Tacoma was created overnight by a Philadelphia millionaire, Charles Barstow Wright (1822–1898). Wright was a high official of the Northern Pacific Railroad when, in December of that year, his company completed laying tracks to Tacoma, thus making this "paper city" the first and only terminus of a transcontinental railroad on Puget Sound. Many residents of Seattle, who hitherto regarded their city as the leading one, now felt their prospects were doomed. It was the discovery of gold in Alaska in 1897 which restored to the city its unquestioned leadership. As a base of supplies for the Klondike Boom, the town prospered beyond all expectations.

Meanwhile, in 1866, Chief Seattle passed away. The death took place in the huge Oleman House at Port Madison, west of the city across Elliott Bay, the same giant Indian structure in which Seattle's father, Chief Schweabe, had lived and died before him. A staunch supporter of the whites, Chief Seattle, in his later years, had become an orator. Shortly before his death, the aged man spoke as follows:

> There was a time when our Indian people covered the whole land as the waves of a wind-ruffled sea covers its shell-paved floor . . . I will not dwell on nor mourn our untimely death nor reproach my pale-faced brothers with hastening it. We too may have been somewhat to blame . . . Your time of decay may be distant but it will surely come . . . We may be brothers after all . . . Let . . . the white people . . . be just and deal kindly with my people. (As translated by Dr. Henry A. Smith, see p. 180, R.F. Watts, *Four Wagons West*, Portland, 1931)

SILVERDALE (H-7)

A down-grading of precious metals took place in evolving the name of this Kitsap Peninsula city, ten miles north of Bremerton. For originally it was called Goldendale; that is, until postal authorities in 1890 forced them to change their original name because there was already in existence a town named Goldendale in eastern Washington.

Goldendale's history, however, goes back farther than this; to the 1830s when the local Indians living at a point of land on nearby Hood Canal were dying of what was called "Boston Fever." Today this point is called Misery Point because of that sad situation. The illness wiped out nearly forty percent of all the Indians in the Northwest. It allegedly began with the anchoring of the brig *Owyhee*, Captain Dominis in command, in the Columbia River off Fort Vancouver in 1830. He had come here to unload a flock of sheep destined for the Hudson's Bay Company farm located across the river on Tualatin Plains. Some of his sailors were ill of what became known to the Indians as "Boston" fever, this name probably owing to the fact that the ship came from Boston, Massachusetts. Pursuant to this disaster, the Northwest Indians nicknamed all Americans living in the Northwest as "Bostons" to distinguish them from the Britishers of the Hudson's Bay Company, whom the Indians dubbed "kinchawgs," translated King George men.

Closeby Misery Point to the west lies the town of Seabeck, originally known to the Indians as "scabbock" or "s'bok." In the 1880s Seabeck was known as "The Metropolis of Hood Canal" boasting "a good library, a Sunday school, a brass band, two hotels, three saloons, a baseball diamond and a traveling show which visited it two or three times per year," recalls one of the town's first settlers, adding "and a preacher once a month."

Dyes Inlet, at the northern tip of which the city of Silverdale now stands, is named after John W. Dyes, a taxidermist member of the U.S. Navy expedition which surveyed Puget Sound in the summer of 1841. Mr. Dyes is remembered for the elegant, though unusual, spelling with which he wrote daily in his journal, as required of all the civilians of the expedition by its commander, Commodore Charles Wilkes. Writing of Puget Sound, Dyes records: "This is one of the most Majestic sheets of Warter I ever saw in my Life" and, commenting upon an occasion that summer when Commodore Wilkes became angry at his crew aboard the USS *Vincennes* for failing to furl a sail properly, Dyes comments "He got out on one of his tantomes."

SKYKOMISH (H-11)

Past this town, forty miles to the east of Everett, flows the north fork of the Skykomish River, the word *skykomish* being an Indian word meaning "inland people." Seatttleites wishing to cross Stevens Pass proceeding to the east side of the Cascade Range drive past Skykomish. Downstream of Skykomish lies the town of Index, named after the spectacular Mount Index which towers above it. The 5,979 foot needle-shaped peak was so named by Persis Gunn in 1889, she said, because it resembled her index finger. The Gunns founded the town of Index after arriving here over the Oregon Trail in 1889.

The next town downstream on the Skykomish River is Gold Bar. Here, in 1875, Chinese wearing coolie hats worked a sandbar in the river in search of gold.

Next door and downstream of Gold Bar is the town of Startup, named for George Startup, manager of the lumber company around which the town developed. He built a water flume four miles long down the side of a nearby mountain, thereby delivering logs to his mill in a rapid fashion.

The first white man to live at Sultan, the name of the next town downstream of Startup, was "an Eastern college dude," according to local historians. His name was John Nailor. After marrying a local Indian girl, he decided to stay here permanently. The real founder of Sultan, however, was an Indian known as Chief *Tseul-tud*. His name being unpronounceable to the local whites, they called him Chief

Sultan; thereby the town which arose where he lived was called Sultan.

In 1792, when railroad tracks were being laid up the banks of the Skykomish, Sultan became the base for this operation. Most of the railroad workers lived in Everett, so three sternwheel steamboats would carry them up the Snohomish and Skykomish rivers to Sultan each morning, returning them by this means after their day's work.

SNIPES MOUNTAIN (N-17)

This landmark is situated in eastern Washington overlooking the Yakima Valley town of Sunnyside, thirty miles southeast of Yakima. It is named in honor of Ben Snipes (1835–1903). Born in Iowa, Ben came west with the Emigration Act of 1852. He was only seventeen years old at the time, and his brothers and parents refused to accompany him. Initially Ben found a job in Willamette Valley as a farm hand. Then he obtained work leading a pack train south to California, carrying potatoes and apples to the hungry gold seekers on Sutter's Creek. Along with thousands of other Americans, Ben then traveled into Canada, joining in the Fraser Gold Rush. In Cariboo country he saw hungry miners eager to pay high prices for beef. Recalling the vast bunchgrass country he had seen east of the Cascades in eastern Washington, Ben conceived the idea of raising beef cattle there. Returning to The Dalles, Ben gave a promissory note to an army officer in exchange for his first steer. From this start Ben developed a herd. He began making cattle drives to the Cariboo gold fields of British Columbia in 1855.

Here the hungry gold prospectors paid him $100 a head for his animals. By 1861 gold discoveries in the Cariboo north of Williams Lake became fabulous, superior even to the best gold mining in California, and Snipes prospered. The cattle empire, which he administered from his crude log cabin on the slopes of this mountain, stretched eastward from here all the way to present Idaho, for there were no fences in all this region.

Ben, at the height of his prosperity, is said to have owned fifty thousand cattle and thousands of horses. It was a day of open-grazing, and natural bunchgrass grew in abundant supply all over eastern Washington. Ben Snipes became one of the earliest and greatest of the Northwest's so-called Cattle Kings.

Unlike the usual prototype of a cowboy portrayed in western movies, Snipes never carried a gun, seldom if ever swore, nor did he smoke or drink. He was a man of modest appearance.

Ben's older brother, George Snipes, followed Ben to Oregon in 1853.

He was a founder of The Dalles. Ben's parents, Elam and Asenath, followed their two sons in 1863, settling in Klickitat Valley where the town Goldendale now stands.

SNOQUALMIE PASS (I-11)

In the early spring of 1853, Mr. Isaac Stevens, soon to become Washington Territory's new governor, was traveling west on horseback leading two hundred surveyors across the northern United States from Minnesota. He was searching out a route through the northern Rockies, making peace with the Indians along the way. His goal was to find a railroad route into Puget Sound. Mr. Stevens, a former army officer, chose one of his West Point friends, George McClellan, to lead an auxiliary party of sixty-six men by ship across the Isthmus of Panama then again by ship to Puget Sound in order to commence, simultaneous with his own westward survey, a similar survey for laying railroad tracks from Puget Sound eastward over the Cascades. It was planned that the two groups would meet up in eastern Washington months later.

This was the same McClellan who, scarcely a decade later, by then commander-in-chief of the Union armies in Virginia, was fired by President Abraham Lincoln for his lack of aggressiveness against Confederate troops threatening to capture the nation's capitol. In hindsight, it is not surprising that the dilatory McClellan, upon landing with his surveyors on Puget Sound, proceeded to spend months organizing them, equipping them, and finally departing.

He led them around the mountains' southern end where the Columbia flows into the ocean. Upon reaching the east side of the mountains he allowed his men to look for gold before commencing a search through the mountains from their east side. The crafty Yakima leader, Chief Kamiakin, having heard of the white mens' plans, advised McClellan that even snowshoes were infeasible in the deep snows which covered the entire length of the Cascade Range in winter. He estimated the snows depth to be over twenty feet.

Much to Mr. Stevens disgust, when the two survey parties met near Spokane late in 1855 (Stevens having successfully found a suitable opening for running a railroad through the Rocky Mountains), McClellan greeted him with the announcement that such a route over the Cascade Range did not exist. He advised Stevens that it would be necessary to lay the railroad tracks southward around the mountains, down the banks of the Columbia River, then north to Puget Sound.

Exasperatedly, Stevens then dispatched Lieutenant Abiel Tinkham, one of his trusted young assistants, to verify McClellan's information. Within a week, Tinkham returned with the good news of having discovered Snoqualmie Pass, the low 3,010-feet opening through which today a six-lane highway allows cars to speed. History does not record the reaction of George B. McClellan upon learning of this development.

The name *snoqualmie* is that of an Indian tribe. The word itself means "moon people," since these Indians believed that their ancestors came from the moon.

SPOKANE (H-23)

This name is derived from the Indian word *spukanee* meaning "sun." *Hust-spukanee* was the expression with which the Spokane Indians greeted each other in the morning, their equivalent of the white men's "good morning" (literally "good sun"). Thus, to the first white people who lived here the local Indians became known as "the Spokanes." It was natural, therefore, that they named accordingly the city of Spokane in 1878, its date of founding.

However, the history of Spokane goes back to 1810—a year before Astoria, the oldest of the Northwest's cities, was established. In the spring of 1810, Mr. Jacques "Jocko" Finlay and fiery-eyed Finan McDonald, two fur trappers of The Honourable North West Company of Montreal, arrived here to become the first white inhabitants.

Directing Jocko and Finan to erect Spokane House, as their fur post was christened, was a Welshman named David Thompson, the great

Canadian explorer. Three years before this, Mr. Thompson discovered the source of the Columbia River, although at the time he did not realize it. It took him another year to solve the mystery of this great river's twists and turns in the regions known today as southeast British Columbia.

Meanwhile, Thompson was commencing a string of North West Company fur posts in the regions northeast of today's Spokane. The first was Kootenae House, located south of Windermere Lake, followed in 1808 by Kullyspell House on Idaho's Pend Oreille Lake, then Saleesh House on Clarks Fork, and finally Spokane House. Thompson's North West Company was envisioning a fur trade which would extend from Montreal westward across Canada, all the way to the Pacific Ocean. The mouth of the Columbia was the ideal terminus spot for the westernmost anchor of the chain but, prior to Thompson, no one had found the source of this mighty river down which they hoped to deliver furs harvested west of the Rockies.

As early as 1807, the Nor'Westers back in Montreal had known that an American named John J. Astor, already wealthy from harvesting furs in New York State and regions south of the Great Lakes, was also coveting the mouth of the Columbia as the site on which to build an American fur post. Lacking experienced American trappers like Finan and Jocko to achieve this goal, Mr. Astor, in 1810, decided to rob the Montreal North West Company of some of their best fur men. Offering them higher wages than their British overseers, Astor then sailed them around Cape Horn. By the spring of 1811, the group had erected Fort Astor closeby the Pacific, ready to receive American furs from upriver on the Columbia. Apparently the former Nor'Westers were not at all ashamed of their recent change in allegiance.

Mr. Thompson's failure to descend the Columbia to the ocean before the Astorians reached there has been portrayed by some historians as a catastrophe. Had this Welshman reached here first, they allege, the present state of Washington would belong to Canada. It appears to this writer, however, that Thompson's chief purpose in descending the Columbia from Spokane House was revealed when he reached Pasco, enroute. Here, where the Columbia and the Snake rivers flow together, he posted his famous notice. Upriver of here, he declared trapping grounds reserved for his Montreal company. Downstream of here, he conceded, were trapping grounds reserved for the Americans. When on July 15, 1811, he reached the site where the city of Astoria now stands, he was not at all surprised to see his former colleagues, now his rivals.

One year later, a band of these former Nor'Westers traveled by canoe from Astoria up the Columbia and Snake rivers, then by horseback up the banks of the Palouse River to visit Spokane House. After greeting their former pals, Jocko and Finan, they doubtlessly startled them by proceeding to erect an American fur post within half-a-mile of Spokane House. They called it Fort Spokane, and the sight of the two posts, one flying the Stars and Stripes, the other the Union Jack, must have presented a colorful site to the bewildered Spokane Indians.

Fort Spokane, however, quickly became their preference for the trading of furs, for the Americans, they soon found, poossessed a far more impressive collection of trade goods than did the British. Hitherto satisfied to receive bits of copper sheeting, cheap glass beads, or calico in exchange for their beaver, fox, and marten pelts, the Spokanes became dissatisfied with such offerings, much preferring the more glamorous items offered at Fort Spokane: looking glasses, for example, horse bells, thimbles, tobacco, and coffee.

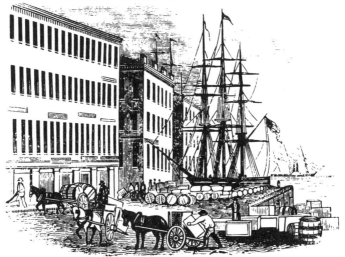

Shortly after Fort Spokane was built, the Americans brought upstream from Astoria animals which the Indians had never seen before: chickens, cows, and pigs, causing the wide-eyed Indians to come from far and wide to gaze upon them. Chief trader John Clarke, also a former Nor'Wester, fascinated the Indians with his strutting style. Invariably when Indians were present, Clarke accompanied himself by a retinue of aides who wore feathers in their hats and obeyed his slightest gesture. Soon the Yankees had won over completely the Indians, and Spokane House languished.

In January, 1813, startling news reached the banks of Spokane River. England and the United States were at war, and a British warship was headed for the mouth of the Columbia to capture Astoria. Gleefully, the Spokane House trappers journeyed down the Columbia to the ocean to witness Astoria's downfall. Weeks passed without the warship's arrival, and in the interim, parleying between these Nor'Westers and their former Nor'Wester pals (now their rivals) took place. Soon they began to rationalize themselves into a deal. After all, the American furs which by now had accumulated in considerable quantity, would soon be seized by the oncoming warship as a prize of war without any compensation to John J. Astor. Why not, they therefore cogitated, sell the furs at Astoria to the Britishers of Spokane House before the warship's arrival. So, when HMS *Raccoon* anchored off Astoria that fall, its captain was disgusted to find that the American post offered nothing to seize. The Astorians and their former British colleagues, in fact, had commenced dispatching Astor's erstwhile furs back to Montreal. When news of the deal reached Astor, he was furious.

With the hoisting of the British flag over Astoria, the former American post was renamed Fort George, honoring the English monarch. Similarly, Fort Spokane, now no longer an American post, was renamed Spokane House and, in view of this post's superior facilities, the older Spokane House was deserted.

For the next decade the North West Company enjoyed a monopoly throughout the regions along the Columbia. Spokane House, itself, became a mecca of luxury. After months of trapping icy streams while dodging Indians, North West Company trappers loved to repair to Spokane House for a rest. Here they found a race track where they could bet on local horses, a dance hall where they could dance with comely Indian girls, and great varieties of food grown in the adjacent gardens. Particularly for the officers-in-charge of this fur post was life enjoyable. As described by one of them, Mr. Alexander Ross in his *Fur Hunters of the Far West* (Norman, 1956):

> The bourgeois [this was his title as Spokane House's officer-in-charge] . . . lives in comfort. He rambles at his pleasure, enjoys the merry dance, or the pastime of some pleasing game . . . his morning ride, his fishing rod, his gun, his dog, or a jaunt of pleasure to the environs in his gay canoe . . . Nor can we pass over in silence one chief object of attraction. Even in this barbarous country, woman claims and enjoys her due share of attention and regard . . . Although descended from aboriginal mothers, many of the females are

> as fair as the generality of European ladies . . . they soon
> acquire the ease and gracefulness of the polished life.

In 1825, this paradise in the wilderness came to an abrupt stop with the arrival of the waspish, energetic, and efficiency-conscious George Simpson, recently appointed as the Canadian Ruler of all fur trapping from the Atlantic to the Pacific. Promptly he declared Spokane House to be "unsuitable for an Indian trading post." Decisively he ordered no more horse racing. No more European luxuries would henceforth be transported here, he ordered, from the mouth of the Columbia. Soon afterward, in fact, he closed down Spokane House, shifting the post to a site on the Columbia River north of here, re-naming it Fort Colvile.

Just prior to Spokane House's demise, however, Governor Simpson directed Alexander Ross to ". . . pick for me a promising Indian boy of the Middle Spokanes . . . to be sent to the Protestant Missionary School at Red River Settlement." Operated by Anglican priests and located near present-day Winnipeg, Canada, this mission school thus became the home of Illim-Spukanee's fourteen-year-old son, for it was he whom his father picked in response to Simpson's order. Here at Red River, the Anglican priests christened Illim-Spukanee's son with the Christian name "Garry," after a deputy governor of the HBC, as he is today remembered. He was taught to speak, read, and write English. Attending, as was required of him, the daily chapel services, Spokane Garry learned about the white man's religion. He was also taught geography, English history, and how to till the soil in the white men's manner.

When he returned four years later to Spokane Falls, dressed in western-style clothes and speaking with a Scottish accent the language of the whites, Spokane Garry became among his own people an instant celebrity and leader. The elders of his tribe persuaded him to set up a school of his own to impart what he had learned at Red River. Built on Spokane's North Hill, this school soon found itself accommodating not only Spokane Indians, but Indians from as far as Nez Perce country southward and Coeur d'Alene country eastward, all eager to learn more about the new "white man's magic." Garry's teachings were eagerly sought throughout many tribes surrounding his own, and he found himself a leading Northwest figure.

With the arrival of the white missionaries, however, Garry's influence waned, as his fellow-Indians rushed to hear about the "talking book," as the Bible was known, from the "black robes" themselves. It was the quarreling of these missionaries amongst themselves and particularly the rivalry between the Protestant and Catholics which disillusioned many tribes, and caused Garry himself to lose some of the enthusiasm he had gained from his years at the Red River Anglican School.

By 1840, he began returning to his native ways, joining with his fellow tribesmen in riding east annually to hunt buffalo in Montana and to fight with the Blackfeet. In 1844, he joined fifty of his fellow Indians in making a trip into Spanish California seeking cattle, driving a large herd of horses with which to employ in exchange. At Sutter's Fort they were ill-received, falsely accused of being thieves. In a squabble over these accusations, one of thier chieftain's sons was killed. A group of Californian Indians captured their horses. They then returned bitter at their experience, particularly at the whites who had killed the youngest of their number.

With the commencement of war upon the whites by Chief Kamiakin of the Yakimas, nonetheless, Spokane Garry advised this leader to be cautious, aware as he was of the white men's power. At the Walla Walla Peace powwow convened by Washington Territory's Governor Stevens in 1855, he neither advocated cooperating with white demands upon the 5,000 Indians there to surrender their lands in return for the proffered material gains, nor against these demands. When, however, it became apparent that Stevens was not fulfilling his part of the treaty agreement, Garry angrily reproached him.

Garry's advocacy of moderation on the part of the war-like Indians nonetheless gained their contempt, and Garry's popularity waned. In the Indian Wars which followed he was torn between conflicting loyalties, those of his fellow tribesmen and those of his Christian teachings.

Spokane Garry was sixty-two years old in 1863 when Mr. James Glover (1837–1921), the founder of today's city of Spokane, arrived to take up free land. A shrewd businessman who, previous to this, had made money selling apples from his native Salem to the gold prospectors in California, Glover picked this site knowing it would eventually become an important one. Here he erected a store selling, as he described it: ". . . cheap blankets, shawls, calico, beads, paints, tobacco, sugar, tea, coffee, cutlery and all sorts of groceries." He continues: "I never carried powder and lead and had no firearms. I frequently loaned a shot gun to the Indians however and they would occasionally bring in deer for its use." Glover also erected a grist mill at The Falls. Some idea of the original town which developed around Glover's store can be appreciated from the following account by one of its first citizens, as recounted in a Works Progress Administration book titled *As Told by the Pioneers (1917)*:

> It was October 1878, fifty-three years ago when I first saw the town of Spokane Falls . . . the original name of Spokane . . . We had been six days on the road coming from Walla Walla. The family traveling in a covered wagon drawn by two horses was accompanied by a large schooner wagon drawn by six horses. The site for a town was magnificent to look at as we approached the business part . . . but in that day it had only one store, a small flour mill, a sawmill and a blacksmith shop. There were nine families here and we made the tenth.

The Northern Pacific Railroad tracks finally arrived in 1881. It was, however, the discovery of gold in the Coeur d'Alene Mountains east of Spokane which caused Indian fighting to intensify. With the defeat of the Nez Perce Indians in the Chief Joseph War of 1877, virtually all the Northwest's Indians, including the Spokane tribe, found themselves in a deplorable plight, Spokane Garry included. His last years were spent with his blind wife, Nina, in abject poverty, rejected not only by the whites but also by his fellow-tribesmen. In general, they disapproved of Garry's later mediation attempts on their behalf to gain for his people whatever crumbs of aid the whites would give them.

Just before his death, the white men robbed this venerable old leader of the land on which, in his younger years, Garry operated a prosperous farm. The school and church which he had erected at North Hill were also gone. Likewise departed was the wealth Garry had reaped from the operation of his farm. He died in 1892, at the age of eighty-one, and was buried in a pauper's grave. The citizens of Spokane have since erected a fitting monument to his memory in the city's Greenwood Cemetery, and Chief Garry Park in the city is also named in his honor.

STEILACOOM (J-7)

In early times there lived an Indian leader at the site where Steilacoom now stands, nine miles southeast of Tacoma. His name was Steilacoom, better known as Tail-a-koom. South of here Tailakoom and his fellow Indians loved to hunt for deer on the vast prairies which extend from the Nisqually River's mouth eastward to the snow-capped Cascade Range.

Each spring, Tailakoom's Indians dug the camas bulbs here which provided them with food enough to last for a year. The only persons living on these flatlands were British who, in 1834, built a fur trading post called Fort Nisqually at the entrance of Nisqually River into lower

Puget Sound. When in 1838, Fort Nisqually changed its mission from trading for furs to growing food supplies to be shipped to the Russians in Alaska, the British post changed its name to Puget Sound Agricultural Company, then commenced grazing thousands of cattle and sheep on Tailakoom's prairie land.

Friction arose between these Britishers and Tailakoom's band of Indians when the British sheep began spoiling the Indians' root-digging for the camas bulbs. It increased when Tailakoom, still hunting deer on these prairie lands, angered the Sandwich Island sheepherders of the PSAC by allowing his favorite hunting dog to chase the sheep. When the sheepherders shot at Tailakoom's dog, the Indian leader responded by shooting at the herdsmen.

For this, Tailakoom was thrown in the PSAC'S jail. Here Tailakoom languished, his hands and feet manacled, until word of the incident reached the PSAC's officer-in-charge, Dr. William Fraser Tolmie, a kindly Scot who loved the Indians. Still manacled, Tailakoom was brought before Dr. Tolmie who, instantly recognizing the Indian as one of the old-time Indian friends, not only ordered Tailakoom to be released but presented him with a gift of Brazilian tobacco. The story is told in Mrs. E.E. Dye's *McDonald of Oregon* (Chicago, 1907), a book based upon first-hand information personally derived by her from persons involved. Tailakoom, she writes, thereafter worked at the British post, serving as a faithful employee, until his death.

The commencement of an American settlement at the site of Steilacoom began with the building here in August, 1849, of a U.S. Army post. Chief Patkanim had led an army of Indians the previous year in an unsuccessful attempt to capture nearby Fort Nisqually, the British post a few miles to the south. Governor Joseph Lane, then the ruler over Puget Sound country as well as Oregon, established Fort Steilacoom to prevent further Indian outbreaks around Puget Sound. Such outbreaks, however, soon followed—causing outlying white families from as far south as White River Valley and as far north as Bellingham to flee here for protection.

Close on the heels of Fort Steilacoom's establishment, moreover, there arrived on Puget Sound the future founder of Steilacoom, Captain Lafayette Balch. Unlike most of the whites now pouring into Puget Sound who came here via the Oregon Trail, Balch did so by sailing ship. Well-to-do, he sailed his ship, named the *George Emory,* here from his home in Maine, carrying aboard the vessel a cargo suitable for setting up a store somewhere around Puget Sound.

Initially he tried to obtain a site for it at Olympia, closeby here to the south. He was unable to do this because of a store already established here by Michael Simmons, recently the founder of the settlement called Tumwater. Captain Balch then decided to build his store near the army post here at Steilacoom. Hopes for his store's success ran high not only with the arrival of persons wishing to live closeby the fort, but also with news that the U.S. Congress was appropriating funds to build a wagon road from Walla Walla westward over the Cascade Range into Puget Sound, with the site of Port Steilacoom (as the town was originally known) as the road's terminus.

Heretofore the flood of emigrants (who by now were arriving on Puget Sound, being unable to surmount the Cascade Range) were forced to take the much longer route down the Columbia almost to this river's mouth before they headed up the Cowlitz River's banks to Puget Sound. Elated that his settlement was soon to become the Oregon Trail's salt water terminus, Balch began touting his new community as Puget Sound's future leading city. This, however, failed to materialize, perhaps due in no small measure to Captain Balch's attempt to get rich seeking gold in the regions to the north of here around the Queen Charlotte Islands. This necessitated his being absent from his town at a crucial time when Steilacoom's rival settlements, namely: Olympia, Port Townsend, and Seattle were assiduously promoting themselves.

A towering figure in Steilacoom's early history was Colonel George Casey, the first commander of Fort Steilacoom. From his U.S. Army headquarters at Fort Vancouver on the Columbia, Colonel Casey's superior in the chain of command, General John Wool, made clear to him that, insofar as possible, Colonel Casey was to leave the Indians alone. The cause of their unrest, Wool believed, was the unfair peace treaties which Governor Isaac Stevens had imposed upon them.

Governor Stevens, however, demanded that Casey use his Regulars to the fullest in assisting Puget Sound's Volunteer Militia (ill-trained men in the eyes of General Wool, who represented little more than a mob of vigilantes). Although torn between these two officials, Colonel Casey did, indeed, cooperate to the fullest with the governor's civilian fighters. However, when they captured Indian Chief Leschi, insisting that he be tried as a murderer, Casey disagreed, insisting that this Indian leader was not a murderer, and that he should be tried as a prisoner of war, given the full rights then accorded all opponents in honorable battle. When, in January, civilian courts found Leschi guilty of murder, and sentenced him to be hung, Colonel Casey refused to allow the scaffold on which the hanging was to be accomplished to be erected on the U.S. Army's grounds at Fort Steilacoom.

STEPTOE BUTTE (K-63)

Surrounded by ferocious Indians on top of this landmark, forty miles south of Spokane immediately south of Rosalia, Captain E.J. Steptoe and his one hundred fifty-eight men, three companies of mounted cavalry and a platoon of infantry, narrowly escaped annihilation. Steptoe and his men had fled south here from the site where the present town of Spangle is situated.

They reached here at the end of daylight on May 17, 1858. A bad night ensued, the Indians repeatedly attempting to crawl to the crest of this butte to kill the whites, the latter outnumbered at least four to one. Drinking water became scarce, ammunition low. Twice the Indians charged up to overwhelm the whites, many employing bows and arrows at the shorter range, and narrowly succeeding.

About midnight the Indians again charged, this time to find the whites had gone. Somehow they and the animals of their pack train had managed to run the gauntlet and make a dash for the Snake River. Friendly Indians ferried them across this stream, enabling them to reach the safety of their base, Fort Walla Walla.

Before coming west, Major Steptoe served with distinction in Florida's Seminole War and in the Mexican War. Prior to his assignment as commanding officer at Fort Walla Walla, he was offered the governorship of Utah Territory, but he declined. Well might he have, in retrospect, regretted this decision, for his humiliating defeat here in Washington Territory brought upon him widespread condemnation from his army superiors. Soon after this episode, Steptoe resigned from the U.S. Army to live abroad. He died in Lynchburg, Virginia in 1865, at age forty-nine.

STEVENSON (Q-9)

Now that the waters of the mighty Columbia River have been tamed by hydroelectric dams, it is difficult to realize how tempestuously this river flowed in early times past the five-mile stretch here on the north bank of which today's town of Stevenson stands, forty-five miles east of Portland. "The Cascades" was the name given to this stretch of the river.

In the fall of 1805, the Lewis and Clark party, all thirty of them traveling by canoes, were forced hastily to beach their craft when they saw this stretch of white water ahead, in order to portage around it.

Prior to the construction of a canal and locks here, commenced in 1879 and completed in 1914, the only way cargo could be shipped upriver past here was by loading it on the backs of mules who transported it over the adjacent Cascade Range of mountains, or later a horse-drawn tramway carried cargo upstream here on wooden tracks.

Recognizing the vulnerability of the whites in shipping supplies to their army posts in the interior caused by this obstruction, the wily Yakima chieftain named Kamiakin, leader of the combined tribes east of the mountains, launched an attack upon this critical stretch of the Columbia at the outbreak of the Indian Wars. On the morning of March 26, 1856, he deployed about two hundred fifty warriors along the northern cliffs overlooking the cascades.

At this time there were living in the vicinity of Bradford's store, at the upper end of these narrows, a handful of whites, unaware of the fighting that was about to take place. Tied up at the boat dock in front of Braddock's Store was the steamboat *Mary*, not yet departed on its daily trip upstream. At the store itself, Mr. Bradford had not yet begun his business of the day. Two miles downstream, U.S. soldiers were just waking up in the U.S. army's blockhouse, located at the middle cascades, unaware of the crisis about to break.

Suddenly, from the heights above Bradford's Store, flaming arrows began to fly, directed not only at the store itself, but also at the bridge of the *Mary* where the engineer below decks was getting up steam in the vessel's boilers. It was Kamiakin's intention to prevent the vessel from departing the dock to spread the word of the impending Indian onslaught. Flaming arrows began to lodge themselves on the roof of Bradford's store. People ran from nearby cabins. Four of the *Mary's* crew found themselves in hand-to-hand combat with Indians in war paint attempting to climb aboard. Boldly rushing from the fireroom up the *Mary's* ladder to the pilot house, Mr. Hardin Chenoweth, the vessel's engineer, lying flat on the pilot house's deck in order to escape the shower of arrows, managed to back the small craft into the stream to go for help.

Attempts to set fire to the store continued. Burning pitch was dumped by the Indians on the second floor's roof. Downstream, meanwhile, the U.S. soldiers at the middle Dalles were likewise repelling attack upon their blockhouse. On the second day of the siege, food ran low and drinking water both inside the blockhouse and in Bradford's store became scarce, remedied partially by persons inside boldly rushing down to the river with buckets.

On the afternoon of the third day, soldiers in the blockhouse heard the sound of a bugle, signalling the arrival of help. Soon afterward U.S. cavalrymen from Fort Vancouver, led by Lieutenant Phil Sheridan, later of Civil War fame, arrived. During the skirmishes which followed, Sheridan received his baptism of fire when a Klickitat Indian's bullet grazed his nose, killing the soldier beside him. Within hours, the steamboat *Mary* returned to Bradford's Landing, its decks loaded with additional troops. The crisis was over. White casualties were seventeen killed, twelve wounded. Indian casualties were probably greater.

Mr. George Stevenson, after whom the town of Stevenson takes its name, was a pioneer Columbia River fisherman who arrived here from Missouri in 1880. Mr. Stevenson served as a lawmaker for years in the legislatures of both Washington Territory and of Washington State before he founded this town bearing his name in 1889.

STRAIT OF JUAN DE FUCA (E-3)

This is undoubtedly the most famous of the Pacific Northwest's place-names. The opening into Puget Sound is named after a Greek explorer who, in 1592, is alleged to have sailed *through* the North American continent. It was he and this myth which induced the numerous searches by European explorers to find this short cut. His real name was Apostolos Valerianos, but he called himself Juan de Fuca to please his Spanish superiors.

The first person who alleged De Fuca's existence was one Michael Lok, an Englishman who claimed that in 1596 he chanced to meet De Fuca at a sidewalk cafe in Venice. De Fuca confided to Lok at this time that he really was a Greek posing under this Spanish name. He said his real name was Apostolos Valerianos; that he had adopted the Spanish name while piloting sailing ships in the New World (around Mexico) for the Spanish Viceroy of Mexico City. Lok states that De Fuca told him of serving aboard a Spanish galleon which was robbed of sixty thousand ducats.

According to one modern historian engaged in trying to prove Juan de Fuca was not a fictitious person, the ship *Santa Ana* seized by the English buccaneer Cavendish off Cape San Lucas in 1857 may have been this ship. Juan advised Lok that after he became a captain of one of the Spanish ships, he sailed north up America's west coast in search of the waterway leading through the continent into the Atlantic known to the Spanish as the Strait of Anian, and that while doing so, alleged De Fuca, the crew of his ship mutinied. Mexican archives, according to this modern historian, recently unearthed, tell of such a Spanish ship on which mutiny actually occurred about the time of this latter allegation by De Fuca to Lok.

Captain John T. Walbran, for many years in command of steamships which operated in the waters inside the De Fuca Strait, was of the opinion that Juan de Fuca really sailed these waters. De Fuca's account, as told to Lok in Venice, tells of sailing past a "tall spire" in a latitude remarkably close to the actual latitude of today's De Fuca Strait, corresponding to the spire which today still stands known on modern charts as "De Fuca's Pillar." It is located closeby the entrance to today's De Fuca Strait, one mile south of Cape Flattery and is one hundred forty feet high.

After passing here and proceeding inside the strait, alleged De Fuca to Lok, he "sayled" past "divers islands" which Captain Walbran surmised were today's San Juan Islands on the American side of the international border, and the Gulf Islands on the Canadian side. De Fuca's account wherein he claims to have found gold, silver, pearls, and other precious items along the way were, Walbran points out, a form of deceit commonly used in De Fuca's day by ambitious explorers in order to interest financiers to support such expeditions as his in exploring the New World. Captain Walbran then surmises that de Fuca may have rounded the north end of Vancouver Island and returned to Mexico down the west coast of the continent instead of along its east coast, as the Greek alleged.

Michael Lok recounted De Fuca's story to both Richard Hakluyt, then England's leading authority on New World geography, and to Sir Walter Raleigh who recently had returned from his discovery of Virginia (*circa* 1857), but neither one was impressed. Thereafter Juan de Fuca's tale would have been classified to be as fictitious as Ponce de Leon's claim to have discovered in Florida the Fountain of Youth had not the British Parliament, in 1745, offered 20,000 pounds in prize money to any English navigator finding De Fuca's passageway.

Accordingly, in 1778, Captain James Cook, remembered in history as "England's greatest navigator," sailed two ships to the Northwest coasts to find the De Fuca opening. Cook flatly declared that it did not exist, at least in the latitude which De Fuca alleged.

Nine years after Cook, however, in July, 1787, a British fur trader, Captain Charles Barkley, sailing in the 400-ton brig *Imperial Eagle,* found "the broad inlet of sea" with the "exceeding high Pinnacle" in the same approximate latitude described by De Fuca. At the time of his sighting, Barkley had on board his vessel an eighteen-year-old girl, Jane Barkley, whom he had married several months earlier on the eve of his ship's departure from Ostend, Belgium. The following is Mrs. Barkley's account of the historic sighting:

> In the afternoon, to our great astonishment, we arrived off a large opening extending to the eastward, the entrance of which appeared to be about four leagues wide, and remained about that width as far as the eye could see, with a clear westerly horizon, which my husband immediately recognized as the long lost Strait of Juan de Fuca, and to which he gave the name of the original discoverer, my husband placing it on his chart.

The following is taken from the only factual document, insofar as this writer knows, relating to the above. It is from Lok's account, as recounted by Samuel Purchas in 1624 in Purchas's *His Pilgrimes:*

> . . . he [De Fuca in 1592] . . . followed his course in that Voyage West and North-west . . . all alongst the coast of Nova Spania and California, and the Indies, now called North America . . . until hee came to the Latitude of fortie seven degrees . . . [the actual latitude of De Fuca Strait is about eighty miles north of this] and finding that the land trended North and North-east, with a broad inlet of sea . . . [the actual Strait of Juan de Fuca is fifteen miles wide and trends southeastward] hee entered thereinto, sayling therein more than twentie days . . . and he passed divers Islands in that sayling . . . And at the entrance of this said Strait there is an exceeding high Pinnacle, or spired Rock, like a piller thereupon . . . [such a unique landmark does indeed still exist today at the Fuca Strait's entrance] Also he said that he went on Land in divers places, and that he saw some people on Land clad in Beat's skins; and that the Land is very fruitful, and rich of gold, Silver, Pearle and Other things, like Nova Spania.

STUART ISLAND (C-5)

The international boundary line between Canada and the United States weaves a sinuous course up Haro Strait past this particular island, first northward, then northeast past this island and then northwestward before reaching the forty-ninth parallel along which it thence goes eastward for thousands of miles to Atlantic waters. Residents of Stuart Island, when they gaze northward, are seeing what the Canadians call the Gulf Islands, though they are really a part of the same archipelago as the American San Juans. Stuart Island's nearest neighbor is the Canadian island called South Pender, located across the waterway called Boundary Pass, and it lies only fifteen miles to the north.

Stuart Island, indeed all of the waters we now call Puget Sound, commencing in 1818, were jointly owned by both the United States and England, pending a settlement at some future date (not then decided) as to how they were to be divided between the two nations.

But for Commodore Charles Wilkes, U.S.N., who named Stuart Island while surveying the Northwest in 1841, all of the San Juan Islands might today lie on the Canadian side of the international border, thanks to the general indifference at this time of then-President Harrison and the U.S. Congress about what was to them a remote part of America. It was Wilkes great fear, in surveying Puget Sound that summer, that England might gain title to these islands by default.

Accordingly, he proceeded to name most of the San Juan Islands after U.S. Navy heroes of past wars, concentrating on those Americans who had fought in the War of 1812, this conflagration being still fresh in the mind of the politicians back East. Stuart Island, however, he named after the Ship's Clerk of his flagship, the USS *Vincennes*. Throughout the four year globe-circling expedition in which Wilkes and his six ships were at this time engaged, Frederick D. Stuart served him faithfully as his secretary and scribe. In preparing his official report to the U.S. Congress of the results of his expedition, Commodore Wilkes depended to a considerable degree upon Mr. Stuart's services.

Through the waters we now call Boundary Pass (separating Stuart Island from its Canadian neighbor, South Pender Island), in early June, 1791, war-painted Indians in huge high-prowed canoes barred the Spaniard Jose Verdia and the sailors of his longboat from exploring further to the northeast. They had to retreat to their mother ship, the packetboat *San Carlos*, which was anchored at Esquimault on Vancouver Island.

However, Senor Francisco Eliza, commander of the *San Carlos*, refused to accept this disappointment, for his orders from his superior, Viceroy Revillagigedo back in Mexico City, were to make every effort to find in the waters inside the Strait of Juan de Fuca the long-sought opening believed to exist in these waters leading through the American continent into the Atlantic Ocean.

SUNNYSIDE (N-17)

The founders of this city, thirty miles southeast of Yakima, were members of a Christian Cooperative Colony. They called their settlement Holy City. In 1893, workers for the Northern Pacific Railroad began digging a huge irrigation canal past here concurrent with their laying railroad tracks. It was at this time U.S. government policy to grant this railroad free land on either side of the land through which the railroad tracks were laid, and so the Northern Pacific, recognizing how valuable this land would be if irrigated, planned, upon completion of the canal digging, to build a town here at Holy City. They christened it Sunnyside because their land here sloped southward, thereby rendering it sunny most of the day.

Sunnyside's history, however, goes back to the year 1850 when Ben Snipes, the Northwest's first cattle king, built a log cabin on the mountain overlooking where the town of Sunnyside now stands, today called Snipes Mountain in his honor. From here Ben administered his cattle empire, his animals ranging over a region larger than all the New England States put together. Most of this vast region was covered with bunch grass, a natural food upon which Ben fattened his calves, producing hundreds of calves annually until Ben's herd was estimated to have numbered over fifty thousand animals. With the discovery of gold about this time on the Fraser River to the north in Canada, Ben

conceived the idea of driving his animals north to feed the hungry prospectors.

Ben's first cattle drive into this region numbered about one hundred animals. Indian cowboys using canoes instead of horses assisted Ben in swimming his steers across the Columbia River, then a swift-flowing stream, at Wenatchee Rapids. Ben himself crossed over by hanging onto the tail of his pony, somehow guiding the animal by this means. Then he and the Indians drove his herd slowly across the Columbia's Big Bend country until, near today's town of Bridgeport, the animals were again driven across the river. Four of Ben's animals drowned in the swift river's current at this crossing.

Ten days were then required to corral the animals up the west side of Osoyoos Lake during which time the animals were plagued by clouds of mosquitoes. There were, of course, no roads as yet built in this region, and rock slides slowed their progress. Another ten days were required in driving the animals up the shores of Okanogan Lake as the group continued north.

Gold, by now, was also being found on the Thompson River. Consequently, by the time Ben reached the site where the city of Kamloops now stands, he had already sold one-quarter of his herd to hungry miners, anxious for their first steak in months. When Ben reached Cache Creek, he found hundreds of prospectors working the sandbars of the Fraser River, thereby enabling him to sell out. The hungry prospectors here reimbursed him for his animals with so much gold dust that he could scarcely carry it all in his pony's saddlebags. On the return trip south, accordingly, Ben was forced to avoid the Columbia River, well knowing that he and his pony would sink beneath the weight of his booty, should he try swimming across it, and be drowned.

The size of Ben's annual cattle drives to the gold fields increased. By 1866, we find him herding nearly one thousand cattle into Montana where new gold fields were opening up. Here he sold beef on the hoof as far east as Deer Lodge at a price of $150 per animal. Soon, however, prices began to decline, rival ranchers having produced an oversupply of beef. A series of severe winters in Eastern Washington drastically diminished Ben's herd.

Always a gambler, however, Snipes continued to increase his business, purchasing herds from less fortunate competitors at depressed prices. It was claimed that by this means, Ben at one time owned one hundred thousand steers. He then branched out into banking.

Even before the Panic of 1893 swept the nation, Snipes had been finding that he had over-expanded. By 1895, one of his former cow hands saw him driving a single cow into Puget Sound's town of Seattle, there to attempt to recover some of the unfortunate investments he had made.

Meanwhile, rival cattle kings had moved into Eastern Oregon. Ranchers there, such as Bill Brown and John Devine, were branding eight thousand or more calves annually from their herds. On his ranch in Donner and Britzen Valley, Peter French had an operation which, upon his death, was valued at nearly $2,000,000.

However by the turn of the century, Mr. Snipes, too, had revived his fortunes. Having brought west from his original home in Iowa his parents, brothers, and sisters, he was again a prosperous and admired man. He died at The Dalles, Oregon, age seventy-one, in 1906.

T

TACOMA (J-8)

No less a personage than George Vancouver, the great British explorer, was the first white man to discover the site where Tacoma now stands, twenty-five miles south of Seattle on Puget Sound. It was in the spring of 1792, and Captain Vancouver's ship *Discovery* was anchored at the southern tip of Bainbridge Island, when early one morning he embarked in his vessel's yawl, then rowed and sailed by members of his crew, he began probing the as-yet undiscovered waterway which lies east of Vashon Island.

The date was May 28, 1792. About noon, they came to today's Dash Point and landed. Here he and his sailors were greeted by Indians whose faces, as he described it, were painted "with Streaks of Red Ochre and Glimmer." They were wearing, he continued, "only animal skins." From here Vancouver looked southeastward and saw the same mountain he had previously seen far away in the distance while sailing into the Strait of Juan de Fuca. Now, he writes, Mount Rainier (as he named this beautiful 14,000 foot snow-capped mountain) loomed overhead seemingly so close one could touch it. It seemed to float in the air, he records.

Then Vancouver invited the Indians to share in the lunch he and his men had brought with them, the main item of fare being the meat of a deer which Vancouver's men had purchased for a sheet of copper from Blake Island Indians who had caught the animal in a net. During the course of this historic luncheon, writes Vancouver, ". . . one of the Chebaulips . . . [this was the name of the local Indians] having taken knife and fork in hand in order to imitate our manner of eating soon found means by which to secrete these items under his garment . . . but upon being detected he gave up the plunder with utmost humour." The Chebaulips' reluctance to eat the deer meat pies, Vancouver then notes with embarrassment, was caused by their suspicion that the pies' contents were cooked from human flesh.

Vancouver continues: "They accompanied us from where we had dined . . . along the beach for several miles." Then, Vancouver concludes, "the two groups separated in the friendliest manner," Vancouver and his sailors presenting the Indians with farewell gifts of "hawk's bells, beads and buttons," the Indians graciously presenting the whites with their "bows, arrows and spears."

Captain Vancouver had come to the Pacific Northwest not only to find the Northwest Passage but also to lay claim to this vast region for King George III of England. The question of Northwest sovereignty, however, was still undecided when in 1841 Commander Charles Wilkes of the American navy led his two ships, the *Vincennes* and the *Porpoise,* into Puget Sound to explore here just as Vancouver had done forty-nine years previous to this.

At this time Americans back east were almost totally indifferent to the remote part of America called the Northwest. "What do we want of this region of savages and wild beasts," Senator Daniel Webster of New Hampshire was orating about this time in the U.S. Senate. Commodore Wilkes had come here not only to survey, but also to make a report which when presented to the White House might change this indifference. Somewhat boldly, he chose to anchor his USS *Vincennes* off Fort Nisqually, just south of Commencement Bay, where the Union Jack flew prominently overhead.

Because Lieutenant Cadwallader Ringgold, in command of Wilkes' second ship, the USS *Porpoise,* officially began Wilkes' survey from the harbor which now serves as the city of Tacoma's seaport, Wilkes named it Commencement Bay. Anchoring his flagship, the USS *Vincennes,* off Fort Nisqually, Wilkes was cordially received at the British post by its chief trader, Alexander Caulfield Anderson, who, at Wilkes' request, provided horses to transport Wilkes and his American entourage south from Puget Sound to visit Dr. John McLoughlin at Fort

Vancouver on the Columbia River. From this capital of the entire region, the white-haired McLoughlin, known as the King of the Columbia, ruled over the Northwest with a firm, though kindly hand.

The city of Tacoma was the creation of the Northern Pacific, and the story of early Tacoma is largely that of this railroad. Ever since 1864 the people of the Northwest had been waiting anxiously for the U.S. government to act upon President Abraham Lincoln's approval that year for transcontinental railroad tracks to be laid across the northern United States into Puget Sound.

When in 1870 the Northern Pacific commenced this project they did so by laying tracks from both ends of the route, and in places in between as well. Almost simultaneously track-layers began their work from Duluth progressing eastward and from Portland proceeding westward. Tracks were laid up the Columbia River along its south bank; also from a point on the Columbia where the Northern Pacific created a town called Kalama northward up the Cowlitz Valley into Puget Sound. Kalama was situated downstream of Portland a few miles on the Columbia's opposite shore.

In order to finance the tracklaying the U.S. government passed laws granting the Northern Pacific free land on either side of the tracks they laid, allowing 25,400 acres of it for each mile the Northern Pacific laid. If there were lands with valuable lumber or mining prospects, the government allowed the Northern Pacific to deviate from a more direct line westward so as to profit accordingly.

Aware that land values boomed wherever they laid the tracks, the N.P. officials frequently, upon approaching an already settled town lying along their path, demanded of its citizens a "donation" which, if refused, would cause the tracks to bypass their town. Aware that the town would thereby become depressed, such town's disappointed residents would find themselves forced to move to some nearby "paper town" created by the railroad overnight, knowing as they did that thereby they would live where the railroad's attendant prosperity would accrue to them.

Even back in 1852, one Nicholas De Lin, aware that a transcontinental locomotive would some day arrive on Puget Sound, came here to claim free land. A skilled artisan and a native of Sweden, Mr. De Lin, previous to arriving where the city of Tacoma now stands, had assisted Michael Simmons, a Kentuckian, in building the waterwheel which ran Troutman's new American settlement to the south of Commencement Bay at Tumwater. De Lin now proceeded to build a similar waterwheel on Commencement Bay. Near the site where Tacoma's Union Railroad Depot still stands De Lin blocked the flow of two small streams with a dam whose flume powered his sawmill. Thus did the city of Tacoma begin. Indians from all over Puget Sound came here to gaze in amazement at De Lin's magnificent operation.

By 1853, De Lin had sawed enough lumber to fill a schooner which sailed that fall from Commencement Bay to the Hawaiian Islands where he sold the cargo at favorable prices. Mr. De Lin prospered. By this time, the U.S. congress was granting three hundred twenty acres of free land to Americans willing to travel over the Rockies to claim Northwest land.

In 1853, accordingly, the Peter Judson family took out a land claim adjacent to De Lin's, thus causing Commencement Bay's south shore to be "populated" all the way to the bay's entrance now called Defiance Point. The Judson family's plot was today's downtown Tacoma. Here they grew wheat and oats.

By then, the ever-increasing influx of whites began to alarm the Indians, particularly after Isaac Stevens, Washington Territory's new governor began forcing these Indians onto so-called "reservations". Soon, several bands of Indians became warlike. After the Battle of Seattle in January, 1856, the De Lins and the Judson's fled Commencement Bay, leaving it in complete possession of the Chebaulips (this being the name of the local band).

Aware that land values would zoom with the approach of the transcontinental railroad, Mr. Job Carr of Indiana came to Puget Sound in 1864, joined soon after by two sons, Anthony and Howard. Recently released from the Union army, all three were veterans of the Civil War just ended. Job had been twice wounded in the fighting, first at Shiloh then at the Battle of Atlanta. Son Howard was captured by the Confederates, and for a year had been jailed in Georgia's infamous Andersonville Prison. Anthony, too, had seen action as a military photographer.

Job's wife, a nurse in the Union army, did not come west with them, she and her husband having recently become estranged. A crystal ball gazer and clairvoyant before becoming a nurse, she is said to have given her clairvoyant powers to her husband when, on Christmas Day 1864, rowing in a small boat in search of a lucky landsite to which transcontinental tracks might be laid, he exclaimed "Eureka, Eureka, this is it!" upon reaching the bluff on top of which the railroad czar Henry Villard was to build his famous hotel in 1877.

Then in 1868, sixty-one-year-old Mr. Morton Matthew McCarver, generally regarded as the father of Tacoma, arrived on Commencement Bay, having ridden here all the way from Portland on an old gray mare. A pompous man of high connections, he liked to be called "General McCarver" by virtue, in years previous, of being head of the state militia in Burlington, Iowa.

Previous to coming here, McCarver had failed in an attempt to lay out a paper town called Linnton (near today's Portland) where, by selling lots, he hoped for riches. Still seeking his pot of gold, he also had failed in attempting to similarly lay out a town in California. This time, here on Commencement Bay, he believed he would hit the jackpot. Backed by Portland bankers, he acquired over fifteen hundred acres.

Meanwhile another transcontinental railroad, the Great Northern, was advancing its tracks westward with view to choosing its terminus on Puget Sound. Residents living where today's cities of Everett, Port Townsend, Anacortes, as well as Seattle began preening their landsite for a sudden city to arise. Lucky Tacoma! Far ahead of its rivals, a railroad train reached this small settlement first. Tantalizingly slow had been the Northern Pacific's railroad workers in laying tracks northward from Kalama, located opposite Portland across the Columbia River, but finally in 1873 a northern Pacific locomotive hissed into the by-now small village.

Hero of all Tacoma's citizens at this point was Mr. George Wright, a Philadelphia Director of the Northern Pacific. Quietly he had bought out Tacoma's former hero, Mr. "Eureka" Carver. It was Mr. Wright's intention to personally embellish his wealth at his future city. Wright's Tacoma Land Company then proceeded to deal nearby Seattleites a severe blow. He would grant any of them free land in his Tacoma if they would move there.

A clever publicist, Wright then proceeded to add further insult. Back east in his native Philadelphia, Wright launched a nationwide publicity campaign inviting all Americans to tour west to Puget Sound to visit the fourteen thousand foot snow-capped mountain which lies between Tacoma and Seattle. To Seattleites' disgust, he proceeded to rename it "Mount Tacoma" on the tourist brochures, thereby desecrating the name Rainier which it had borne ever since its discovery by Vancouver.

Seattleites anger, too, was aroused when, after laying his Northern Pacific railroad tracks up the slopes of Rainier, he refused to allow the tracks to be extended from his Tacoma over the short distance to

Seattle. Gaining control over all the ferry boats on Puget Sound, then
the chief means of transportation in the region, he then arranged the
ferryboat schedules so that any Seattleite wishing to travel to Portland
must take a ferry to Tacoma (so scheduled as to necessitate the traveler
having to spend the night in this hated city before continuing on).
Moreover, the still-Portland-bound traveler, upon arising the next day,
found himself unable to reach Kalama until late in the day, thereby
forced to spend the next night there before finally reaching his
destination on the third day.

Prices for real estate in Tacoma rose to unheard of levels before the
Panic of 1893. But not long afterward, the businessmen of Seattle had
their chance to smirk when the Great Northern Railroad, Wright's
Northern Pacific rival, chose Seattle as its trans-continental terminus.

TATOOSH ISLAND (D-1)

As Captain George Meares (1756–1809) approached this huge high
rock off Cape Flattery at the entrance to Puget Sound on June 30, 1788,
he was seeking sea otter skins of the island's inhabitants. As his tiny
schooner lay off this island, the chief of the Makah tribe, also named
"Tatoosh," put out from the island in a giant canoe paddled by thirty
Makah warriors. Their bodies were bedaubed with black and red ochre
and they were armed with bows and arrows barbed with bone and
large spears pointed with mussel shell, records Meares in his book
titled *Voyages in the Years 1788–1789.* Chief Tatoosh, Meares writes,
proved to be a "surly and forbidding fellow," his face being painted
entirely black "and covered with glittering sand which added to the
fierceness of his appearance," Tatoosh informed Meares that the power
of the Wicanninish nation (who lived up the coast from here on
Vancouver Island) ended here at this island, and that Meares and his
ship were now within the limits of his government which extended
considerably to the south. "On receiving this information," continues
Meares, "we gave him a small present but he did not make us the least
return nor could he be persuaded to let his people trade with us."
Meanwhile, in strange contrast to the unfriendliness of their leader,
Meares' schooner had become surrounded by many canoes, each
holding from twenty to thirty Makahs who, despite their fierce
demeanor, all began to sing "in perfect unison." Continues Meares:

> Situated as we were on a wild and unfrequented coast, in a
> distant corner of the globe far removed from all those friends,
> connections and circumstances which form the charm and

comfort of life, and taking our course, as it were, through a solitary ocean in such a situation, there simple melody of nature, proceeding in unison found its way to our hearts and at the same time awakened and becalmed the painful thought.

From Tatoosh Island, Captain Meares continued sailing southward down the coast trading with the coastal Indians and searching for the long-rumored River of the West, which today we know as the Columbia River. After failing to find it, he then returned north toward Nootka, the base on Vancouver Island from which he had sailed, and which, as headquarters of the fur trade, was the busiest of all the harbors on America's west coast.

Tatoosh Island is named after an Indian deity named Tatoosh; otherwise called Thunderbird. The Mahak Indians worshipped him. So big and powerful was Tatoosh, they believed, that when he flapped his wings he shook mountains and caused earthquakes, and the flashing of his eyes caused lightning. So enormous were his claws that, unlike other birds who caught salmon in theirs, Thunderbird could sweep down from the sky and catch whales.

Tatoosh Island lies one mile north of Cape Flattery. It is the first close-up look at terra firma at which seamen could gaze in entering Puget Sound after weeks or months at sea.

TONASKET (C-17)

Emulating the people of Seattle who named their city after an Indian chieftain, this smaller community, located in eastern Washington (twenty miles south of the Canada border), also chose the name of an Indian leader famous locally in early times. Chief Tonasket first came into prominence during the 1850s when gold prospectors, some of them from as far away as California, were marching by the hundreds past the site where the town of Tonasket now stands, headed into the Fraser River gold fields of British Columbia (then called New Caledonia). As these prospectors passed through the Indian lands around Tonasket they helped themselves to anything they chose, thereby angering the local Indians.

Six miles south of Tonasket, near the small settlement called Janis, is located the famous McLaughlin's Canyon where over two hundred local Indians built fortifications and prepared to ambush an advancing mob of these white men as they headed north. It was following the so-called Battle of McLoughlin's Canyon that Chief Tonasket, then a rather obscure local Indian, came into prominence through the considerable skill which he displayed in treating these whites, thereby restoring peace.

This affair marked Tonasket's rise to the honor of becoming the local Indians' chief. In 1883, Chief Tonasket journeyed with another Indian leader of eastern Washington, Chief Moses of Moses Lake, to Washington, D.C. There the two Indians met with the U.S. Secretary of the Interior and signed documents giving up large amounts of Indian lands in return for monetary and other considerations. Among the latter were a new sawmill, a grist mill, and provisions enabling Tonasket to build an Indian boarding school at the site where Tonasket, the city, now stands.

Thereafter, Chief Tonasket waxed wealthy, owning huge herds of horses which grazed along the banks of the Okanogan River which flows southward past today's city. These animals were so numerous that they could not be counted and, unlike the rest of the local Indians, Tonasket also owned innumerable numbers of cattle as well. When grazing became scarce, Chief Tonasket moved with all his possessions eastward of Tonasket to Curlew Valley, located north of today's town of Republic.

The history of Tonasket, however, goes back to the days when French Canadian voyageurs used to pass by today's city traveling up and down the Okanogan River plying what was then the sole business of white men, namely: the fur trade. Back East in 1810, Mr. John J. Astor, a New York financier and a fur magnate as well, preferring as he did Canadian fur trappers rather than American ones because of their superior experience in the fur trade, lured a group of these Canadians away from Canada's North West Company by offering them higher wages than their Montreal company could afford to pay. Ordering them to go west for him, he directed them to establish the now-famous American fur post called Astoria at the mouth of the Columbia.

Thus the famous Astoria, or Fort Astor, was built in 1811. The following year, having become established there, they decided to tap the interior regions of today's state of Washington of their unlimited supply of beaver, then in great demand back in Europe where beaver hats were stylish. Accordingly, they built for Mr. Astor a fur post where today the town of Brewster now stands, forty-five miles downstream of Tonasket where the Okanogan River flows into the Columbia. Hoisting the Stars and Stripes over it, they called it Fort Okanogan.

Then in 1813, owing to the War of 1812, these same British hirelings of the American Astor, sold their American post at Astoria to some of their former buddies of the North West Company who by now had also come west to establish Spokane House in eastern Washington, their British post. Their excuse for this seeming perfidy (Mr. Astor never forgave them) was that Astoria was about to be captured by a British warship, which in fact did transpire in October of that year.

And so with Astoria's fall to England, its satellite, Fort Okanogan too became a British possession, one belonging to the North West Company of Montreal. In continuing its operation under the auspices of the Union Jack, Fort Okanogan brought a succession of French-Canadian trappers paddling their canoes up the Okanogan River past today's city of Tonasket, heading into the rich fur trapping grounds to the north of here.

Returning with tons of furs carried in bales on the backs of horses, they would again pass the site where Tonasket stands, delivering the furs to Fort Okanogan. Here they would be loaded aboard large Columbia River boats which took them to Fort George, as Astoria was known under the Union Jack. Probably it was one of these French-Canadian voyageurs of that period after whom Tonasket's Bonaparte Creek takes its name, for the great Napoleon Bonaparte was still a hero at this time and consequently his name was popular among Frenchmen.

Located twelve miles northwest of Tonasket is the town of Loomis, so named for Julius Allen Loomis, a former stockbroker from Chicago who in 1885, being "tired of the treachery of bulls and bears," came here to live "the untrammeled life among the wilder, but less dangerous, species." This quotation was written by Mr. Guy Waring who preceded Loomis in living at the site now bearing Loomis' name before moving to establish the town named Winthrop, which lies fifty miles southwest of Loomis.

TOPPENISH (N-14)

"People of the foothills" is the translation of this Indian name. Doubtless, the foothills to which it refers are the Rattlesnake Hills, Horse Heaven Hills, and the Simcoe Mountains which are located closeby this town, twenty miles southeast of Yakima. The Toppenish tribe belonged to the Yakima nation, one of the most powerful of all the Indian groups of the Pacific Northwest. Leader of the Yakima nation was Chief Kamiakin, square-jawed, handsome, and a chieftain who particularly impressed the early white men.

Angered by the trickery used by Washington Territory's diminutive new governor, Isaac I. Stevens, Chief Kamiakin prepared his Yakimas for war. The killing by one of Kamiakin's Indians of Mr. A.J. Bolon, U.S. Indian Agent at The Dalles, sparked the actual outbreak of the fighting. On October 3, 1855, Captain Granville O. Haller marched northward from The Dalles at the head of eighty-four U.S. Army troops into Yakima country. Suddenly, on the second day of the march, Haller and his men found themselves under attack by five hundred or more Yakima warriors, their faces streaked with war paint. The Indians were angered not only over the so-called "peace treaty" which Governor Stevens had wheedled them into foolishly signing, but also at white men seeking gold who by now were trespassing upon the very Yakima lands which the governor promised would be reserved for their exclusive use.

For three days Captain Haller and his whites, despite the superior weapons they possessed, were barely able to fight off their Yakima opponents. Both sides seesawed back and forth between Ahtanum Creek in the north and Toppenish Creek in the south. Then the whites became surrounded by the Yakimas. They also ran out of food and water. Had it not been for the Yakimas' practice of ceasing to fight during the night hours, Haller and his whites would not have been able to make their escape.

News of this humiliation then caused Major Gabriel Rains, senior officer present at Fort Vancouver, to sally forth in revenge, assisted by civilian volunteers. With a force by now numbering seven hundred, the whites under Rains departed The Dalles to attack. Serving under Major Rains at this time was Lieutenant Phil Sheridan and his Dragoons. This was the same Sheridan who later, as General Sheridan, led the cavalry through Shenandoah Valley in the Civil War.

Aware of these superior white forces now opposing him, Chief Kamiakin and his Yakimas laid low, offering the whites only sporadic resistance. Meanwhile, signal fires were being lighted by the Indians along the high peaks of the Cascade Range all the way from Canada south to Spanish California. Indian attacks upon the whites spread south into Oregon. On March 26, 1856, the Indians launched an attack upon The Dalles, the strategic point through which all supplies for whites living east of the Cascade Range were funneled. Only by a narrow margin did this attack fail. Had it been successful, all white settlements in eastern Washington Territory would probably have fallen.

The final defeat of the eastern Washington tribes took place near the site where the city of Spokane now stands. On September 4th, at the battle of Spokane Plains, the combined forces of the eastern Indian tribes were decisively defeated. As a final blow the whites then rounded up and slaughtered about eight hundred of the Indians' horses and livestock. Thereafter, Indian resistance in Washington Territory subsided, only to revive, however, with increased intensity in southern Oregon the following year.

U

UNION GAP (M-14)

Situated three miles south of Yakima (one hundred miles southeast of Seattle) this town was the original site of today's city of Yakima. When, in 1883, railroad officials visited this area preparatory to laying transcontinental tracks past here toward Puget Sound, everyone locally was thrilled at the prospect of seeing their first steam locomotive. To have railroad tracks laid to any Northwest town was a great honor.

Fully aware of this, railroad executives expected generous bribes of the townsfolk toward whose town they were laying tracks. When, in fact, the founding fathers of Old Yakima (today's Union Gap) failed to produce enough, the Northern Pacific officials decided to bypass Union Gap and lay their tracks instead to a site four miles to the north. Here, the railroad officials laid out a "paper town" of their own, subdivided the land into lots, then, well knowing that wherever tracks were laid prosperity followed, they offered such lots free to anyone in Old Yakima willing to move to the newly-created townsite.

Particularly did the merchants of Old Yakima respond with alacrity. Over one hundred buildings, including Old Yakima's sole bank and hotel, were moved to the new railroad town closeby, this move effected by means of trucks and rollers. Old Yakima's several saloons likewise responded, and they conducted business as usual, it is said, while enroute. Old Yakima was left in a state of shock and shambles.

What little remained of Old Yakima after this mass exodus then became known as Union Gap, presumably because of the local gap in nearby Ahtanum Ridge. The word "union" expressed, perhaps, the wish to someday be united with North Yakima, long since renamed Yakima. Today it is hard for a stranger to tell where the city of Yakima stops and Union Gap begins.

The Indians who lived in the neighborhood where Union Gap now stands were members of the largest of the tribal groups who then occupied eastern Washington, namely the Yakima tribe. The Yakimas prided themselves as being "horse Indians" in contrast to the Puget Sound tribes whom they characterized disdainfully as "canoe Indians."

The most impressive of the Yakima leaders was Chief Kamiakin. Impressed with the white men's strange ways, in 1847 Kamiakin requested a lay worker at the Whitman mission station, William Gray, to establish a missionary station on the Ahtanum River which flows past Union Gap. When this request was ignored, Kamiakin welcomed the arrival here of Father Charles M. Pandosy, who erected a Catholic mission closeby Chief Kamiakin's own home on this stream's banks. Kamiakin even attended this mission school.

We know, too, that Chief Kamiakin was friendly to Dr. John McLoughlin, head of the Hudson's Bay Company headquarters known as Fort Vancouver located on the lower Columbia River. In 1840 Kamiakin drove a large herd of his horses across Klickitat Valley to Fort Vancouver where Dr. McLoughlin received him cordially. In exchange for Kamiakin's horses McLoughlin gave the Yakima chief several of the strange (to Kamiakin) animals called steers with which the Indian returned, thereafter to become the owner of large cattle herds three decades before such cattle kings as Ben Snipes, Peter French, and John Devine commenced ranching in the Northwest.

Chief Kamiakin attended the great powwow held at Walla Walla in May, 1855, at which more than five thousand Indians were in attendance. As one of the leading chieftains present, he placed his mark upon the so-called "peace treaty" drawn up by Governor Isaac Stevens, although perhaps he was already aware (along with other Indian leaders present) that Stevens was speaking with a "forked tongue." Historians believe, accordingly, he may have signed the treaty with tongue-in-cheek, for by now the wagon train emigrants of the Oregon Trail were overrunning Indian lands in large numbers.

Kamiakin became angry the following October when white men prospecting for gold overran the Yakima tribe's lands set aside under the provisions of Stevens' treaty for the Indians exclusive use. With the arrival soon afterward of Captain George McClellan (later General McClellan of Civil War fame) at the head of fifty-six surveyors searching for an opening through the Cascade Range over which to lay railroad tracks into Puget Sound, trespassing on the same land Stevens had promised would be barred to white men, Kamiakin became convinced the Indians must fight.

Using harassment and delay tactics rather than decisive confrontation, Chief Kamiakin led his Yakima warriors to decisive victory over Major Haller in the summer of 1855, and in all likelihood he was the initiator of the Indians' brilliant surprise attack upon white settlements at the Cascades which followed. Wisely he avoided confrontation with the overwhelming forces under Major Gabriel Rains which then swept Yakima Valley. They burned Father Pandosy's Mission on Ahtanum Creek and also Kamiakin's beautiful home there. Thereafter, Chief Kamiakin becomes a shadowy figure in the fighting which ensued, although he probably was a leader in much of it. Unlike other Indian leaders, Kamiakin managed to escape death by fleeing into the Rockies.

The first whites to live at Union Gap were the John Nelson family of Indiana. They moved to Missouri before deciding to travel to the remote region where land was being given away called "Oregon." They crossed the Rocky Mountains in 1847 with the largest wagon train as yet attempting the three-month trip by ox cart, some 4,700 men, women, and children making the journey that year. Initially they resided in the Willamette Valley.

Then in 1864, since this area had in their opinion become too overcrowded, the Nelsons moved north of the Columbia River, at this time a region inhabited only by Indians. They built a log cabin where Richland now stands. Here, however, the Indians stole their horses and threw tomahawks into their cabin's door. So they moved to the site of the present town of Moxee, the first white settlement in Yakima Valley. Surprised to find two log cabins already erected here occupied by the Fielding Thorpe and Moses Splawn families, they then moved to the site where Union Gap now stands, wishing to occupy land still farther away from white neighbors. Here they continued for generations.

VANCOUVER (Q-7)

This is perhaps the most historic city in all the Pacific Northwest. It is situated on the right bank of the Columbia River opposite Portland. Captain George Vancouver, after whom the city of Vancouver takes its name, never viewed the site of this metropolis but his chief assistant, Lieutenant Commander William Broughton did.

Rowed by sailors of his sailing ship, the armed tender *Chatham,* 135-tons, Broughton passed the site where Vancouver now stands on 28 October, 1792, the first white man ever to reach this far upstream. Somewhere near the mouth of what we now call Sandy River on the eastern outskirts of Portland, Broughton and his oarsmen landed, then held formal ceremony claiming as a possession of King George III of England not only the Columbia River itself but also all of the river's surrounding regions.

It was a rather brazen act for, as Broughton at this time well knew, a Yankee fur trader named Robert Gray five months prior to this had been the first white man to enter the Columbia River. While, being a fur trader, he probably never held a ceremony such as Broughton's, he could have done so, rightly claiming the Columbia River and all its surrounding regions for George Washington, then the President of the United States.

Captain Gray and Commander Broughton, as well, had sailed here from a place up the northwest coastline, located on Vancouver Island, then believed to be a part of the mainland, for as yet there were no maps in the region. It was called Nootka. Here in the summer of 1792 Broughton's superior, Captain George Vancouver, had spent weeks negotiating with Senor Bodega y Quadra, a Spanish naval officer, over the question of how Spain and England were to share Nootka, then the capital of the Pacific Northwest. In this effort they had been unsuccessful and therefore they had agreed that their only course of action remaining was to send back to their respective headquarters in Madrid and London for further instructions as to how to proceed.

Within weeks following Commander Broughton's sally up the Columbia and his claiming of the river for England, he traveled overland by donkey across Mexico to Vera Cruz and then by sailing ship back to England, carried Vancouver's request for further instructions from The British Foreign Office.

This Columbia River city is named for the same George Vancouver after whom both Vancouver Island and British Columbia's city of Vancouver are also named. One of the great explorers of the world, George Vancouver was born at Kings Lynn, located one hundred miles north of London in East Anglia, in the year 1857.

Kings Lynn, at the time, was England's third largest seaport and doubtless the many sailing ships young Vancouver saw tied up here influenced him in his choice to make a career for himself in the British Royal Navy. Young Goerge was of Dutch lineage, his grandfather's name being Van Couiverden. It is believed that a friend of Vancouver's father, Dr. Charles Burney, was responsible for young Vancouver's appointment.

In 1771, Dr. Burney chanced to go from Kings Lynn to London where he was a guest of the Earl of Sandwich, then First Lord of the Admiralty. Here he met Captain James Cook, recently returned from his sensational trip to Tahiti and the South Seas during which he observed the transit of Venus, then surveyed New Zealand before returning home via the Cape of Good Hope to a welcome comparable to that received by modern astronauts after visiting the moon.

It was through Cook's influence, as a result of this visit, that at the age of fourteen George Vancouver commenced his sea career as a seaman aboard Cook's ship the *Resolute* on the great explorer's second foray into the Pacific's southern waters.

As young Vancouver soon discovered, it was to be a career of great hardship involving absence from loved ones for years at a time and involving many months at a time spent at sea. Tempers flared and discipline was severe under the rigorous conditions involved. Sleeping quarters below the decks of the small ships then used were lit only by candles and ventilation was poor. During the nine months required to reach Tahiti, six were spent at sea. Scurvy was common and, as Vancouver was later to discover in the West Indies, yellow fever caused hundreds of deaths.

Nevertheless, doubtlessly Vancouver felt lucky in his chosen career, for it was a day when distant lands awaited discovery and fame for accomplishing it, and appointments such as his were eagerly sought by members of England's upper class. With Captain Cook, on this voyage young Vancouver discovered the Cook Islands, the Marquesas, Tonga, and New Hebrides.

Again with Captain Cook, now having received promotion to the rank of second lieutenant, young George sailed from England in 1776 on Cook's "Third Voyage," this one to be his last. After again stopping in Tahiti, they discovered the Sandwich Islands before sailing to the coasts of then-remote Northwest America. It was following Captain Cook's search in sailing up these northwest coasts to find an opening through the American continent that he was killed by Hawaiian natives on the Kona Coast.

Upon the return of the two ships to England under the command of Captain Clerke, young George served on the West Indies Station, then a hotbed of warfare between England and France. On board His Majesty's Ship *Fame,* Vancouver saw action in the Battle of Saints.

Lieutenant Vancouver then returned to England and was appointed to HMS *Europa,* a two-tiered ship carrying fifty guns. In this vessel he returned to the West Indies. Here serving under Captain Alan Gardner, Vancouver achieved a reputation as an outstanding surveyor. It was largely due to Gardner's high regard for him that in April, 1790, Captain Vancouver, now promoted to this rank by virtue of his forthcoming assignment, sailed from Falmouth, England, at age thirty-three, with orders to proceed to the still largely unexplored northwest coasts of America. His mission was not only to fill in the gaps in mapping this remote region's coatlines left unfinished by Captain Cook, but also to carry out a very delicate diplomatic mission.

Recently Spain and England had nearly gone to war over Spain's seizure (along these coasts at a place called Nootka) of three English ships, which, anchored in Nootka's harbor, had disobeyed the orders while there of a mad Spaniard named Estevan Martinez, thereby incurring his disfavor. Refusal by these English fur traders to comply with Governor Martinez' orders had caused a war between the two nations to be imminent. In the Treaty of Nootka which prevented open eruption of violence between the two nations, it was agreed that each nation would send a representative to Nootka to arrange how this base would be shared equally by the two nations.

Arriving on this mission at Nootka in the late summer of 1791, having spent a year in the interim since leaving England in exploring more regions of the South Pacific, Vancouver in his flagship HMS *Discovery* accompanied by the armed tender *Chatham*, commanded by Lieutenant Commander Broughton, arrived and dropped anchor in Nootka's harbor, called Friendly Cove. Here Vancouver, as expected, found a Spanish representative, Senor Bodega y Quadra, awaiting him with new provisos which the Spanish viceroy in Mexico City had superimposed during the year Vancouver had been enroute here. Vancouver, in addition to dividing Nootka equally between the two nations, must also agree, he was told by Quadra, to the establishment by Spain of a naval base at the entrance to Puget Sound. It was at this point that Vancouver decided to dispatch one of his officers, Lieutenant Mudge, back to England to request further advice from the British Foreign Office. Senor Quadra, too, sent a courier back to Mexico City to advise the viceroy of New Spain of their disagreement.

Agreeing, however, that during the interim period while awaiting further instruction from their superiors friendlier relations should be established with the local Nootka Indians, Vancouver and Quadra were successful enough that the leading Nootka chieftain invited them to a party. The writer of the following description of this affair was Edward Bell, one of Vancouver's subordinates who accompanied Vancouver and Quadra on this occasion. Herewith he is describing entertainment which followed the dinner itself:

> Maquinna, dancing, now entered, dressed in a very rich garment of Otter skins with a round Black Hat and a Mask on and with a fanciful petticoat or apron, around which was suspended hollow tubes of Copper and Brass and which, as he danced, by striking against each other made a wonderful tinkling noise. After dancing thus some time in the course of which he play'd some Pantmimical [sic] tricks with his hat and Mask, he returned and two more songs were sung by the Performers, to which they danced. (Bell, Edward, *A New Vancouver Journal on the Discovery of Puget Sound, by a Member of the Chatham's Crew.* Edited by E.S. Meany, Seattle, 1915)

Through the summer of 1792, both Quadra and Vancouver waited to receive from their respective superiors their instructions as to how to proceed. Then in the fall of 1792, no responses having been forthcoming, Senor Quadra departed south back to his headquarters in lower California; not, hoever, before arranging to meet with Vancouver at a later date at Monterey. On the eve of his departure Quadra asked Vancouver "to commemorate our meeting and the very friendly intercourse that has taken place between us" by placing upon British maps ". . . some port or island named after both of us." To this request Vancouver responded by giving to the island where Nootka still stands today the name "Quadra's and Vancouver's Island." Later the name was shortened by the Hudson's Bay Company to "Vancouver Island." The island is now the site of Victoria which is the capitol of British Columbia.

It was not until 1795 that Captain Vancouver and his expedition returned to England, the interim having been spent surveying Alaskan waters and returning to Hawaii to survey there each winter. In these islands Vancouver became a good friend of King Kamehameha, gaining his favor by bringing him sheep, cattle, and other domestic animals from California, ones never seen before in the Hawaiian Islands. In response to this generosity Kamehameha offered to cede the Hawaiian Islands to England, an offer which Vancouver accepted.

Meanwhile, Senor Quadra having died and the Spanish viceroy in Mexico City having replaced him with one Jose Manuel de Alava, word was received soon after by Alava from the Spanish viceroy that the Nootka dispute had been settled back in Europe. Reassured of this news while in Monterey, Captain Vancouver then led his expedition homeward.

Napoleonic Wars now preoccupied the British government; indeed England declared war upon France even as Vancouver and his two ships were nearing England. Despite the colossal task he had accomplished, Vancouver's reception at London was a cold one. Back in 1794, while anchored off Hawaii, Vancouver had ordered off his flagship a young nobleman, Midshipman Thomas Pitt, for refusing to obey orders and for creating disturbances aboard this ship. By the time of Vancouver's arrival in England, Lord Pitt (having returned before him) had stirred up trouble for his former commanding officer, and at the highest governmental levels.

Vancouver's health, as a result of his months of surveying in open boats under the severest weather, was failing. Bitter over the treatment accorded him by his superiors in London, unable even to obtain governmental funds with which to complete the publishing of his expedition's report, Captain Vancouver died in obscurity, age forty-one. Even today Vancouver's surveys and maps of the intricate coasts of the Pacific Northwest are regarded as masterpieces of accuracy, particularly considering the instruments available in his day. He was unquestionably one of the greatest of England's navigators.

The city of Vancouver traces its history back to 1825, when Sir George Simpson, governor of all Hudson's Bay Company activities in Canada, established a fur post called Fort Vancouver here. The following is Sir George's description of the ceremonies attending this occasion:

> Sat. Mar 19th—At Sun rise mustered all the people to hoist the Flag Staff of the new Establishment and in the presence of the Gentlemen, Servants, Chiefs & Indians, I Baptised it by breaking a Bottle of Rum on the Flag Staff and repeating the following words in a loud voice: "In behalf of the Honble Hudson's Bay Co'y I hereby name this Establishment Fort Vancouver God Save King George the 4th" with three Cheers Gave a couple of Drams to the people and Indians on the occasion . . . The object of naming this fort after that distinguished navigator George Vancouver is to identify our claim to the Soil and Trade with his discovery of the Columbia River and the Coast on behalf of Gt Britian . . . If the Honble Committee in London do not approve the Name it

can be altered. At 9 o'Clock A.M. took leave of our Friend
[Simpson here refers to the venerable Dr. John McLoughlin
whom he left in charge of Fort Vancouver], embarked and
continued our Voyage. Put up for the night 20 miles below
Cascade Portage. (George Simpson's Journal as contained in
Frederick Merk's, *Fur Trade and Empire*, Cambridge, 1968)

At this time, England and the United States were sharing sovereignty
over all of the Pacific Northwest pending some future date when they
could agree how to divide the region. Believing as he did that the
Northwest would eventually be divided by giving England all the lands
north of the Columbia, the Americans to own all territory south of this
stream, Governor Simpson chose the site for Fort Vancouver, situating it
on the north bank of the river, in the hope it would serve to emphasize
this belief.

As the first chief factor of Fort Vancouver, Sir George chose Dr. John
McLoughlin (1784-1867), a handsome, white haired giant of a man with
such leadership qualities that he soon became known as "King of the
Columbia". Under McLoughlin's rule, Fort Vancouver became the
collection point to which furs from as far north as Russian Alaska and
as far south as Spanish California were transported on the backs of
horses and by canoe. From Fort Vancouver these furs were shipped
overseas to England and to China.

Fort Vancouver boasted a population of over six hundred souls when
commencing *circa* 1840. American homesteaders began pouring down
the banks of the Columbia River to take up free land in Willamette
Valley which lies to the south of McLoughlin's Fort Vancouver a few
miles. Many of these wagon train folk, having spent three months in
reaching here from the East via the Oregon Trail, were destitute, some
starving and many without the wherewithal to survive in this new part
of the world. For Dr. McLoughlin's compassion in providing them with
these necessities, he was criticized by his superior in the HBC, Sir
George Simpson. The latter's orders to McLoughlin were to discourage
all American settlement in the Pacific Northwest. In 1845, Dr.
McLoughlin, angered by this criticism and a bitter man, was forced to
resign as Fort Vancouver's ruler. Building himself a house just south of
Fort Vancouver at the site where Oregon City now stands, he became a
U.S. citizen.

With the signing by the United States and England of a Boundary
Treaty dividing the Pacific Northwest into two regions, one north of the
forty-ninth parallel of latitude belonging to England, the other lying

south of this borderline belonging to the United States, the Hudson's Bay Company moved Fort Vancouver north to the site where British Columbia's city of Victoria now stands.

By 1852, a U.S. Army post called Vancouver Barracks had replaced McLoughlin's original Fort Vancouver. Its first commanding officer was the famous Benjamin Louis Eulalie de Bonneville, about whom the author Washington Irving writes in his famous book *Adventures of Captain Bonneville* (Boston, 1977). In the years which followed, Vancouver Barracks served as the duty station of many other distinguished U.S. Army leaders, among these: Ulysses S. Grant, Commander of Union Forces in the Civil War and later President of the United States, Phillip H. Sheridan, another distinguished Union general in the Civil War, famous for his intrepid cavalry rides through Shenandoah Valley against Confederate General Jubal A. Early; George B. McClellan, another distinguished Union general in the Civil War who was fired by President Abraham Lincoln for his lack of aggressiveness; George Armstrong Custer, who along with his two hundred and sixty-four soldiers died in the Battle of Little Big Horn, killed by Sioux Indians; General E.R.S. Canby, killed through the treachery of Chief Keintpoos of the Modoc tribe in Southern Oregon; and, in later years, George C. Marshall, Chief of U.S. Army troops in World War II.

The city of Vancouver which grew from this U.S. Army post was initially called Columbia City. Commencing *circa* 1852 and continuing for nearly a decade Columbia City was the leading commercial center of Washington Territory, even after the territorial capitol was transferred to Olympia. The name Vancouver was applied here *circa* 1853.

VASHON ISLAND (I-8)

Puget Sound, in which this island is situated is an amazing composition of bays, passages, and cul-de-sacs set against the Olympic Mountains for a background. This particular island, eleven miles long, lies just south of Bainbridge Island—with which it shares honors in its role today as a bedroom community where Seattle business people retire after each day's work. Ten miles long it lies between Seattle and Tacoma separated from the mainland by a waterway called East Passage.

Down East Passage toward the present city of Tacoma in May, 1792, sailed George Vancouver, captain of His Majesty's sloop-of-war *Discovery,* a vessel of 330 tons with a fifteen foot draft. The *Discovery* at this time was anchored at the southern tip of Bainbridge Island which lies immediately north of Vashon Island. Several days prior to this Vancouver had dispatched from the *Discovery* Lieutenant Peter Puget, also to proceed south into these as-yet unexplored waters, with Master Joseph Whidbey and a crew of the *Discovery's* sailors, to see where they led. Now Vancouver in the *Discovery's* yawl had decided to also explore these mysterious waters to see for himself what they contained.

Captain James Vashon (1742–1827), after whom Vancouver named this island, had recently been Vancouver's commanding officer. Prior to becoming commander of the exploration to these northwest coasts, Vancouver had been serving aboard Captain Vashon's warship in the waters off Jamaica, West Indies. This warship, HMS *Europa,* 50 guns, was one of the finest in the British navy and it served as flagship for Admiral Alan Gardner, the man who had selected Vancouver to become the leader of the exploration in which Vancouver was now engaged. Today the city of Everett's harbor is called Port Gardner after Admiral Gardner.

Captain Vashon's career in the British Navy was also a long and distinguished one, from 1755 when he entered His Majesty's service at the age of thirteen, until 1814 when he was retired with the rank of Admiral, age seventy-two. Vashon's wife was a sister of Admiral Peter Rainier after whom, about the same time as he named Vashon Island, Vancouver named Mount Rainier, the 14,000 foot mountain which looms up to the southeastward of Vashon Island, forty-five miles away. Vashon's niece, moreover, was the wife of Lieutenant Joseph Baker after whom also about this same time, Vancouver named 10,750 foot high Mount Baker which lies ninety-five miles northeastward of Vashon Island.

At the southern end of Vashon Island is Maury Island, so named for William L. Maury, an officer of the Wilkes Expedition which followed the Vancouver Expedition in exploring Puget Sound forty-nine years later (in 1841). Like Vancouver's British expedition, Commodore Wilkes' American expedition was a globe-circling one. While in the Fiji Islands in 1840, young Maury led a contingent of U.S. sailors in burning a Fijian village; this in order to avenge the Fijians' killing the day before of Midshipman Wilkes Henry of the Wilkes Expedition by these Fijians. Young Henry was a nephew of Commodore Wilkes.

In May, 1841, Commodore Charles Wilkes of the American navy likewise sailed southward past Vashon Island and anchored his flagship, the USS *Vincennes,* a sloop of war of 780 tons displacement, off Nisqually Flats lying southward of Vashon Island. He then assigned his own personal boat, normally used only by himself, called a gig, to be used by one of his subordinates, Lieutenant George Sinclair, to survey the waters adjacent to Vashon Island. It was while so engaged that Lieutenant Sinclair discovered and named Gig Harbor after the boat in which he was exploring. Gig Harbor lies westward of Vashon Island's southern end.

Colvos Passage is the name of the waterway which runs along Vashon Island's west side. It separates the island from what is known as The Great Peninsula which, but for a narrow neck of land at our present town of Belfair, would constitute a huge island, almost fifty miles in length and in some places as much as twenty-five miles wide. The person after whom Wilkes named Colvos Passage was really named George W. Colvocoressis, called Colvos for short.

In surveying Colvos Passage, Midshipman Colvocoressis also used a small boat of the USS *Vincennes.* Of his experiences while surveying Colvos Passage, he writes: "On leaving the Vincennes we were warned to be on the watch for the Puget Sound Indians, as they were arrant thieves, but I am not aware they ever attempted to take anything from us, except one of the eye pieces to our theodolite."

Midshipman Colvos goes on to state that this eye piece was recovered through the kindness of "a Mr. Anderson," the same Alexander Caulfield Anderson after whom present Anderson Island, seventeen miles south of Vashon Island, is named. Mr. Anderson, a fur trader of the Hudson's Bay Company, was at this time in charge of the British fur headquarters called Nisqually House. Colvos continues: "I observed the Indian men were well supplied with muskets, fowling pieces and knives which they procure from the Hudson's Bay Company at Fort Nisqually in exchange for furs. They also had bows and arrows, and the latter were pointed with iron."

Mr. Colvos, a native of Greece, was raised in Vermont before joining the U.S. Navy. During the Civil War he fought in the Union Army.

Quartermaster Harbor, formed by the proximity of Vashon Island's southernmost end to Maury Island, also was named by the American explorer Wilkes in the summer of 1841. Although "quartermaster" is originally an army name, used to designate a soldier who is involved in logistical matters, in the U.S. Navy a quartermaster is a sailor who steers the ship, adjusts compasses, and assists generally in matters related to the navigation of his vessel.

There were, in all, six ships in the Wilkes Expedition, only two of which, however, visited Puget Sound. In bestowing the name Quartermaster Harbor here, Wilkes was honoring all the expeditions' quartermasters, and to the two promontories guarding the entrance to Quartermaster Harbor he gave the names Neill Point and Point Piner, Neill and Piner being the names of the two quartermasters serving aboard his flagship.

VENDOVI ISLAND (C-7)

Of the many islands in Puget Sound this one is probably one of the least known. It lies at the entrance to Bellingham Bay and is named after a Fijian chieftain named Vendovi. Commodore Charles Wilkes, U.S.N., captured Vendovi while the Wilkes globe circling expedition was exploring the Fiji Islands in 1840. The Fijians at this time practiced cannibalism and Vendovi, one of these islands' leading chieftains, probably participated in this practice. However, Commodore Wilkes chose to punish Vendovi because, as he learned from the natives soon after anchoring in these islands, Chief Vendovi had murdered all of the American crew members of an American sailing ship named the *Charles Daggett* eight years prior to Wilkes arrival here when the *Daggett* was anchored off Vendovi's island headquarters.

At the time (1841) when Wilkes applied Vendovi's name to this Bellingham Bay island, the Fijian chieftain was being held a captive aboard Wilkes' flagship, the USS *Vincennes,* and was being taken by Wilkes back to the United States to be tried for the murder of the whaling ship *Daggett's* captain and crew. At this time Chief Vendovi, though a prisoner, was still regally defiant. Before his arrest by Wilkes, he had been one of the most powerful of all the Fijian chieftains, and possessed fifty wives and slaves as members of his retinue. Chief

Vendovi died of pneumonia in 1842, three days after the Wilkes Expedition reached New York City.

Also while Wilkes was visiting the Fiji Islands in 1841, he burned down a native village on Malolo Island because he suspected that members of this village had stolen one of the USS *Vincennes'* boats. It was probably in revenge for this act that these villagers, several days later, killed Commodore Wilkes' teen-age nephew, Wilkes Henry by name. On the eve of the expedition's start in the States, in 1838, Wilkes' sister had begged her brother to allow the boy, her son, to go on the globe-circling trip. Young Henry was killed by the natives while beaching his boat to sightsee on one of the nearby islands. In honor of the young lad, Wilkes applied the name Henry Island in 1841 to another small island in Puget Sound. Henry Island is also the name of a small atoll in the Fiji Group where Henry lies buried.

W

WAIILATPU (O-21)

This is the place where lived Dr. Marcus Whitman (1802–1847), who is credited with having "saved Oregon from the British." Today we know this to be an exaggeration of history but it is not at all without justice that Dr. Whitman is now enshrined in the rotunda of our national capitol in Washington. Perhaps more historical research will reveal that Dr. Whitman in fact, through interviews with President Tyler, Secretary Daniel Webster, and others, prevented the cession to England of the American claim to Oregon, thereby preventing today's Pacific Northwest from being traded for a codfishery on Newfoundland.

Located eight miles west of Walla Walla in southeastern Washington, *Waiilatpu* in the Indian tongue means "place of the rye grass." Here in the fall of 1836 Dr. Whitman and his twenty-eight-year old wife, Narcissa, commenced their attempts to bring Christianity to the local Indians. On Whitman's first trip west in 1835, the members of the caravan with which he traveled became ill of cholera, but thanks to Whitman's medical skills (he was a doctor before becoming a missionary) all but three of the party with which he was traveling survived.

At the annual fur trappers' rendezvous which was held that year at Green River (in today's state of Wyoming), Dr. Whitman is remembered for his removal of a three-inch barbed Indian arrowhead from the back of Jim Bridger, the famous mountain man, thereby awing the Indians with his skill as a "medicine man." The following year, Dr. Whitman was accompanied on his trip west by his bride, the beautiful blue-eyed blonde of shapely figure who soon became the center of such widespread appreciation, particularly by the Indians who had never seen a white female before; also by the grizzled white men of the Rockies, known as mountain men, who had been away from civilization here engaged in trapping furs for years.

Intense hardship awaited the Whitmans upon their choice of Waiilatpu on which to erect their buildings. Unwittingly, the site chanced to be on land belonging to the local Walla Walla chief, and for their failure to ask of him permission to build upon it he proved unfriendly. Here at Waiilatpu they built a church, an Indian school, a small hospital, and a grist mill; also raised horses, cattle, pigs, and sheep. Also, they grew rye, oats, and barley. But insofar as their attempts to bring Christianity to the natives, their efforts were not successful. In 1839 their first-born child, Alice Clarissa Whitman, accidentally drowned in the nearby Walla Walla River.

Commencing in 1843, there began arriving each summer at their mission a long succession of Oregon Trail emigrants, passing through in their covered wagons enroute to the Willamette Valley on the lower Columbia. Not only did these visitors heavily tax the Whitmans' limited facilities and supplies, but they also angered the local Indians who feared they would soon settle upon local lands as well. These newcomers, moreover, brought with them the dreaded illness called cholera, and it soon spread among the local Cayuse.

Among these new arrivals at Waiilatpu was a part white-blooded Indian named Joe Lewis. Bitter at the treatment he had been accorded back East in Maine by the whites, Lewis spread discontent even further among the local Cayuse. Soon he was telling them that Dr. Whitman, in his frantic attempts to save the Indians from cholera, was not really doing so but instead was deliberately poisoning them. In the eyes of these Indians moreover any "medicine man" who failed to save their lives must himself die.

The climax came on the early afternoon of Monday, November 29, 1847. At the time of the tragedy nearly seventy whites, most of them Oregon Trail emigrants, were crowded into the small Whitman compound. At this moment, Chief Tilokaikt and a fellow Cayuse knocked on the Whitmans' door and asked for medicine. As Dr.

Whitman turned his back to go and obtain it, he was struck over the head with a hatchet, and the bloodshed commenced. Narcissa Whitman, hit by an Indian bullet, lay wounded while innumerable Cayuse swarmed onto the mission grounds, shooting, butchering and setting fire. When the carnage was over, fourteen whites including Narcissa lay dead. Another forty-seven whites, mostly children, were taken prisoner by the Indians. Only ten managed to escape.

On the day before this tragedy, a fellow missionary of Dr. Whitman, Reverend Henry Spalding, had arrived at Waiilatpu from his own mission station to the northeast of here called Lapwai, near today's city of Lewiston. He had come here with his ten-year-old daughter named Eliza to place her in the Whitman school. It so happened on the same day of Spalding's arrival that Dr. Whitman received word from Indians southwest of Waiilatpu near the mouth of the Umatilla River (near present Hermiston) of a sick Indian girl in need of emergency medical attention. At this same location a rival Catholic mission had recently been established by Father John Baptiste Brouillet. It was decided that Reverend Spalding would accompany Whitman on the trip to assist the Indian girl; also so that the two Protestant missionaries might visit with Father Brouillet and inspect his recently established mission.

While riding together from Waiilatpu to the Umatilla River, Reverend Spalding's horse stumbled causing him to suffer a fall. The damage to his leg which resulted was so severe that when Dr. Whitman returned to Waiilatpu on the following day, having administered to the sick Indian girl, Henry Spalding remained behind to recuperate. Thus was Spalding spared a terrible death on the afternoon of the twenty-ninth, the following day, when the Whitman massacre took place.

When news of the terrible event reached Father Brouillet, at the risk of his own life he rushed over to Waiilatpu to help. Aware that there was little of an immediate nature he could do, Brouillet then rushed back to his own Umatilla mission to warn Reverend Spalding that his life was in danger. By now the entire Cayuse tribe seemed to be on the warpath. Despite his injured leg Reverend Spalding mounted a horse and headed back to his own mission station at Lapwai, fearful for the safety of his wife, also named Eliza, and the two remaining children.

Forced to take a circuitous route, one night Spalding was hiding in the darkness from the Indians when his horse wandered away. Accordingly the last leg of his journey to Lapwai found him wandering through deep snow in a crazed condition. At Lapwai, he found his wife and children safe. Friendly Lapwai Indians had hidden them in their own home.

Weeks later, Spalding's daughter, Eliza, who had survived the Whitman massacre, was returned to the Spaldings, thanks to a British official of the Hudson's Bay Company at Fort Vancouver. Upon hearing of the tragedy, Mr. Peter Skene Ogden of this organization, at the risk of his own life, had journeyed up the banks of the Columbia River to serve as an intermediary between the Cayuse and the Americans. For the return of Spalding's daughter, Eliza, and the other Americans whom the Cayuse had taken captive, Mr. Ogden paid the Cayuse sixty-two blankets, sixty-three cotton shirts, twelve Hudson Bay rifles, six hundred loads of ammunition, seven pounds of tobacco and twelve flints.

The Cayuse War continued for more than two years. Finally in June, 1850, Chief Tilokaikt and five of his fellow-Cayuse were hanged at Oregon City following a trial presided over by Oregon's Supreme Court Justice Orville C. Pratt.

WALLA WALLA (O-21)

The name of this southeastern Washington city used to be the butt of a cheap joke made by Eastern dudes visiting this recently-discovered part of the United States. "Walla," they exclaimed in visiting here, "Why repeat such a silly-sounding word twice?"

That "walla walla" is basically an onomatopeic name is borne out by etymologists who believe it imitates the sound of the Walla Walla River which flows by the town. Further substantiating this is the fact that in China the motor taxis used in transporting persons between Hong Kong and nearby Kowloon are called "walla wallas" simulating the sound of the churning waters made by these boats in plying between the two points. According to Father Charles M. Pandosy, one of the earliest of the missionaries of Washington, the name Walla Walla comes from the Indian word *wana* which means "river" and repetition of the word *(wana wana)* diminuizes the word; hence "little river," given locally to the Walla Walla River. To the white men's ears *wana wana* sounded like *walla walla,* and thus this city's name has come into being.

As thousands more whites continued to pour into the Pacific Northwest the Indians feared they would soon lose all of their land to these newcomers. Then in May, 1855, Washington Territory's recently appointed territorial governor, Isaac Stevens, held a famous conference with the Indians which was held at the site where the city of Walla Walla now stands. Over five thousand Indians attended, representing virtually all of the tribes of Eastern Washington. One of Governor Stevens' young military aides, Lieutenant Lawrence Kip, has left us the following description of this dramatic affair:

Wednesday, May 23, 1855—At two o'clock P.M. we arrived at the ground selected for the Council . . . one of the most beautiful spots of the Walla Walla Valley, well wooded and with plenty of water. Ten miles distant is seen the range of the Blue Mountains stretching away along the horizon into the dim distance . . . [and on the following day] About 2,500 of the Nez Perce tribe have arrived. It was our first specimen of this Prairie chivalry and it certainly realized all our conceptions of these wild warriors of the plains. Their coming was announced about ten o'clock and, going on the plain to where a flagstaff had been erected, we saw them approaching in the distance on horseback in one long line. They were almost entirely naked, gaudily painted and decorated with their wild trappings. Their plumes fluttered above them, while below, skins and trinkets and all kinds of fantastic embellishments flaunted in the sunshine. Trained from early childhood to live upon horseback, they sat upon their fine animals as if they were centaurs. Their horses too were arrayed in the most glaring finery. They were painted with such colors as formed the greatest contrast; the white being smeared with crimson in fantastic figures and the dark colors streaked with white clay . . . Beads and fringes of gaudy colors were hanging from their bridles while plumes of eagle feathers interwoven with the mane and tail fluttered as the breeze swept over them, and completed the wild and fantastic appearance . . . When about a mile distant they halted, and half of dozen chiefs rode forward and were introduced to Governor Stevens and General Palmer, in order of their rank. Then on came the rest of the wild horse-men in single file clashing their shields and singing and beating their drums as they marched past us. Then they formed a circle and dashed around us, while our little group stood there, the center of their wild evolution. They would gallop up as if about to make a charge, then wheel around and round, sounding their loud whoops until they had apparently worked themselves up into an intense excitement. Then some score or two dismounted and, forming a ring, danced for about twenty minutes while those surrounding them beat time on their drums. After these performances, more than twenty of the chiefs went over to the tent of Governor Stevens where they sat for some times smoking the "pipe of peace", in token of good fellowship, and then returned to their camping ground. (Kip, L., *The Indian Council in the Valley of Walla Walla*, San Francisco, 1855)

Within ten days after the treaty making commenced, most of the assembled tribal leaders had succumbed to Governor Stevens' blandishments. They were about to surrender huge portions of their tribal lands in return for the governor's promise of forthcoming rewards from the Great White Father in the national capitol when suddenly into the assemblage galloped Chief Looking Glass of Asotin (Apash Wyakaikt) with a large retinue of followers. They had been hunting buffalo east of the Biterroot Mountains on the Montana Plains when word reached Looking Glass of the Walla Walla meeting.

By riding full tilt back in order to participate, the seventy-year-old leader and his followers had covered the intervening 300 miles in seven days. Looking Glass' arrival on the scene was a dramatic one. As they approached the conference group from the distance, riding their ponies full tilt, each rider displaying scalps of Blackfoot Indians suspended from their poles, they caused a great stir among the treaty-makers.

Upon being apprised of the treaty developments, Chief Looking Glass is said to have exclaimed: "My people! What have you done? While I have been gone you have sold my country . . . There is not left me a place on which to pitch my lodge!" Although the treaty soon after was signed, it was not a success. Within months after its execution, war between the two races broke out on both sides of the Cascade Range.

Governor Stevens had failed to make clear to the Indians that the rewards promised under the provisions of the treaty would be long in arriving, thanks to the slowness of the legislators back in the national capitol who had to approve of the treaty. Meanwhile, gold was being discovered on these Indians' lands and white men seeking it were overrunning the very lands which Governor Stevens had promised would be reserved exclusively for Indians use. Fighting broke out and spread.

To combat the Indians, U.S. Army forts were built, one of them being Fort Steptoe, the structure around which today's city of Walla Walla began. It was named after Lieutenant Colonel Edward Jevnor Steptoe, the post's firm commanding officer. Later its name was changed to Fort Walla Walla.

Initially, gold was discovered to the north of Fort Walla Walla, and in leading U.S. troops from his new fort to aid the white men seeking gold around Colville, Colonel Steptoe suffered a humiliating defeat by combined Indian forces blocking his way. In 1860, the gold rush spread to central Idaho on the Clearwater River. Five thousand whites invaded the gold fields fifty miles upriver of the site where the city of Lewiston now stands, known as the Orofino Mines. They yielded gold worth $2,756,128 between the years 1861 and 1867.

The search for gold then spread south into the wild and rugged Salmon River country. Here a settlement called Orogrande attracted fifteen hundred whites. In a mining camp called Florence near today's town of Riggins, over nine thousand prospectors, in 1862, found gold in Baboon Gulch, so named for a Mr. Baboon who made the initial strike here. Baboon's arrival at Walla Walla, where by now a settlement had arisen around the fort, carrying seventy-five pounds of gold dust in his saddlebags, signalled still another gold rush which, according to the historian H.H. Bancroft, netted about 3500 prospectors here in an average of $4,000 each (multiply at least by four for modern values). Gold, too, was discovered south of Fort Walla Walla in Owyhee River country.

Because it was located at the hub of all these gold discoveries, the site where the city of Walla Walla now stands became the focal point from which radiated trail routes leading to the north, east, and south. Upon the backs of mules and horses, virtually all supplies for the miners were transported from this new town. One of the more famous of the many pack train operators who based out of early Walla Walla was Mr. Jack Splawn, who later became the first mayor of Yakima. He has left us the following description of a typical pack train. As recorded in Splawn's book *Kamiakin, Last Hero of the Yakimas* (Portland, 1944):

> The average load for a mule was 300 pounds; charge for freight was a dollar a pound when carried a distance of not more than 200 miles . . . The boss of the pack train was called a *cargadero* . . . *arrieros* were the men who did the packing and the "belle mare" was called *mulara.* The whole train was known as *caballada* . . . When all the packs were satisfactorily adjusted, the arrieros would break into a song, the music bending with the rattle of the bells on the old *mulara*"

The sight of a column of fifty of the animals, winding their way through deep forests along and around steep mountains on paths blazed by the Indians was a memorable sight. On the inbound trip, food and general supplies were transported to the mining camps. On the outbound trip, the animals were loaded with the precious gold ore. To prevent robbery by bandits, each member of the train including the cook, carried a shotgun, rifle, or revolver. Mr. Splawn describes making camp at night:

> The cook, besides riding the *mulara* on the trail, was expected to have his meals on time. The minute camp was

reached, he made a grab for the kitchen animal, unloaded it
and built a fire. By the time the rest of the animals were
unloaded he generally had a meal ready. If he failed to be on
time, he had to endure the ridicule of the *arrieros* for the
remainder of the day.

By 1860, Walla Walla was a raucous supply town, full of saloon
keepers and "ladies of the night." Writes one contemporary: "It was a
straggling and disorderly place. The dirty streets were crowded with
freighting wagons, teams of pack animals, and a considerable army of
rough men. One would naturally conclude, to judge from the numerous
places where gambling was in progress, that this was the chief
occupation."

By the 1860s, paddlewheel steamboats were transporting supplies for
the miners up the Columbia River to Wallula. Conestoga wagons then
carried them up the banks of the Walla Walla River to the town which
had grown up around Fort Steptoe. By now a new form of
transportation, namely; stage coach, was spreading all over the West
and Mr. Ben Holladay, the stage coach king, had made Walla Walla one
of his more important stops.

One of the early leaders of Walla Walla was Dr. Dorsey Baker. He was
an ex-Illinois physician whose local riches were acquired through
raising cattle. By 1865, the growing of wheat on the rich soils around
Walla Walla was accelerating, and when the gold mining boom
declined, Baker began shipping wheat from Walla Walla down the
banks of the Walla Walla River to the Columbia, down which it was
shipped by barge to Portland.

When, however, the local wagoneers charged Mr. Baker excessively
high fees for delivering the wheat to Wallula, he conceived the idea of
building a railroad to supplant them. Indicative of how hard Baker was
pressed in financing this plan was the lone steam locomotive he
purchased for his 30-mile long railroad. It was a tiny second-hand
contraption which he found while shopping for one back East. From
Pittsburgh he shipped it to Walla Walla by sailing it in a schooner
around Cape Horn. Unable to afford steel tracks on which to operate it,
Mr. Baker laid wooden ones. However, even though the locomotive
weighed only seven and one-half tons, this weight soon proved to be
causing excessive wear on the wooden tracks. Baker then resorted to
covering the wooden tracks with pieces of strapiron.

Mr. John Murphy, an Englishman who was touring the west in 1875
has left us the following description of his ride on Baker's unique

railroad line. Eastward bound at the time, he had come up the Columbia River to Wallula by steamboat, and now was heading overland as best he could. Records Murphy:

I went ashore at Wallula . . . intending to go to Walla Walla in Eastern Washington Territory . . . but on landing I was informed that the stage coach had left and that the only means of reaching Walla Walla was to secure a seat in a goods truck attached to a miniature train that ran into the interior on a wooden line of rails. Having secured an interview with the president, secretary, engineer and brake-man . . . all in one person . . . he informed me that he would book me as a passenger upon the payment of two dollars, and that sum being paid, I was placed on some iron in an open trunk and told to cling to the sides and to be careful not to stand on the wooden floor if I cared anything about my legs. I promised a strict compliance with instructions. The miserable little engine gave a grunt or two, several wheezy puffs, a cat-like scream, and finally got the car attached to it underway. Once in motion it dashed along at the headlong sped of two miles an hour, rocking like a canoe in a cross sea. The gentleman who represented all the train officials did not get on board but told the engineer to go on and that he would overtake him. Before we had proceeded half a mile I now saw why I had been told not to stand on the floor for suddenly a piece of hoop iron which covered the wooden rails curled into what was called a 'snake-head,' pushed through the

wooden floor with such force that it nearly stopped the train
. . . Enroute prairie schooners drawn by six or eight mules
had the temerity to challenge us to a race with them . . . At
the end of seven weary hours . . . my eyes made sour with
smoke, my coat and hat nearly burnt off with the sparks . . .
we arrived at the station marked Walla Walla . . . a rude
shanty through which the wind howled. (*Rambles in
Northwestern America from the Pacific to the Rocky
Mountains*, Murphy, J.M., London, 1879)

By 1858, Walla Walla was the largest settlement in all of Washington
Territory, a region which then stretched from Puget Sound all the way
east to the Continental Divide and from Canada south to Utah,
excluding Oregon. By then, the citizens of Walla Walla, in view of their
greater population and their more central location, believed that the
territorial capital should be shifted from Olympia on Puget Sound to
their community. After all, they argued, there were more votes in
Eastern Washington, counting the thousands of miners then gold
mining around the town's eastern flanks, than west of the Cascade
Mountains where Olympia stood.

However, the wily politicians at Olympia quickly responded. They
proposed establishing a new U.S. Territory of Idaho, thereby gerry-
mandering the miners' votes into this new jurisdiction. With far greater
influence in the nation's capital than the citizens of Walla Walla could
muster, the new Territory of Idaho was then established. All hopes of
Walla Walla's becoming the territorial capital of Washington vanished.

As the base from which the Inland Empire's wheat was shipped
down the Columbia River overseas, however, Walla Walla prospered in
the ensuing years. By 1910, Walla Wallans were being characterized as
a fat and prosperous lot of people, and their town was being described
as one of "complacency and superiority." Probably still applicable
today is the description of Walla Walla given about this time by one
writer: "It is an old, well-settled, rich, intelligent, prosperous, happy, and
up-to-date community, knowing the good things of life and determined
to have and enjoy them."

WASHINGTON

Often called "Washington State" to avoid confusing it with
Washington in the District of Columbia, this name dates back to the
sixth century when there was a village in northern England called
"Wass-ton," after the town's leading family whose name was Wass. Six
hundred years later, the town of Wass-ton boasted as one of its people

a gallant knight whose name was William and, as was then the custom for famous persons such as he, William began calling himself William Wass-ton after the name of his native village. Seven hundred more years then transpired, during which several of Wass-ton's descendants also became famous and the name gradually was changed to "Washington."

Among them was John Washington, a distinguished clergyman whom the Puritans began attacking for his more traditional religious beliefs. To escape their persecution, John Washington then moved his home to Virginia in the remote continent called America, and it was from John Washington's great grandson, George Washington, that the state of Washington takes its name.

There are some one hundred and twenty towns and cities bearing the name Washington today in the United States. First use of the name was during the American Revolution when Fort Washington was built in today's New York City between 181st and 186th Streets, an area still called Washington Heights. Located at the highest point on Manhattan Island, Fort Washington was an important military post for the Continental Army whose commander-in-chief, General George Washington finally forced the surrender of the British forces under General Lord Cornwallis in January, 1777. Later, as the first president of the United States, George Washington became known as the father of his country.

In 1852, four years after Oregon Territory was created, the white settlers of this territory who lived north of the Columbia River were so dissatisfied with their lack of representation in Oregon Territory's Legislature at Salem that they petitioned Congress to create a new territory for them. Thus came into being the U.S. Territory of Washington, established in 1853.

The first governor of Washington Territory was Isaac Ingalls Stevens (1818–1862). President Pierce, who appointed Stevens as governor, had served with Stevens in the Mexican War. It was characteristic of the dynamic Stevens, a Massachusetts-born West Point graduate who was trained as an engineer, that he asked for and received from Pierce additional duty in Washington Territory as its U.S. Indian Agent, a position which was to give the young governor so much grief. Enroute westward to Washington Territory, at Stevens further request, he was given command of 243 surveyors assembled to map a northern railroad route across the Rockies into Puget Sound.

Despite a boyhood injury which forced him to wear a truss

throughout the remainder of his life, not to mention an injury he received in the Mexican War caused by a bullet which splintered his ankle and thereafter necessitated his wearing of a special shoe, the short-statured Stevens exulted in traveling with his map-makers across the Rockies to his new assignment.

During the trek Stevens narrowly missed being stampeded by buffalo. He became toughened to riding for days on horseback and endured the hardships of fording swift rivers and crossing over unknown mountain passes. Vigorously, upon his arrival at Olympia, the future territorial capitol town, he organized the legislature, urged the Britishers who, prior to the Boundary Treaty of 1846 had monopolized this region, to depart, and commenced familiarizing himself with the geographical features of his domain, one which included today's Montana and Idaho as well as the present state.

To hasten the laying of railroad tracks from the East into Puget Sound, Stevens then traveled via sailing ship back to the national capital in 1854, then returned to Washington Territory with his family. Four thousand white settlers by now had arrived in the territory, attracted by the Donation Land Act granting one square mile of free land to each of them. Without any concern for Indian rights to the same land, the U.S. Congress had thus created for Stevens an impossible task, namely, to persuade the Indians and the whites to live amicably notwithstanding.

Stevens embarked on a whirlwind series of visits to the various tribes of his domain urging their leaders to affix their marks to so-called "peace treaties" he had drawn up. Under these treaties' provisions the Indians surrendered much of their land to possession by the whites; this in return for promises of reimbursement from "The Great White Father" back in the nation's capitol.

Still hopeful of peace throughout his realm, Stevens was thus engaged in parleying further treaties with Blackfoot and Flathead Indians east of the Rockies when a messenger from his legislators back in Olympia arrived, nearly exhausted from many days of travel here from Puget Sound by horseback. He bore a message advising the governor that from British Columbia south to Spanish California virtually all Indians appeared to have gone on the warpath. They further warned Stevens that it would not be safe for him to return to Olympia by retracing down the Columbia River. He must return to the territorial capitol by going down the Missouri River and the Mississippi River to New Orleans and thence proceed by sailing ship to Panama where, after crossing the isthmus, he should return by ship north to his headquarters.

Characteristically, the bold Stevens disregarded the warning. Risking his life, he descended the Columbia River, enlisting some support from friendly Indians enroute. At Fort Vancovuer the Commanding General of U.S. troops in the Northwest, General John Ellis Wool, turned a deaf ear to Stevens' request for U.S. troops to assist in quelling the Indian unrest. According to the seventy-one-year-old general Wool, the whites were to blame for the outbreak. He refused to assist the volunteer militia which Stevens proposed to organize.

Adding to Governor Stevens' troubles were the white settlers themselves, some of whom sympathized with the Indians while others complained that the Indian Reservations on which Stevens had arranged for the Indians to live were located too close to their own homes. Even the governor's legislators in Olympia complained of Stevens' imposing martial law under circumstances they considered unnecessary. The White House, too, condemned the peppery governor for exceeding his authority.

By 1857, however, General Wool had been replaced, and army commanders in the field began to realize the necessity to quell the still-continuing Indian unrest. In July of this year the earlier censure of Governor Stevens by his territorial legislators was officially revoked and a memorial was dispatched to the U.S. Congress by them commending Stevens and his leadership of the volunteer militia. Soon afterward, Stevens was elected by the citizens of Washington Territory to become their first delegate to the U.S. Congress.

Living in the nation's capital, Stevens became increasingly involved in national politics. He would doubtlessly have gone on to become a national leader but for volunteering at the start of the Civil War to join the Union Army. He was killed at age forty-four while leading the 79th New York Regiment in a charge against Confederate emplacements at Chantilly, Virginia, September, 1862.

WASHOUGAL (Q-8)

Had today's residents of this Columbia River city been living in the late summer of 1843, they would have witnessed a most memorable sight, namely: hundreds of emigrants, men, women, and children, drifting down the river on crude rafts, huddled together attempting to guide their craft in the swirling waters which then flowed past this site, at the same time trying to prevent the goods they carried on board from falling overboard, for they represented all the worldly goods these emigrants possessed.

Just a mile upstream of today's town of Washougal ended the worst stretch of these waters, known as The Cascades. When traveling down this fifteen-mile portion of the Columbia, the emigrants' rafts sometimes overturned and some drowned. At a spot which thereafter became known (as it still is) under the name "Cape Horn," nearly two hundred of these emigrants, mostly women and children, became marooned by high winds, and faced starvation and freezing before the British chief factor at Fort Vancouver (fifteen miles downstream of Washougal) finally rescued them.

Fort Vancouver, about this time, was the capital of the entire Pacific Northwest. Living at this palatial fur post, with the Union Jack flying overhead, was white-haired, handsome, Dr. John McLoughlin (1785-1857). McLoughlin disliked the arrival of these Americans into his fur-trapping realm but, being kind-hearted he nonetheless felt the need to rescue them, and later to feed them when, as many did, they reached Willamette Valley with no resources.

In the fall 1844, the year after the Cape Horn tragedy, still more American emigrants headed for Willamette Valley rafting down the river past the site where today's Washougal now stands, and among them was a thirty-year-old Kentuckian named Michael Simmons. After passing with his family the site where Washougal now stands, he beached his raft and made camp on land just outside the high walls surrounding McLoughlin's headquarters. It was a bold and defiant act since all emigrants knew that all land, as decreed by McLoughlin, lying north of the Columbia, was taboo to Americans. When, probably at Dr. McLoughlin's direct order, Simmons was told to move to the south shore, he refused. He advised McLoughlin that his wife was about to have a baby, and insisted, therefore, he must stay.

Despite his iron-bound policy requiring Americans to live in Willamette Valley, the King of the Columbia made an exception to it. The Kentuckian and his family might stay until their new child was born. But Simmons, still defiant of anyone British, then struck out into the region north of the fort, his goal being to reach Puget Sound where he had resolved to settle his family. There being no roads whatsoever by which to reach Puget Sound, after ten days of desperate struggle, Simmons was forced to return. When the "White Eagle," as Dr. McLoughlin was also known, then insisted that Simmons cross the Columbia like the rest of his Americans, Simmons again defied him by moving to the site where Washougal now stands, sixteen miles upstream of today's city of Vancouver.

Here Simmons spent the winter making shingles from the local cedar trees which he then sold to McLoughlin's Hudson's Bay Company downstream, thereby enabling the Kentuckian to keep his family from starving. Also, however, during that winter Simmons spent much time organizing more Americans to rise up against Dr. McLoughlin and to go with him the following spring on a second attempt to reach Puget Sound.

Exulting, thereby, in twisting the British lion's tail they marched north en masse in the spring of 1845 to establish the first American settlement on Puget Sound. Called New Market, it was located at the site near present Olympia, Washington, today known by the name "Tumwater." Thereafter, hundreds of Americans followed Simmons into this new region and by 1850, they had placed the British there in a shadow, outnumbered and largely subdued.

WENATCHEE (I-15)

The first white men to view the site of this city, twenty-eight miles northeast of Ellensburg, were fur trappers, Alexander Ross of John J. Astor's trading post at Astoria being their leader. In May, 1811, as they were paddling by canoe up the Columbia River they decided to stop here where the mouth of the Wenatchee River joins the larger stream. Being very hungry, they decided to ascend the Wenatchee into its upper regions to find some deer. While thus engaged they came upon some Wenatchee Indians who themselves were hunting for deer too. Generously, these Indians presented Ross and his men with several haunches of venison which they had just killed. Around a campfire that evening they became good friends.

Three years later (May, 1814), Ross and his followers found themselves again passing the site where Wenatchee now stands. By this time, Ross had successfully established a fur post upstream of Wenatchee where Brewster now stands, called Fort Okanogan, and to this trading post large quantities of furs were being brought from the rich fur country to the northward around Kamloops in Canada. So successful, in fact, was Ross in obtaining furs that by now he badly needed horses in order to transport the pelt on these animals' backs.

And so, on the occasion of his renewing acquaintance with the Wenatchee Indians, Ross and his men were heading south down the Columbia River into Yakima Indian country. Here he hoped to procure a number of these animals, for the Yakima Nation were famous for the large numbers of horses which they possessed.

While they were encamped for the night at Wenatchee, Ross and his men found the Wenatchees as friendly as they had been on the previous visit. However, upon learning from Ross that he and his men were headed for Yakima country, they warned Ross that they would all be killed. Disregarding this, his need for more horses so acute, Ross decided to continue south.

In the book which Mr. Ross later wrote (*Fur Hunters of the Far West*, Norman, 1956) he recalls that on the following night after their departure from Wenatchees, he lay sleepless, worrying about the warning given him by his Wenatchee friends, aware that he was now approaching enemy territory. Suddenly he became aware that people were approaching the tent where he slept. Much to his relief he found them to be the same Wenatchees whom he had left the previous evening. They had come to warn him again not to continue southward. As described by Ross in his book:

> The zealous couriers reached our camp late in the night. My men were fast asleep. I was too anxious and heard their approach. I watched their motions [not knowing who they were] for some time with my gun in my hand, till they called out in their language, "Samah! Samah!" (Turn back, turn back, you are all dead men!) It was no use however, for we must continue [into Yakima country] at any hazard.

Ross continues:

> On the second night after our friends left us we entered
> beautiful "Eyakema Valley," so called by the whites. But on
> the present occasion there was nothing beautiful or inter-
> esting to us. For we had scarcely advanced three miles when
> a camp of the true Mameluke style presented itself—one of
> which we could see its beginning but not the end! This
> mammoth camp could not have contained less than 3,000
> men, exclusive of women and children, and treble that
> number of horses . . . it was a grand and imposing sight
> covering more than six miles in every direction . . . The din
> of men, the noise of women, the screaming of children, the
> tramping of horses and the howling of dogs was more than
> could be well described.

The moment Ross and his followers dismounted among the mob, they knew they were prisoners. As they commenced trading for horses, it became evident that the Indians were playing with them as cats with a mouse. "As soon as a horse was acquired through trade," writes Ross, "it was driven instantly out of sight amidst jeering and yelling." Two nights and days passed "without food or sleep," and his men became despondent of their ever coming out alive. Overwhelmed and surrounded by the huge mob, they began to despair.

On the third day, one of Ross' men was cutting some venison they had acquired for a meal, (the first one since their arrival three days prior to this), when a fierce-looking Yakima chief snatched the knife Ross' man was using out of his hands, causing the man to lunge at the chief in an attempt to recover it. A crisis was clearly at hand.

Quick-wittedly Mr. Ross, grasping his pistol, walked between the two, and slowly taking his own elaborately-carved hunting knife from his sheath, he offered it to the chief saying: "Here, my friend, is a chief's knife, I give it to you!" Ross, in his book, then describes the awesome moments during which the Indian leader hesitated, obviously trying to decide the white mens' fate. Finally, he exclaimed in a loud voice, turning to his people: *She-augh, she-auugh, me yokal waltz!*" which meant, "Look, look, my friends at the chief's knife." These words he repeated over and over to the delight of his followers, all admiring the toy.

Then in an excess of joy, the Indian chief harangued the crowd. He urged them to be friendly to the whites. The crisis was over and five days after, Ross and his trappers were back safe at Fort Okanogan, twenty-five horses having been acquired at the Indian fair.

Alexander Ross (1783-1856) was no ordinary fur trapper. A native of Scotland, he came to Montreal in 1804 where he taught school. In 1810 he commenced his trapping career with the North West Company. He was among this British company's trappers whom the American John J. Astor lured away from this British organization to establish the American fur post, Astoria, in 1811 at the mouth of the Columbia.

In the years subsequent to his service at Fort Okanogan under Astor, Mr. Ross was Donald McKenzie's chief assistant at Fort Nez Perce, then himself led fur brigades into Snake River country until, incurring the wrath of Governor George Simpson, head of the Hudson's Bay Company, Ross was retired in 1825 to Red River (near today's Winnipeg) where he wrote and taught school until his death. Mr. Ross's wife was an Okanogan Indian.

The Indian word *wenatchee* means "great opening in the mountains," a reference to local Tumwater Canyon due west of today's city of Wenatchee. Here the waters of Wenatchee River coming from the nearby mountains of the high Cascade Range plunge with great ferocity on their way down Wenatchee River to enter the Columbia River at the site where the city of Wenatchee stands.

WHIDBEY ISLAND (E-7)

But for New York City's Long Island, Whidbey Island, located just inside the Strait of Juan de Fuca, would be the longest one in the continental United States. Whidbey Island is named in honor of Joseph Whidbey (1755-1833) of His Majesty's Ship *Discovery*, ninety-nine feet, two inches long, 340 tons, commanded by the dour Captain George Vancouver in the spring of 1792 when the explorer was commencing his famous survey of Puget Sound. Mr. Whidbey, unlike his associates aboard the *Discovery*, Lieutenants Peter Puget and Joseph Baker, came up through the ranks. He had risen from the rank of seaman to his present position of sailing master, being thirty-seven-years-old, six years older than Captain Vancouver himself. Captain Vancouver had previously served with Sailing Master Whidbey in the West Indies, and when Vancouver was selected by the Board of Admiralty to command the forthcoming exploration to the then-remote northwest coast of America, he particularly asked that Sailing Master Whidbey accompany him on the long voyage.

It was on May 30, 1792, that Captain Vancouver dispatched Mr. Whidbey from the *Discovery* to probe in the *Discovery's* longboat the outlines of Whidbey Island. Previously, Spanish explorers must have seen Whidbey Island at a distance, but they failed to recognize it as an island, nor were Vancouver and Whidbey aware that the land Whidbey was exploring at this time was an island.

Equipped with a week's supply of provisions and carrying instruments for taking angles and the making of maps, Whidbey and his sailors approached the island's southern tip. As the shoreline grew more distinct they were surprised to see so many Indian dwellings on shore. Whidbey surmised that as many as six hundred Indians lived here. As they rowed and sailed their way northward up the eastern shore, Whidbey and his crew were followed by over one hundred curious Indians walking up the beach as they progressed. Obviously, the natives had never seen white men before, nor witnessed the invention of the sail.

Vancouver's journal of these events describes the moment when Whidbey, accompanied by three of his sailors, decided to risk setting foot ashore. "The situation on the spot where they landed," records Vancouver, "was delightful, being composed of hills, dales, and extensive lawns. This," he continues, "together with the cordial reception they met . . . induced Mr. Whidbey to continue his examination on shore." As he continued northward, walking ashore with the Indians, they began "expressing a great desire," as Vancouver tells it, "to be satisfied as to the color of Whidbey's skin. They believed," continues Vancouver, "that only Whidbey's hands and face were white. By openinng his waistcoat," concludes the explorer, "Mr. Whidbey convinced the Indians of their mistake. Their astonishment was inexpressible."

Whidbey and his boatmen continued sailing and rowing northward up presently-named Saratoga Passage until they reached the site of today's Penn Cove. Then they turned back and rejoined their ship which, by then, was anchored in the waters off the site of the city of Everett. After holding formal ceremony ashore here claiming all the surrounding lands for England, Vancouver sailed the *Discovery* northward up Whidbey Island's west side through Admiralty Inlet until he reached Strawberry Cove off Cypress Island in the San Juans, just north of Whidbey Island.

From here Vancouver again dispatched Sailing Master Whidbey in a small boat southward with a boat crew with orders to further explore Whidbey Island, not knowing as yet it was, in fact, an island. On this trip Mr. Whidbey discovered that the narrow waterway which Captain Vancouver previously called Deception Pass, mistakenly believing it to be a cul-de-sac, was in fact a throughway. Through it Whidbey and his men sailed into the same Penn Cove which they had reached on Whidbey's earlier exploration. Thus it was discovered that the land they had been surveying these past days was, indeed, an island. It was at this time that Captain Vancouver, in recognition of Whidbey's efforts, gave to the land south of Deception Pass the name "Whidbey's Island."

Captain Vancouver, it should be mentioned, had not come from England to these Northwest coasts simply to survey its waters. Three years prior to this, Spanish warships entered a place, on what we now call Vancouver Island, called Nootka. Here they seized several British fur trading ships because their British skippers refused to salute Spanish colors hoisted over Nootka's harbor, called Friendly Cove. When England's Prime Minister Pitt heard about this, he mobilized the British fleet.

Fortunately, war between the two nations was avoided by their signing of a so-called Treaty of Nootka, allowing England henceforth to share Nootka with Spain on an equal basis. To arrange the details of how Nootka was to be shared, not long after naming Whidbey Island, Vancouver in the *Discovery* arrived at Nootka to meet with his Spanish counterpart, sent here from Mexico, Senor Bodega y Quadra.

Upon anchoring in Nootka's harbor, known as Friendly Cove, Vancouver was pleased to find anchored here the third ship of his expedition, the supply ship *Daedulus* commanded by Lieutenant Richard Hergest, long overdue from the Sandwich Islands. The delay, Vancouver was saddened to hear, was caused by Captain Hergest's death in the islands, murdered by Hawaiian warriors. Owing to this loss, Vancouver appointed Sailing Master Whidbey to become the *Daedulus'* new commanding officer.

This was a distinct honor for Mr. Whidbey, for although he was doubtlessly more skilled than the commissioned officers under Vancouver in the practice of navigation, he was not of noble lineage and therefore normally would have been ineligible to command the vessel. Captain Whidbey now sailed the *Daedelus* south to Monterey in California, surveying enroute the body of water now known as Grays Harbor. Doubtless, because he needed Mr. Whidbey for the more important task of surveying, at Monterey Whidbey was replaced as commander of the *Daedulus* by one Lieutenant James Hanson.

With Vancouver, in the *Discovery,* Whidbey then sailed for the Hawaiian Islands to conduct surveys there. During the winters of 1793 and 1794 such surveys continued, alternated in the summer months by surveying in Alaskan waters. Many of the landmarks north of Vancouver Island on British Columbian and Alaskan coasts were discovered by Mr. Whidbey, among these being the Skeena and Stikine rivers; also the site of present Petersburg.

By 1815, we find Mr. Whidbey, by now retired from the British navy, busily supervising the building of the breakwater which still guards the harbor of England's city of Plymouth on the Devon Coast. Whidbey's death occurred at Somersetshire in 1833, age seventy-eight.

Little remembered today are the many Spaniards who probed the waters around Whidbey Island in 1790 and 1791; among these: Galiano, Valdes, Eliza, Quimper, Narvaez, and Carrasco. It remains a mystery as to why at least one of them did not discover the existence of lower Puget Sound, as Vancouver did, for they were aware of the waters lying west of Whidbey which Vancouver christened Admiralty Inlet. They called it *Boca de Caamano,* apparently believing this body of water was a bay rather than a throughway.

In choosing the name Admiralty Inlet in 1792, Vancouver was expressing his gratitude to the British navy's highest group, the Board of Admiralty, for their having recently promoted him to the rank of captain then dispatched him as leader of the exploration to this northwest coast of America to become famous.

The First Lord of the Admiralty back in London at this time was The Honourable John Pitt. He was a brother of William Pitt, then the prime minister of England. A first cousin of both of these prestigious gentlemen, when Vancouver gave the name Admiralty Inlet, was a young midshipman named Thomas Pitt serving aboard Vancouver's ship. His presence aboard Vancouver's *Discovery* was a disaster from the very start of the long voyage to America, for the fourteen-year-old youth, aware of his prestigious relatives, behaved poorly, refusing to abide by the ship's rules. In the year following Vancouver's discovery of Whidbey Island, Captain Vancouver expelled Midshipman Pitt from his ship because of the young man's insubordination. This act returned to plague Vancouver upon the conclusion of the exploration when Vancouver reported back to naval headquarters. In fact, the great explorer's last years were spent defending himself against ungrounded charges made by this young nobleman.

Whidbey Island's Point Partridge, situated on the island's northwest coast, was so named in June, 1792, by Vancouver to honor one of the relatives of Vancouver's brother, John Vancouver. Back in England, at the city called King's Lynn, East Anglia, where Captain Vancouver was born, Vancouver's brother John was married to Martha Partridge of Hockham Hall, and doubtless this name was given here on Whidbey Island due to this relationship.

WHITMAN COUNTY (K-23)

The name of this eastern Washington county, located immediately south of Spokane County, honors Dr. Marcus Whitman (1802–1847) who founded the missionary station called Waiilatpu which was located just south of Whitman County in Walla Walla County.

Dr. Marcus Whitman was a medical missionary sent west by the American Board of Missions of Boston in 1836. Whitman's seven years of heart-breaking effort at Waiilatpu ended in his death at the hands of the very people he was attempting to help. The gap between Whitman's Christian culture and that of the Walla Walla Indians whom he was trying to help was just too great to bridge. A chief factor in Whitman's misfortunes, too, was his choice of location. Although he could not have foreseen it, Waiilatpu became an important stop for the thousands of Americans who poured over the Oregon Trail into Willamette Valley. With them, these emigrants brought measles, a disease which spread to the local Walla Walla Indians. Within a short time, nearly half of these Indians were wiped out from the disease. Believing that Dr. Whitman's medicine had poisoned them, they attacked and killed him.

Dr. Whitman first arrived in the Pacific Northwest in 1835, in the company of a fellow-missionary, Reverend Samuel Parker. The following year, after returning east, Dr. Whitman again arrived in this new region of the world with his bride, Narcissa. Again in 1842, Whitman traveled east to ask for reinforcements from his American Board of Missions in Boston. His final trip west in 1843, was as leader of the Great Migration, so called because it was the first of the many massive waves of American emigrants, which for over a quarter of a century poured into "Oregon country," thereby taking over by sheer numbers a region larger than all of the New England States plus New York, one which hitherto was claimed by England. Due to these trips as well as to his tragic and dramatic death, Dr. Whitman became a national hero, hailed for years as "the man who saved Oregon from the British," although today most historians regard this largely as a myth.

Probably this belief was based largely upon the trip back east from Waiilatpu which Whitman made in 1843 in the thick of winter, unaccompanied except by one traveling companion, Asa Lovejoy, a man six years Whitman's junior. Departing Waiilatpu on October 3 of that year, the pair traveled up the Snake River to Fort Hall on horseback in the remarkable time of ten days (Fort Hall stood where the city of Pocatello now stands).

Snow in the Rockies then forced them to detour south into the more clement weather of today's New Mexico before heading northeastward to Bent's Fort in present Colorado. By this time, having traveled in freezing weather over trackless wilderness, the younger Lovejoy (later the founder of Portland) was exhausted and Dr. Whitman, his face permanently scarred from frostbite, found himself proceeding alone toward St. Louis, which he reached on March 9, 1844.

Penniless and exhausted, he there looked up a friend who enabled him to continue to Cincinnati. Still a mystery even to this day is Dr. Whitman's diversion of his journey at this point to Washington, D.C. In fact, the journey from Waiilatpu was made by Whitman in order to return to his missionary headquarters in Boston, Massachusetts, there to persuade his missionary superiors to cancel their order to close down his mission station. Accordingly, Dr. Whitman's arrival in the nation's capital was, indeed, far off from his original course.

Whitman arrived in the nation's capital still wearing the dirty buffalo robe and leather leggings of his long trip. That he met with the secretaries of War and Treasury is certain, and perhaps President Tyler also gave him an interview, as Dr. Whitman pressed not only for more Americans to pour west to Oregon but also urged the establishment of U.S. Army forts to facilitate the emigrants' travel and protect them from Indian attack.

From Washington he traveled to New York City, where he was welcomed by Horace Greeley, then the nation's leading newspaperman. Journeying thence to Boston, Whitman was successful there in persuading the American Board to rescind their earlier order.

Heading back to Waiilatpu, Dr. Whitman found himself leading over eight hundred men, women, and children over the Rocky Mountains, advising them what trails to take, encouraging them not to abandon their covered wagons despite the roadless trail beyond Fort Hall, and generally inspiring the huge group with his confidence. This was Dr. Whitman's third trip west.

Perhaps the most memorable of such trips, however, took place in 1836 when in April, Dr. Whitman and his beautiful blonde wife, Narcissa Whitman (their marriage having just recently been consummated) departed St. Louis accompanying a caravan of fur trappers in the charge of the famous mountain man Tom "Broken Hand"

Fitzergerald. Also accompanying them were another pair of newlyweds, like themselves American Board missionaries; namely: Reverend Henry Spalding and his wife, Eliza. Fitzgerald's long line of pack mules were carrying supplies to the Rocky Mountain fur trappers at their annual summer rendezvous to be held this year at Horse Creek on Green River in Wyoming. Here, as was customary at such affairs, the lonely mountain men, after a long winter of trapping beneath icy Rocky Mountain streams, brought their accumulated beaver pelt in order to swap with St. Louis merchants the necessary supplies with which to continue another winter of trapping in the wilds.

Back in St. Louis, while preparing for this long journey, Dr. Whitman had purchased a yellow-wheeled Dearborn wagon in which the two wives were to ride. There being no roads westward, this purchase was indeed a bold one, and it caused the mountain men accompanying them to laugh in ridicule.

The terrain being very rough even at the start, these wagons proved a most uncomfortable mode of travel for the two ladies, and soon they took to horseback. Riding side-saddle, as was the customary way for females of that day, they created a spectacle which particularly amazed the Indians they encountered along the way. Flocking from far and wide, they followed the group for days, for neither had they seen the invention of the wheel before, and the sight of pale-faced females riding in such a strange manner left them goggle-eyed.

Writes Narcissa to her mother about this time, describing the daily routine which was followed as they slowly progressed at the rate of about sixteen miles per day:

> Just think of me . . . at the word "Arise" we spring from our beds . . . while the horses are feeding we get breakfast in a hurry and eat it. By this time the word "catch up, catch up" rings through the camp for moving . . . we are ready to start usually at six, travel 'til eleven, encamp, rest, feed, then start again at two and travel 'til six . . . then . . . camp for the night. My Husband, the best the world has ever produced, is always ready to provide a comfortable shade from the noonday sun when we stop. With one of our saddle blankets stretched across the sage brush or upheld by sticks . . . our resting is a delight . . . Dried buffalo meat and tea for breakfast lunch and supper . . . (Journal of Mrs. Whitman for 28 August 1836, T.C. Elliott, *The Coming of the White Women.*)

As they approached Wyoming's Green River country, having by now been on the trail for over two months, they were welcomed by a cavalcade of horsemen from the fur trappers' rendezvous on Horse Creek where news of their approach had been received, brought them by Indians traveling in advance of the caravan. Firing pistols as they galloped toward the caravan, they were initially believed to be attackers, particularly since included among this welcoming contingent were four bands of Indians dressed in full war paint, friends of the trappers. Circling the missionaries' caravan they fired their pistols into the air, whooped and hollered, then brought their animals to a sudden halt, followed by a parade around the wide-eyed newcomers. William H. Gray, a missionary assistant to the Whitmans and the Spaldings, describes the scene as follows:

> Of the number assembled, there must have been not far from one hundred Americans, hunters and trappers; about fifty Frenchmen belonging principally to the caravan; some five traders; about twenty citizens or outsiders, principally our mission party. The Snakes and Bannocks mustered about one hundred and fifty warriors; the Nez Perce and Flatheads about two hundred . . . The procession commenced at the lower end of the plain down Horse Creek . . . the Indians all painted in their gayest uniforms, each having a company of warriors in their war garb; that is, naked except a single cloth . . . and . . . bearing implements of music such as skins drawn over hoops with rattles and trinkets to make a noise . . . When the cavalcade, amounting to full five hundred Indian warriors (though I noticed quite a number of native belles in beads) commenced [approaching] those of us who were not informed as to the object of the demonstration began to look at our weapons and to calculate on a desperate fight. (Gray, W.H., *History of Oregon,* Philadelphia, 1870)

According to Joe Meek, one of the more famous of the mountain men who attended the Horse Creek rendezvous that year (such affairs were held annually each summer), there was less drunkenness than usual this time thanks to the presence of the two white females. As he recalls, the mountain men contented themselves with promenading before the tent of Mrs. Whitman. She was a beautiful, flaxen-haired, blue-eyed woman of full figure. Others attending the affair recalled later that Joe himself was totally smitten by her, even attending the prayer meetings held at the rendezvous by Reverend Spalding despite the general drunkenness and debauchery. At these prayer meetings, they recall, Meek was preoccupied in gazing at Dr. Whitman's wife, totally oblivious to the religious aspects.

The Indian women who always attended such rendezvous as well, on the other hand, were singularly attracted to Mrs. Spalding. They smothered her with kisses, upon the caravan's arrival, as they had been told by the mountain men that this was a standard white persons' form of salutation. They also curiously examined the clothes Eliza wore.

Equally curious were the male Indians at the sight of Dr. Whitman's Dearborn wagon, by now quite dilapidated having been dragged, pushed, and pulled for weeks through the trackless terrain. The Indians quickly dubbed the strange contraption a "land canoe". Many Indians followed the Whitman-Spalding caravan as it continued.

Tension mounted in the severe heat encountered during the slow leg of the journey down the Snake River of Idaho. Nearly three months had elapsed since leaving civilization. Tempers flared. In 1835, prior to the marriage of either couple, Narcissa, then a recent graduate of a girl's finishing school, and Reverend Spalding had met each other back in New York State. On this occasion, Spalding had proposed marriage to Narcissa, an offer she rejected.

Now Narcissa's presence, after months of weary travel, was embittering Spalding through his recollection of this earlier rejection, causing him to be irritable not only to Narcissa, but also to Whitman. When the cavalcade reached the mouth of Boise River, the Whitmans decided to ride ahead of the main group. As the pair commenced their climb into the cool Blue Mountains, weeks of heat and stress behind them, Narcissa expresses in her diary her delight at finding themselves at last alone:

> 28 August 1836 This morning lingered with Husband the greatest in the world on top of the hill which overlooks Grande Ronde, for berries . . . Having no distressing apprehensions now referring to her previous constant fear of Indian attack . . . we have entirely passed the dangerous country."

Little did Mrs. Whitman realize the dangers that lay ahead; she and her husband would lose their first born child through drowning in the Walla Walla River, and in 1847 both of them would be killed by Indians.

James Willis Nesmith (later Chief Justice of Oregon's First Provisional Government), who made the trip westward with Dr. Whitman in 1843, writes of Dr. Whitman, recollecting this famous crossing:

> He spent much time in hunting out the best route for the wagons, and would plunge into streams in search of practical

fords, regardless of depth and temperature . . . then . . . he
would spend the night on going from one party to another to
minister to the sick. He was a quiet, unassuming man of great
purity of character.

WILLAPA BAY (L-3)

Located in southwestern Washington, this body of water, just north of
the Columbia River, is still largely unspoiled by human habitation. But
for the narrow twenty-five-mile-long tongue of land projecting north
from Cape Disappointment, called Long Beach Peninsula, Willapa Bay
which parallels this peninsula on its east side would in fact be a part
of the ocean. The only entrance to Willapa Bay is around its northern
tip.

Willapa Bay was famous among the early Indians of the Northwest as
a place where Indian slaves might be purchased. Long before the
arrival of white men on these coasts, Nootka Indians from Vancovuer
Island, traveling in their high-prowed giant canoes, came to Willapa
Bay to obtain these slaves. The first white man to view Willapa Bay
was Captain John Meares (1756–1809), a British fur trader. Sailing in his
tiny schooner named the *Felice Adventurer,* he tried in the summer of
1788 to enter today's Willapa Bay but changed his mind when, from the
top of his vessel's mast, he saw that the bay was shallow. Accordingly,
he gave to Willapa Bay its first name which was Shoalwater Bay.

Although Captain Meares did not enter Shoalwater (Willapa) Bay in
1778, he encountered some of the bay's Indians who paddled out to the
open ocean past Leadbetter Point with furs in their canoe to swap with
this Englishman. From the Indians about this time, Meares was
obtaining sea otter skins then worth about a hundred dollars apiece in
Macao by giving these Indians a few nails or a handful of colored
beads per skin.

Today Captain Meares is remembered by historians as a scoundrel,
fond of stretching the truth to suit his own ends. Being a prolific writer
of his adventures along these coasts, Meares (by inference) records that
soon after visiting off Shoalwater (Willapa) Bay he discovered the Strait
of Juan de Fuca; this despite his full knowledge at this time that a
fellow fur trader, one Captain Barkley, had preceded him in this
discovery. In fact, Meares had employed Barkley's map sailing into the
De Fuca Strait. As Meares sailed past the entrance to Willapa Bay, he
records the amazement of the Indians at the tremendous size of his
giant canoe. It was obvious, he writes, that these Indians had never
before witnessed the invention of the sail.

Before arriving on these northwest coasts, Meares had been serving in the British navy in Calcutta in India with the rank of lieutenant. It was here that he quit his active duty in the British navy in order to proceed to then-remote America to seek his fortune. Sea otter skins, he had heard, were so thick at a place called Nootka (today a deserted spot on Vancouver Island but then the Northwest's chief harbor) that the Indians used these pelt to roof their houses as well as to pave the sidewalks.

The vessel in which Meares sailed being too small to cross the Pacific Ocean directly to Nootka, Meares sailed it up the China coasts, thence along the Kurile and Aleutian chain of Islands to Prince William Sound which lies off Anchorage. Here he and his ship and crew became locked in the ice for the winter. They attempted to survive this ordeal by liberal use of alcohol. When in the spring of 1787, two fellow British sailors came upon them, twenty of Meares' crew were dead, and they were not impressed with the awful condition of the survivors, including Captain Meares. They also found Meares to be falsely alleging himself to be a Portuguese trader; this in order to evade the rather large trading fees legally required of all British fur traders.

According to James G. Swan (1818–1900), a handsome New Englander who was the first white man to reside on Willapa Bay's shores, there were only two or three Willapa Indians living here when he arrived in 1853, the remainder of this tribe having become extinct. Mr. Swan was a Bostonian whose aversion to domesticity caused him to leave a wife and small children there in order to come here and live with the Indians. In 1857, Swan wrote a book about this region of Washington, the first book of the Pacific Northwest to win national recognition. Titled *The Northwest Coast, or Three Years Residence in Washington Territory,* it contains the following description of the pristine condition of Willapa Bay when he arrived:

> The turbot and flounder are caught while wading in the water by means of the feet. The Indian wades along slowly and, as soon as he feels a fish with his feet, he steps quickly on it and holds it firmly till he can reach hold if it with his hand, when he gives it a quick jerk, and away it flies far into the flats. This process is repeated till enough fish are caught, when they are picked up, put in a basket, and carried to the canoe—usually quite a number are engaged in the sport, and their splashing, slipping, screaming and laughing make a lively time . . . the largest I have ever seen weighed twenty pounds.

About 1850, a large oyster industry began on Shoalwater Bay. It was centered around Bruceport, a long-since abandoned site located on the mainland side of Willapa Bay at the mouth of Willapa River. When the name "Shoalwater" became a handicap to local oystermen in attracting San Francisco schooners to venture into these waters to purchase oysters, this older name for the bay, given by Captain Meares back in 1778, was abandoned in favor of the name Willapa Bay.

Today the name "Nootka" means little or nothing to most citizens of the Pacific Northwest. Although Nootka is now a deserted spot on Vancouver Island, in Captain John Meares' day it was the capital of the entire Northwest. In Nootka's harbor, called Friendly Cove, sailing ships of many nations anchored. All over the world, Nootka was famous as the headquarters of the sea otter trade.

Meares chanced to be back in China selling sea otter pelt in Macao when news reached him that a Spaniard named Estevan Martinez had arrived with Spanish warships at Nootka and seized the village's harbor (called Friendly Cove) in the name of King Carlos IV of Spain as henceforth a Spanish possession. Martinez, too, had forbidden all non-Spanish ships (including those of English fur traders) from henceforth entering or leaving Friendly Cove without his permission. Worst of all, in the eyes of Meares, was news that the mad Spaniard had seized some lands which (according to Meares) he owned, having purchased it from the local Nootkan chieftain; also a house which Meares had built on this land, also a ship which Meares had built and launched at Friendly Cove (the vessel was named the *Northwest America*).

Angered at all this news, Meares departed Macao for England to complain to British authorities. Upon reaching London, he reported the seizures to the British Parliament; then skillfully, by means of pamphleteering and speech-making, Meares managed to arouse the English public to indignation over the incident.

Forced by public demand, Prime Minister William Pitt mobilized the entire British fleet, then threatened war upon Spain. When at the last minute, largely through the diplomatic skills of England's ambassador in Madrid, Lord Saint Helens (after whom Mount Saint Helens, lying to the east of Willapa Bay, is named), Spain backed down and agreed to make recompense. The terms were included in a so-called Treaty of Nootka. Under the treaty's provisions both nations henceforth would share Nootka and Friendly Cove equally, and Spain was required to pay restitution money to Captain John Meares for the property he lost.

Suddenly, Meares' property at Nootka which the Spanish had seized, a plot of land which he probably obtained from Chief Maquinna in exchange for two pistols, became worth an amazing amount of money. The sea otter pelt which Meares had left in Nootka became an incredible number of skins and, moreover, the ship which Meares' Chinese laborers had built for him at Nootka (the first ship ever constructed on the northwest coast) required, according to Meares, a reimbursement to him by Spain of 653,000 Spanish dollars. In terms of the present value of U.S. money as finally decreed in the Treaty of Nootka, Meares received over 180,000 dollars as a result of his efforts.

Further enriching himself, Meares then wrote a book about the incident, one which proved a best-seller of the day. Then in 1793, Meares was reinstated to active duty in the British navy and with a new rank; namely: commander, two steps above the one he held eight years previous to this when he embarked on his northwest adventures.

Leadbetter Point, which guards the south side of Willapa Bay's entrance, opposite Cape Shoalwater, commemorates Daniel Leadbetter, the U.S. Army soldier who surveyed the coast of Washington in 1850.

Toke Point and the town of Tokeland, located on Willapa Bay's north shore commemorates "Old Toke," a Chinook chief whom Mr. Swan found living here when he arrived. Swan describes Chief Toke in his book as "full of tales of Indian prowess and legends . . . one of the best men in the bay for handling a canoe." Doubtlessly, Old Toke had much influence upon Swan in this author's subsequent writings, particularly those prepared by Swan for the Smithsonian Institute.

Y

YAKIMA (M-13)

This eastern Washington city, located one hundred miles across the Cascade Range from Seattle, is named for the once-powerful Yakima nation of Indians, one of the largest among the tribes who lived in the region now constituting the state of Washington. Estimates of its size range from four to six thousand. A wide variety of translations are ascribed to the tribal name *e-ya-kima,* as this name was first spelled, among these: big belly, runaway, lake water, well-fed people, and black bear. The Yakima River, in early times, was called *tapteal.*

Some idea of the vigor of the early Yakima Indians is described by Mr. A.J. "Jack" Splawn (1845–1917), one of the first white men to live among the tribe. He later became the first mayor of the city of Yakima. In Splawn's book titled *Kamiakin, Last Hero of the Yakimas* (Portland, 1917) Splawn recalls one of the festivals he attended, an affair the Yakima tribe held annually each spring:

> It was a representative gathering, not only the men, but the squaws and papooses gambling among themselves, dogs fighting and snarling, drums beating and old women wailing for loved ones long since gone. In the village stood a 100-foot lodge covered with mats. Here they held ceremonies and they made an imposing sight in beaded buckskin suits, haiqua shells and wampum hung around their necks, faces painted both red and yellow, going through their drills and dances, keeping time to the music of songs, beating of sticks and the sound of the pum-pum . . .

Chief Kamiakin, the most famous of the Yakima's chieftains according to Mr. Splawn, was one of a group of leading Northwest chieftains who assembled at Grande Ronde Valley (Oregon), in the summer of 1854, to formulate a grand plan for the Northwest tribes to stop the giant tide of white men pouring into the Northwest about this time to take over the region from the Indians.

In the summer of 1853, the author Theodore Winthrop, a recent graduate of Yale College, paid a visit to Kamiakin at his home on Ahtanum Creek, located closeby today's city of Yakima. In the book which he later wrote titled *Canoe and Saddle* (Portland, 1913) he describes Chief Kamiakin as "a majestic man . . . tall, very dark with a massive square face and a grave reflective look . . . quiet, dignified . . . every inch the king." Chief Kamiakin was an eloquent orator. He is remembered, too, for the dramatic costumes he wore. Young Winthrop states that on the occasion of his visit to Kamiakin, the great chief "wore a long tunic of fine green cloth." On other occasions the whites remember that Kamiakin used to wear a Hudson Bay Company broadcloth coat with red trimmings and brass buttons.

Chief Kamiakin was uniquely qualified for the leadership role which he exercised during the Indian Wars, not only over his Yakima nation of Indians, but also over most of the Indian tribes of Eastern Washington; for his grandfather was a Nez Perce and his father was a Spokane chief. As a boy, moreover, Kamiakin was raised among the Palouse Indians. He was married to a Yakima girl whose parents and grandparents were hereditary Yakima leaders. In explaining in later years why he placed his mark on Governor Stevens' peace treaty in

1855, one which gave away over 45,000 square miles of Indian lands to the white men, Kamiakin said it was to keep peace with his wife's powerful relatives, they having succumbed to Governor Stevens' blandishments.

Probably however, Kamiakin did so with tongue-in-cheek and as a tactic to give more time to prepare for the widespread Indian uprisings which followed a few months later. Indian leaders from all over the Northwest, according to Jack Splawn's book *Kamiakin,* had assembled the year prior to the Walla Walla Peace Council, in Grande Ronde Valley to discuss means by which to drive the whites away, and Kamiakin on this occasion, was one of the key formulators of the grand strategy by which to accomplish this goal. Soon after the Walla Walla conference, Indian signal fires were said to have been lit simultaneously along the high peaks of the Cascade Range signaling the commencement of the Indian wars upon the whites.

As a military leader in these wars Kamiakin's performance was mixed. Although he defeated Major Heller and his volunteers at Toppenish Creek in 1855, he was defeated the following year by Major Rains in their attack upon his home at Ahtanum Creek. In 1858, he and his Indian followers forced Colonel Steptoe from invading Spokane country to resupply whites around Colville. But the Battle of Four Lakes and the following fighting on Spokane Plains were defeats not only for Kamiakin, but for all the tribal leaders of Eastern Washington. Soon afterward, Chief Kamiakin moved with his wife and children east across the Bitterroot Mountains to live with the Kootenai Indians. Later he moved with his family to Crow Indian country, still defiant of the whites and encouraging these tribes to resist. In 1859, Governor Stevens asked Kamiakin to return to his home country to lead the Eastern Washington tribes to a meeting at Fort Vancouver, where the governor hoped to reconcile the Indians with white supremacy. Kamiakin refused. He refused, too, to accept the U.S. Government's offer to him of blankets and other supplies due him under the Walla Walla Peace Treaty's terms. At the time of his death in 1883, Kamiakin was probably eighty.

The first whites to take up land claims in Yakima Valley were the Fielding Thorpe family, who came here from Salem, Oregon. There Fielding's father, Major John Thorpe, had claimed free land in 1844. In 1856, Fielding drove a herd of cattle to the site, located just southeast of Yakima, today called Moxee City. Fielding had recently acquired these cattle in Klickitat Valley near the present town of Goldendale, where he had lived briefly. Soon after Fielding Thropes' arrival with his family at Moxee City, several more white families arrived in Yakima Valley, among these, three members of the Splawn family, the youngest of whom, Jack Splawn, was later to become the city of Yakima's first mayor.

Gold was discovered about this time in British Columbia on the Fraser River. When Fielding Thorpe's father, Major John Thorpe, decided to leave his family in Salem in order to seek his fortune in the Fraser River gold country, he asked young Jack Splawn to accompany him there, and the eighteen-year-old Jack was quick to accept. Their plan was not to dig for gold in the Cariboo, but rather to sell beef to the miners there.

Accordingly, they commenced the long drive north driving a sizeable herd of cattle, planning to slaughter them when they arrived to sell to the miners. Two Indians accompanied them as they swam their animals across the swift Columbia River northward past Okanogan Lake, covering the vast distances involved at a snail's pace due to the always burdensome task of herding.

Swarms of mosquitoes plagued them, the trails were difficult to follow, and as autumn set in apprehension over the freezing winter ahead caused them all concern, their clothing being inadequate. Winter snows became so deep they could progress no further when they were scarcely half way to their destination, near Cache Creek, forty miles west of the present city of Kamloops. At this point the two Indians deserted, and Major Thorpe, having business to attend to back in Yakima Valley, left young Splawn alone to keep himself and his cattle herd alive as best he could until spring. For seventy days, records Jack Splawn again in his book *Kamiakin, Last Hero of the Yakimas,* he lived on "beef and icicles," forced to slaughter an animal in order to survive.

Returning in the spring of 1861, Major Thorpe found Jack still alive and his herd intact. They then resumed their march up the Fraser River northward toward Barkersville. Again, however, they found themselves overtaken by the next winter's snows, still not having reached Williams Creek, the point where the miners were concentrated. Killing the entire herd, they then proceeded to sell the carcasses to passing prospectors at high prices. The following spring (1863) they returned to Yakima, their saddlebags loaded with over eighty bags of gold dust.

For the next two decades Jack Splawn continued making cattle drives, another to the Cariboo, others to Montana's Blackfoot Mines, the Boise and Orofino gold fields, and to Canyon City. He also drove cattle

over Snoqualmie Pass into Seattle and from the Okanogan south to
The Dalles, on several occasions swimming his animals across the
swift-flowing Columbia in the midst of heavy snowstorms. Splawn's last
drive, made in November, 1896, involved 680 steers from Omak to
Wenatchee. By now fifty-one years old, Splawn decided to give up his
life on the range in order to enter politics. He was elected Mayor of
Yakima in 1884.

Originally the city of Yakima was located several miles to the south
of its present site, where the town of Union Gap now stands. When in
1884 the founders of "Old Town" demanded too high a fee for allowing
the Northern Pacific Railroad their requested right-of-way through the
town, officials of this railroad decided to retaliate by laying their
railroad's tracks several miles north, eliminating "Old Town"
completely.

Here they proceeded to lay out a new township (today's city of
Yakima) promising Old Town's residents free land at the new site as
well as free transportation for their homes to the new site. Aware by
now of the error they had made in attempting to defy such a powerful
group, the whole town of Old Yakima then moved en masse to the new
Yakima. Horse-drawn flatcars and rollers enabled storekeepers and
banks to conduct their businesses as usual from their buildings while
being moved.

YELM (K-7)

This town lies on the prairie southeast of lower Puget Sound. It is an
extensive prairie, one which stretches eastward all the way to the
slopes of Mount Rainier. Here, in 1842, the British decided to raise
sheep and cattle to ship to the Russians in Alaska. For some time the
supply of furs in the Northwest had been declining and the profits of
the HBC were dwindling. Accordingly, the Hudson's Bay Company at
Nisqually House beggan converting their trappers into cowboys and
sheep herders. It was at Yelm that they would eat and sleep, while at
the nearby site where the town of Roy now stands, they erected a
slaughterhouse for killing the animals.

By 1845, however, it had become apparent that these plans were to
be short-lived, for in that year the boundary between England and the
United States, having been drawn to the north of Yelm along the 49th
parallel as it is today, placed these lands under American jurisdiction.

By 1853, when the first American settlers arrived at Yelm, England
had already abandoned hope of retaining their agricultural activity

here. Also in this year, Mr. James Longmire settled at Yelm, the first American to do so. Traveling west over the Oregon Trail with his wife and family, Mr. Longmire took a new and bold way to reach Puget Sound.

Heretofore the wagon trains bound for Puget Sound country had drifted down the Columbia by raft to its mouth before then proceeding overland north to Puget Sound. Instead of this circuitous route Mr. Longmire proposed to attempt a shortcut, one which a group of 172 of his fellow emigrants agreed to attempt with him. Crossing the Columbia to its opposite shore near the site east of the Cascade Range where Pasco now stands, Longmire led his group northward up the right bank of the Yakima River preparatory to making his bold attempt to cross these snow-capped mountains.

Successfully they floated their covered wagons, all twenty-seven of them, across the swift-flowing Columbia at Pasco. As they followed the Yakima River hundreds of Indians came to view them, amazed at their "land canoes," as the Indians called them, for it was the first time they had witnessed the invention of the wheel. At the point where the Naches River flows into the Yakima, Longmire then led them up this stream into the mountains, hoping to find a pass through which they could cross over, then descend into Puget Sound.

The twisting Naches River forced them to cross it some twenty-six times before reaching six thousand-foot-high Naches Pass where, in crossing the summit, 14,000-foot Mount Rainier seemed close enough to touch.

In descending the mountains' western slopes they found themselves confronted by steep cliffs impossible to bypass, thereby forcing them to adopt a most unusual means by which to continue. Killing several of the oxen used to pull the covered wagons, they used these animals' hide to cut strips of leather, tying them together into ropes. In Longmire's own words:

> One end of the rope was fastened to the axles of our wagons, the other thrown around a tree and held by our men. Thus one by one the wagons were gradually lowered a distance of three hundred yards, when the ropes were loosened and the wagons drawn a quarter of a mile with locked wheels. All the wagons were thus lowered except one which was crushed by the breaking of the rope . . .

Following down the twisting banks of Greenwater River, they found themselves forced to pull and drag their wagons across this stream's swift-flowing waters sixteen times. Similarly the White River (which also flows into Puget Sound) had to be crossed six times.

After settling his family at Yelm in the log cabin which he constructed, Mr. Longmire became fond of exploring into the slopes of Mount Rainier. He was not long in discovering the place now called Longmire Springs where he loved to visit. This site is now the entrance to Mount Rainier National Park's southwest corner. Moving with his family from Yelm to Longmire Springs, Lomgmire spent his later years riding his famous horse, named Nisqually, with whom he discovered many portions of Mount Rainier never before seen by white men. For many years the site where Yelm stands was the outfitting and starting point for those attempting to climb Mount Rainier.

BIBLIOGRAPHY

Akrigg, G.P.V., *British Columbia Chronicle 1778–1846.* Vancouver, B.C., 1975.
Anderson, Bern, *The Life and Voyage of Captain Vancouver.* Seattle, 1960.
Anderson, E.G., *Chief Seattle.* Caldwell, Idaho: The Caxton Printers, Ltd., 1950.
Bancroft, H.H., *History of Oregon.* Vols. I & II. San Francisco, 1888.
Binns, Archie, *Sea in the Forest.* Garden City, N.Y., 1953.
Carey, Charles H., *General History of Oregon.* Portland: Binford Mort, 1971.
Chittenden, H.M., *The American Fur Trade of the Far West.* Stanford, 1954.
Clark, Malcolm, *Eden Seekers.* Boston, 1981.
Cline, Gloria G., *Exploring the Great Basin.* Norman, Oklahoma, 1963.
———*Peter Skene Ogden.* Norman, Oklahoma, 1963.
Cook, Warren L., *Flood Tide of Empire.* New Haven, 1973.
Cutright, P.R., *Lewis and Clark, Pioneering Naturalists.* Urbana, Illinois: University of Illinois Press, 1969.
Denny, Arthur, *Pioneer Days on Puget Sound.* Seattle, 1868.
De Voto, Bernard, *The Course of Empire.* Boston, 1953.
Fargo, Lucile F., *Spokane Story.* New York, 1950.
Goetzmann, W.H., *Exploration and Empire.* New York: Norton, 1967.
Johnson, R.C., *John McLoughlin.* Portland, 1935.
Josephy, Alvin M. Jr., *The Nez Perce Indians.* New Haven, 1965.
Lavender, David, *Land of Giants.* Garden City, N.Y.: Doubleday & Company, 1956.
McCurdy, J.G., *By Juan de Fuca Strait.* Portland: Binford and Morts, 1937.
Meany, E.S., *Vancouver's Discovery of Puget Sound.* Portland: Binford and Morts, 1942.
———*Origins of Washington Geographic Names.* Portland, 1923.
Morgan, Murray, *Puget's Sound.* Seattle: University of Washington, 1979.
Morton, A.S., *Sir George Simpson.* Portland, 1944.
Richardson, David, *Pig War Islands.* East Sound, Washington: Orcas Publishing Co., 1971.
Ross, Alexander, *The Fur Hunters of the Far West.* Norman, Oklahoma, 1956.
Ruby, R.H., *The Spokane Indians.* Norman, Oklahoma: University of Oklahoma Press, 1970.
Sheller, Roscoe, *Ben Snipes, Northwest Cattle King.* Portland: Binford and Morts, 1957.
Snowden, Clinton A., *History of Washington.* New York: Century History Company, 1911.
Speidel, William C., *Sons of the Profits.* Seattle, 1967.
Splawn, A.J., *Kamiakin—Last Hero of the Yakimas.* Portland, Oregon, 1944.
Terrell, J.U., *Black Robe.* New York, N.Y., 1964.
Tyler, David B., *The Wilkes Expedition.* Philadelphia, Pennsylvania, 1968.
Warren, Sidney, *Farthest Frontier.* New York, N.Y., 1949.
Watt, Roberta F., *Four Wagons West.* Portland, 1931.
Wing, R.C., *Peter Puget.* Seattle, 1979.

Winther, O.O., *The Great Northwest.* New York, N.Y., 1950.
——— *The Old Oregon Country.* Stanford, California: Stanford University Press, 1950.
Winthrop, Theodore, *Canoe and Saddle.* Portland: Binford and Mort, 1913.
Wyeth, Nathaniel Jarvis, *Correspondence and Journals.* Eugene, Oregon, 1945.

INDEX